CHEWING GUM
in Holy Water

CHEWING GUM
in Holy Water

A Childhood in the Heart of Italy

Mario Valentini
Cheryl Hardacre

ARCADE PUBLISHING
NEW YORK

FIRST NORTH AMERICAN EDITION 2007

First published in Australia in 2006 by Allen & Unwin PTY LTD

Map on page xii © 2006 by Cheryl Hardacre
Illustrations on pages ii, 195, and 261 © 2006 by Mario Valentini
Illustrations on pages 5, 12, 27, 53, 83, 113, 151, 226, and 295 © 2006 by Cheryl Hardacre

Photograph on page vi: Religious festival in Abruzzo with the bishop (under canopy), Mario's uncle, Don Ruggero (in white smock at front), and young Mario, center foreground
Photograph on page 321: Mario's uncle, Don Ruggero, and young Mario in front of a waterfall
All photographs courtesy Mario Valentini

Library of Congress Cataloging-in-Publication Data
Valentini, Mario.
  Chewing gum in holy water : a childhood in the heart of Italy / Mario Valentini and Cheryl Hardacre. —1st North American ed.
      p. cm.
  ISBN 978-1-55970-837-1 (alk. paper)
  1. Valentini, Mario. 2. Children—Italy—Biography. 3. Abruzzo (Italy)—Biography. 4. Abruzzo (Italy)—Social life and customs. I. Hardacre, Cheryl. II. Title.
  CT1138.V323A3 2006
  945'.71091092—dc22
  [B]   2006101356

Published in the United States by Arcade Publishing, Inc., New York
Distributed by Hachette Book Group USA

Visit our Web site at www.arcadepub.com

10 9 8 7 6 5 4 3 2 1

EB

PRINTED IN THE UNITED STATES OF AMERICA

For our wonderful sons,
Tommy and Jason

CONTENTS

HOW THIS BOOK WAS CREATED

For years I've found myself grappling for a pen and paper every time my partner, Mario, started telling me yet another amazing tale from his childhood. At times I drove him crazy, as he could never finish a story without me continually interrupting, asking him to slow down or repeat a particular name, place or situation. The end result was hundreds of pages of notes about an extraordinary boyhood, a boyhood we both came to realize might just make a wonderful book.

To bring these stories to life, we decided to work together in a way that would draw on each of our creative strengths. Between us we would map out a story in point form and I would then write it from the point of view of the young Mario—attempting to re-create the humor, irony and emotion of each situation through the words and actions of the characters. Mario would then review each of these, using his skill with narrative—developed during his years as a film script editor with Cinecitta in Rome—to suggest changes that would strengthen the storyline and ensure it captured the cultural ambience of his youth.

The result is a journey that (we hope!) will sweep you, the reader, up into these wonder-filled adventures, and have you alongside the young Mario experiencing, moment by moment, the exasperation and humor of being trapped in a war of wills with his cantankerous aunt; witnessing the quick-wittedness required to explain to an outraged priest how gum came to be in the church font; experiencing Mario's awe while gazing from a *palazzo* window for the first time at his ghostly princess; and sharing the rush of adrenaline and sheer terror as our young hero—moments from death—tries to outrun a ferocious bull in a dare undertaken for love.

We hope that you will enjoy these stories as much as we enjoyed bringing them to life for you.

C. H.

FIRENZE

Giulianova

TERAMO

PESCARA

ADRIATIC SEA

ITALY

Abruzzo
Molise

Collemare

Gran Sasso

L'AQUILA

Ateram Pescara River

Aterno River

AVEZZANO

Popoli

The Majella

Sangro River

VASTO

TERMOLI

ROMA

Sulmona

Roccaraso

APPENNINI MOUNTAINS

Castel di Sangro
Capracotta
Vastogiradi

S. Giovanni

Trigno River

MOLISE

Biferno River

Trivento

©Cheryl Hardacre.2005

ISERNIA

Castropignano

CAMPOBASSO

NAPOLI

INTRODUCTION

I magine a childhood hunting wolves with slingshots in the snow-encrusted Abruzzo mountains; snatching hot chestnuts and pizza from the communal stone oven; playing with ancient swords in ruined castles where you and your friends dared each other to jump wells three hundred feet deep; eating fried zucchini flowers, quince pudding with its exploding red fruit in crisp dough, and *confetti*—almond sweets—made by the nuns who spoiled but never scolded you, for your uncle was the priest; where getting drunk meant collapsing, intoxicated, in a wine-soaked barrel the size of a small house; where love is first stirred by an aristocratic young girl who appears in the window of the medieval *palazzo* in which you live, challenges you to a knife-throwing duel, and then disappears as quickly as she came...

Imagine this boy, aged four, crying into his bowl of *orzo* on the morning he is swept from his mother's arms. In a shattered postwar Italy, with his father working in Germany and his mother unable to support three children, Mario is taken away by his uncle—a priest—to be educated and roam the world outside his small rural village. What began as grief became wonder as the boy was transposed to a world of freedom, privilege and adventure, traveling from town to hilltop village in the luxury of that rare commodity, a car; living in palaces, manors, convents; witnessing, firsthand, the intimate life of the village through the eyes of his uncle; coming face to face

1

with wolves, haunted nuns, wild bulls, and the transience of love. Imagine him returning, yearly, to the open-eyed wonder of the children he left behind in his village, who would sit in the hayloft hanging on his every word: words that spun the magic of movies never seen, places never dreamt of, adventures never before told.

The stories in this book are true: they are the real-life adventures of a boy born in an ancient stone hilltop village in the Abruzzo region of postwar Italy; a village that was perched, with a string of other tiny villages, atop the magnificent spine of Italy—the Apennines. The spectacular geography of this region, with valleys at three thousand feet and peaks towering twice this distance above them, helped preserve a breathtaking wilderness, but it also meant isolation for its inhabitants. Before expressways and modern roads, such villages were, if not inaccessible, very difficult to reach. Distance was a lesser problem than the dangerous, winding roads that twisted and turned back on each other in a succession of *tornanti*—tight hairpin bends—the narrow, poorly kept tracks luring drivers to their death on the valley floor if they erred on the side of haste. The mountain villages of this region were so isolated from each other by the intervening deep valleys that, while the inhabitants could often view each other on neighboring peaks a short distance away as the crow flies, they developed separate dialects, cuisine and ways of life.

This was a time when geographical isolation and the deprivations caused by years of war meant that the skills and daily practices of the villagers belonged more to the 1850s than the 1950s. It was a magical time when, for just over a decade, people pulled together in a way that would never occur again. A time when—with fewer men around as a result of war casualties or exile to other countries to find work—male relatives would drop by, and end up staying a full day to assist the women and children with the more arduous

2

tasks; when people preserved every resource—grew their own food, made their own cheese, pasta, wine, and kept their eggs in liquid lime and ash—so that their families would not starve. A time when money was almost nonexistent and work was paid for with a wheel of pecorino, honey, a loaf of bread, a prosciutto, homemade pasta, scoops of corn. A time when children had to walk a mile to a creek with their mother to wash clothes with ash from the fire, for soap was not available; when soccer balls were made of paper, rags and rope; when a car was so rare the village would come to a standstill to take a look; when women grew the flax to make linen, spun the fibers, and from this made the clothes; when shoes—*ciocie*—were made by hand from rags.

This was a time when, once again, bullock pairs worked the land instead of tractors, and wheat was cut by hand with a scythe. When, at harvest time, large teams of people could be seen working together in the moonlight before dawn, moving from field to field, until *all* in the village had harvested their crops: the men singing as they cut the wheat, the children jumping into the *covoni* (wheat stacks) and laughing as they collected the sheaves, the women watched for as they came later in the day carrying large baskets on their heads full of wine, cheese and fresh pasta. A time when all the wheat was taken back to the *aia*, the village communal ground, for processing and each family competed to build the best *mucchia*—wheat stacks made into the shape of a little house, which were laid out like a miniature village. When, at the end of the long, arduous day of harvesting, someone would pull out a piano accordion and, drawing on the last drop of their energy, the villagers would begin dancing, singing and storytelling, while the children—giggling all the more from the fresh homemade red wine—ran in and around the magical wheat houses until the moon rose high in the sky. Perhaps this period was all the more wonderful because change was coming...

For this short window of time poverty meant community, surviving meant cooperating, and the skills and practices of the previous century were revived in order to survive. Soon, though, tractors could be seen across the valley in neighboring towns, jobs became available in the larger towns and people left the land; more and more the outside world—in all its modernity—arrived. By the mid-1960s, Italy had all but "caught up" with the rest of the western world—suddenly everyone had a television, radio, washing machine, fridge and, more often than not, a car.

But let us return to these magic years, the years when, in the hilltop town of our young storyteller, "going out to play" meant pushing your way through a flock of sheep at your front door, your stomach full of fried polenta and *orzo*; flattening yourself—slingshot around your neck and wooden gun at your side—against ancient houses in alleyways to avoid the passing bullock teams, your nostrils filled with the acrid smell of dung mixed with the aroma of warm pecorino and ricotta being wrung out in kitchens you passed; dodging mules and donkeys pulled by laughing and yelling cigar-smoking farmers in black felt hats and clacking boots—their soles punched with nails to reduce wear; through the ancient piazza, its clock tolling the time, full of boys playing *zizzola* and *battimuro*; rummaging through your secret stash of swords—genuine, as they were found in a nearby castle well—and knives that you hid in the top of a deserted barn; racing across the *aia* with its carpet of bean pods—the farmer threshing the pods with a simple stick-and-chain implement and welcoming your fleeting steps as they crushed more pods underfoot; and finally climbing atop the highest wall of the castle ruins with your best friend, the immense valley spread out below, and yelling out that you have just seen Hannibal and his elephants approaching.

For this was the childhood of Mario Valentini, and these are the stories . . .

La Suora THE NUN

The smell of bubbling quince and roasting nuts wafts from the main kitchen as we pass: today the nuns are making jam and chestnut *torta*.

Barely eight, I follow the floating robes of my uncle across the courtyard with its broken flagstones, through the arched portico, into a large hall, and up several more steps to the dining room.

Sunday mass and lunch in the convent dining room to follow: my uncle, the priest, always the guest of honor. Mother Superior and several nuns greet us, feed us, and politely entertain. Today—Epiphany Eve—the village matrons, the local doctor and some of the poorer families join us: lots of distraction.

We are early. The room we enter overlooks the atrium; stone floor, several scrubbed tables. It is a large room, and we eat at the table next to the *armadio*; plates filled with antipasto, bruschetta, fresh ricotta, *sfrizzoli* and *uva passita*—pork crackling and dried grapes—adorn its worn surface. The room is light and dark—heavy shutters allow in slats of light. The thick glass panes seal it against the chill of January, and the shutters are closed but for a vertical gap as wide as my hand that allows each window one long strip of light, an irreverent intruder from the world outside: a world of *zizzola*, soccer, swimming naked in the Sangro, and words that could never be uttered within these walls.

I follow one such strip of light. Along the floor, across my uncle's foot, along the table, striping the bosom of one of the younger nuns (is she aware the light plays there?), up the wall, resting, befittingly, on the gentle face of the carved Madonna high in her stone alcove. I glance back at the young nun. She has moved, ever so slightly. No reason to look there—the curve of her bosom—the light has struck the thick, dark robes covering her arm. The light and I are thwarted.

Something catches my attention at the end of the long hallway to my left. Red metal and discordant color peek around the base of a doorway at the end of this vista: it is the entrance to the converted chapel, now the nuns' reception room. I crane my neck: a mound of metal, wood and plastic three feet high cascades to the door and a thrill sweeps through me. Toys! The nuns' annual gifts at Epiphany to the village children. My mind races: which one is mine?

The lavatory is at the end of this hallway. I make a mental note to be in need at the end of lunch.

The hall is cool, dark, and moist, away from the winter fires burning in the dining area. With each step the temperature drops. I swing my arms and spin, breathing in the cool air, trying to look casual should anyone be watching. I glance back down the hall. A clatter of plates from the nearby kitchen; nuns bustle past the visitors, serving, clearing dishes; my uncle and Doctor Roversi chat with their backs to me—there's a polite conversational hum. I do not exist. One more spin and I whirl myself into the converted chapel—the room of treasures.

A pile of toys but, oh! My gaze is locked on a large red metal bus which takes two hands to lift: black rubber tires, a large silver key to wind up and send my bus (for it is *mine!*) hurtling across the room, the *cortile*, the street. And the envy of the boys in the piazza: this bus, my dream!

I inspect the nametag—not mine, of course. Epiphany toys are for the poor, but some of the *chierichetti*—altar boys—such as myself also receive gifts. But the toys are scaled to balance advantage; my uncle is a comparatively wealthy man, and my gift will be a lesser one. I search. "Mario Valentini": *confetti*—almond sweets—and a rubber ball. The tags are easily swapped—could I? I would have to move quickly...

I shiver again as I finish peeing, hot body fluid striking the chill air. The smell is pungent but not unpleasant. I exit to the hallway, at ease as I return from the direction of the toilet, past the converted chapel—eyes rigidly ahead—my body relaxing with every step I take closer to the dining area. There is the sound of chatter, children laughing. Mother Superior catches my eye and smiles. My uncle is still in conversation with the doctor. My friend Ottavio—a fellow *chierichetto*—yells my name and signals to me. The heat of the fire greets me as I reach the end of the hall and I run toward him.

Something blocks me. For a moment I don't know what has happened. I am blocked by something soft, and solid, and blue. I recognize the clean smell of starch and the texture: nuns' vestments. My usual experience of this comes with cuddling, soft words, warm biscotti—at worst, good-natured reprimands. But here the familiar

7

blue is rigid, with no give at all. I look up into the face of Sister Angelina.

Blue eyes, rounded cheeks a ruddy pink, and perfectly formed lips: she is the closest thing to the Raphael angels I have seen in my uncle's books. Her face is framed in a fiercely starched wimple, and I see nothing past the middle of her brow, the curve of her lower lip; the stiff sides clamped to the very edge of her eyebrows. A small square of face. No chin, no neck, no wisp of hair. She seems neither young nor old, and is less like a nun than the others: she talks to us about things that aren't church-related, gives us extra cookies, and smiles a lot. But right now she isn't smiling.

Adrenaline pumps through me. I try to read her face. It is expressionless. Perhaps my fears are unfounded: she wants me to do a chore, my uncle has asked for me... She grips my hand like a vise. My heart sinks.

"Come with me. I know what you did."

She spins me back in the direction of the chapel, her stride forceful, her grip unrelenting. I stumble along beside her, my mind racing with thoughts of the shame I have brought to my uncle, and the punishment that awaits me: being confined to my room for days, my friends in the piazza without me, my dignity lost. The long hallway suddenly seems short with only fifty feet to go. I look up at her stern profile.

"You're beautiful," I say.

"We're all beautiful in our own way." Clipped, curt. No change in pace.

From instinct I nuzzle into her waist, grasping her skirts, pulling in against her body.

"You look like my mommy. I miss my mommy."

I pull back and look up. She strides onward, her feet not missing a beat. But was that a slight easing of her grasp?

"I never see your hair. I'd really like to see your hair because you look like my mommy."

Definitely a slight release of her grasp, a slackening of her hand, and a slowing of pace. She strides onward, the chapel doorway looms, but something has changed. I know not to utter another word. Not one other sacred, profound, violent or beautiful word. My instinct tells me enough has been said, but I still don't know what will happen.

Six feet to go. I can see the red bus protruding from the pile through the doorway. How could I have left it so far to the front, so obvious? With a mixture of calm and horror I realize there is no escape. We reach the doorway.

I am pulled suddenly to the right instead of the left, this unexpected tack tipping me off balance. We enter a small, disused prayer room opposite the converted chapel: old books line one wall and a pigeon flutters from the floor to the window.

Sister Angelina hesitates and then grips me by the shoulders, looking into my eyes: "Mario, you are very naughty—"

"My mommy's hair...it was yellow..." I begin, but the words catch in my throat.

The nun releases her grip and steps back. Silence. The pigeon rattles the window casement as it escapes. I watch it fly off. When I look back, I see Sister Angelina fiddling with her wimple—she is *removing* it! A distant bell, muffled sounds from the kitchen, we stand facing each other. No words are spoken.

The rigid wimple cracks in the silence. I can hear her breathing, and I realize I have stopped breathing myself, my body tense. There is a further snapping of starched linen, indents on her face from the stiff edges, the soft swish as she removes her veil, eyes brimming. Cropped blond hair is revealed, hacked short at the fringe and sides. But when she turns two golden yellow braids nestle in to the sides of her head at the back. She releases them. Soft gold cascades to her shoulders, past her shoulders—crinkled, twisting, unraveling of its own accord.

I gasp. "You are beautiful like my mother."

A tear spills down her pink cheek. Her eyes look at me, through me, beyond the stone wall behind ... I know she is not in the convent at this moment.

A bell tolls in the tower above us, and the ringing vibrates through my body. Startled, I step back, awkward. Another step back toward the door. She watches, but makes no attempt to stop me. I take the last step backward and escape, down the hall, past my uncle, skimming the stone steps to the atrium—the sunshine.

The dawn breaks. It's Epiphany. The dim, golden sun rises over snow-encrusted peaks; soft, icy flakes spit and dissolve against my face as I open the casement window, watching for my aunt. The freedom of fresh air. The valley below is still, a soft, white cloud hiding the river, the trees, the cluster of houses nestled there. The vale embalmed by soft white. I am alone with the muted sun, the mountain peaks, the ancient hilltop village.

My uncle has already left. I am spared six a.m. mass. I will go to the later mass that precedes the ritual of Epiphany gift-giving.

Bustle and noise emanate from the converted chapel, the chill room of yesterday now warm, well lit, and full of voices. Children's hands are slapped as they pull at the pile of toys. Others, not old enough to break the front line of toy gazers, focus on the Nativity scene behind: several of the figures are already missing. The culprit, barely two, is found with Balthazar, a donkey and baby Jesus in a far corner, the great Persian priest and the Messiah sticky with dribble and *confetti*.

Adults mill. *Caffe* and panettone are served, and gifts of biscotti, mandarins and *confetti* are handed out, tied in doilies that have been crocheted by the nuns. My uncle moves toward the pile of toys. The room quietens and the ritual of name-calling begins.

I fidget, resigning myself to the long wait: my surname, Valentini, runs close to last on any alphabetical list. Marco—red fire truck; Romano—bow and arrow; Guillermo—a drum; Renato—a book (he asked for that, always sucking up to the nuns, pushing ahead of us to show how well he can read the missal); Giuseppe—a wooden rattle (I'm sure he preferred the donkey). No one gets coal. We're all threatened with a chunk of coal at Epiphany if we're naughty, so we wait, more to see if *someone else* gets it.

Feeling miserable, I spy the object of my desire jammed at the back against the wall, looking more red, more beautiful, bigger than any other toy in the room—its new nametag is in place. This is too cruel! I make sure my eyes do not meet Sister Angelina's.

"Tallermo...Tanti..." Four toys remain and still the bus sits there, cajoling, taunting. I look around with jealous eyes. Who is about to receive that which I *so* desire?

"Vaini...Valenti..." Still the bus. The bus and a small spinning top. I look around in a panic. Who, besides me, remains? I am alone.

My uncle checks the nametags—twice. He looks confused. One of the nuns approaches and they confer.

My uncle's voice rings out. "Your name is on both of these, Mario, there has been some mistake. We ask that you make a choice."

All eyes are upon me. So this is it: the cruelest choice of all. The red bus is mine in a word, but I am my uncle's apprentice. Epiphany is for the poor: humility and honor dictate that I take the lesser toy. I look at my uncle, the faces around me, back at the red bus. Agony.

There is a sudden movement behind me and Sister Angelina comes forward, carrying the toddler Giuseppe. She cradles him with confidence against her breast, sliding him to her hip before she bends and places him on the floor between the two remaining toys.

"Peppino has broken his toy. Let him decide on one of these."

Don't look at the bus. Please, *please* don't look at the bus. He does. Fascinated by its size, the wheels, its color, he reaches for it.

Suddenly, there is the sound of whirring metal. Giuseppe stops and turns. Sister Angelina is spinning the top. The toddler stares, entranced by the flashing metal, the spiral of color skidding across the stone floor, and he loses his balance as he grabs at the top, delighted.

The graceful nun stands, handing me the red bus. Our eyes meet. A smile, almost imperceptible, crosses her lips. I fumble with the bus. Guilt, joy and remorse all mingle—and there's the sting of tears.

I look into her eyes: they are gentle, reassuring. In that moment I know that Raphael did paint from life.

I stare at the white outside my bedroom window. It's now a week since Epiphany, and the snow has come in thick. Too deep to walk, no bus for the teacher, and a classroom with poor heating means no school today, and my aunt has forced me into my bedroom to read. I try to follow the words, but the shadows of the spitting flakes keep running down the page—the dull sun illuminating them from behind—and this draws my eyes upward, out of the window, and beyond...

I was four years old the day my uncle came to get me.

I remember sitting on the bottom step of the staircase that led up to the one small bedroom of our house, sobbing and trying to finish the bowl of *orzo* I was told I had to eat before my long journey with my uncle. He stood near the fire in his long priest's coat while my mother tried to calm me, the baby in her arms writhed, and my two-year-old brother watched silently.

We were all downstairs in the kitchen: our house had one room on each level. It was one of the small village houses that stood on the edge of an allotment of land. A few steps from our house we had a barn for the animals to shelter in during winter. I remember how many steps it was because when it was too cold to go to the distant outhouse toilet, we would go to the barn instead. I remember peeing and grunting in the warm straw, its sharpness tickling my bottom as I squatted, and the sounds and smells of the animals around me—I liked it.

Near us lived my grandparents, Nonno Cesare and Nonna Custodia, in the *portone*, the great communal house that belonged to our family—the Valentinis—and another family, the Antonellis. It had the number "1693" on a large beam as you entered the main doorway; when I asked Nonno Cesare what this meant, he told me this was when it was built and that it was a long, long time ago. I asked him if the knights built it. He said it wasn't quite that old, and explained that our village of Collemare had begun hundreds of years ago with five or six families building houses on land that belonged to a nobleman. The nobleman could not afford to pay people to farm such a great area of land—the feudal era, when such labor was free, was over—so some families were given permission to live on and farm the land as long as half the produce was given to the owner. The small houses of the farmers became larger houses— or *portone*—as their extended families grew, and as the centuries passed and the strength of the aristocracy faded, the land was granted to the families who farmed it, along with the houses.

These great *portone* lined the one road on our hilltop: two stories high, they had enormous archways through the center that led from the street front through to the fields behind the house. Four, five or more families lived upstairs while the areas downstairs were used as stables for animals, and storage. My *nonno* said that eventually, as individual members of a family wanted their own home, people would build little houses alongside the *portone* until they all joined up to create a village. That was how we came to be in a small house three doors from Nonno Cesare, who, being the eldest in his family since his brother had died, lived in and was in charge of the *portone* and all the surrounding Valentini land.

Although my mother said he *wasn't*. In charge, that is. I heard her say it to a neighbor. I listened carefully, because I knew it was secret talk when my mother lowered her voice and kept glancing across to see if I was listening. So I kept playing, and listened.

She began by saying how my grandmother, Nonna Custodia, ruled the roost and took charge of all the food supplies and the land allotments, and made all the family decisions that should have been made by my grandfather, and she said that my *nonno* needed to "take her in hand." She then told tales about how my grandmother bullied all the women in the family, locking the food in cupboards so that they had to beg for it, giving more soap (made communally by all the Valentini women) to those she favored, letting me—as a young baby—roll in the ash near the fire the one day she had to mind me, and generally causing problems with chickens and vegetables by continually changing allocated land boundaries among the clan. Finally my mother whispered fiercely that Nonna Custodia even bullied the younger men of the family, then she and the neighbor went back to talking out loud. I was disappointed that this was the secret, because I already knew.

I loved my grandfather. Nonno was big, talked loudly and wore colorful braces and a straw *paglietta*—on Sundays it was a suede *cappello* with a blue feather tucked in its band. He would put me on his shoulders, show me his knives and promise me a slingshot and hunting lessons when I was bigger. But I didn't like Nonna. She made my mother cry.

My uncle, the priest, was Nonno Cesare and Nonna Custodia's son too, just like my papa. That was why he visited Collemare, to see his mother and father and then to see us. I think he was sad that his brother, my papa, was not there to help my mother and her children, so he was very kind to us. I liked it when he came: he would talk about a place called Rome that had lots of people, lots of houses and no land. My mother was upset whenever he said this. She said she didn't understand how the people in this place called Rome survived; she said *everyone* needed land, or how else could you feed your family, grow linen for clothes, or produce extra grain and poultry for barter?

The day my uncle came for me, he stood by the fire in the downstairs room that was our kitchen and sitting area. Downstairs I knew as happy, warm and full of activity: my mother heating water, sweeping, stoking the fire, and pushing, kneading and pounding a great slab of something on the wooden table—polenta, pasta dough, pastry. There was always the aroma of onions, garlic, tomatoes and fresh herbs; the tangy whiff of hanging prosciutto; the piquant, salty smell of warm pecorino being wrung out in linen. The large copper *conca* that held our water sat under the window, and we would regularly dip in the *coppino* and sip the fresh, cold liquid. Twice a day I would watch as my mother wound fabric around the crown of her head, coiling it until there were high, soft sides and an empty center—this they called *cipolla*, or onion. She then placed the *conca* on top of the *cipolla* on her head, balancing the large vessel this way even on the return journey when it was full, and went into the street to join her neighbors, talking and singing with the other women as they walked the mile to the village spring to fetch water.

The day my uncle came for me, I sat on the step struggling with my breakfast because we only had two stools, one for my mother and the second for any visitor. Burlap bags full of potatoes, dried beans, grains and other foodstuffs lined each side of the narrow wooden steps, and I leaned against a large, musty-smelling sack of chickpeas as I tried to balance the bowl on my knees. The tears made bubbles as they fell into my *orzo*, and I remember the taste of salt. I was four years old the day my uncle came to get me, and I knew I wasn't coming back.

With a loud *thump!* a lump of ice breaks away from the eaves and strikes the windowsill: startled, I go back to my book. The sentence seems familiar. I've read it before—many times. In the last few minutes. Shutting the book, I slide my hand over its soft cover, and absently start flicking the top corner back and forth with my finger as I stare at the drawing of Saint Peter on the front. Schoolbooks make things dull, unlike the books about Caesar, Garibaldi and Alexander the Great in my uncle's study: their pages are filled with exciting pictures and words—they have blood and swords and heroes and great battles...

The room has become cold. I put one hand to my cheek. It's icy. I could tell my aunt that I couldn't finish my schoolwork because I was in danger of being frozen in my chair: I would have frozen into a curve, and if I'd stood straight I would have snapped in two like the brittle icicles that hang off the edge of our roof! I leap onto the bed and wriggle under the *trapunta*—my warm quilt—shoes and all. In view is the shelf on the opposite wall with its motley assembly of books, ornaments and toys. My aunt tells me to keep the shelf neat or she will throw my things out. I try to keep it neat, but it always ends up messy, and now I have to keep checking just in case anything is missing... She's not my aunt anyway, and the red bus is broken.

I miss my mother. She gave me a cookie to stop me from crying the day my uncle came. A cookie to stop me from tearing up and down the stairs in terror after I had been told I was leaving. My four-year-old mind searched desperately for somewhere to hide. I looked upstairs to the bedroom with panic-stricken eyes, and then down and out the front door past my uncle, but I knew there was nowhere. A cookie to stop me from screaming out that I didn't want to go; a cookie that could tempt my small hands away from my mother's skirts, which they clutched again and again each time she pulled them away; young hands that clutched and clutched as my kind uncle nervously wrung his. But I couldn't eat.

A cookie was a rare treat—even a brittle, month-old biscotto that could not be bitten without first being softened in warm milk—and my brother and I would snatch them eagerly. But this day I could not eat. Tears dropped onto the cookie floating on the surface of my bowl of milky barley.

I didn't think my uncle would come. My mother had told me I was going, but I didn't think he would come. It wasn't that I didn't like my uncle: he was kind, he brought us gifts. *He had a car.* No one in our village had a car—it was rare for anyone, anywhere, to have a car, and people would run out to look whenever he arrived. It wasn't that I didn't like my uncle; I just didn't want to go away.

Our village sits high up in the Appennini mountains, and its name means "mountain-sea." I asked my *nonno* why this was when all the other villages around us seemed to be named after a saint, and he replied it was because when he was a boy there had been a great sea around Collemare! For a long time I thought it was true because people found shells up here in the mountains. Then someone told me that there *had* been a sea here, but it was millions of years ago. Our village is so high up that everywhere else seemed a long way away. My uncle said in some ways this was true, because even though big towns and cities were not too far "as the crow flies," the steep, narrow, winding roads through the mountain peaks—sometimes there were fifteen hairpin bends within a mile or so—made traveling dangerous and *everything* far away.

I asked him how his car stayed still on the sloping road outside our house, and why he wasn't afraid that it would roll all the way back down the mountains, so he explained to me about brakes. Before that I wouldn't get in the car. Uncle had a car for his preaching work but most people couldn't afford cars, he said, and even if they could, there was little gasoline anyway, because of the war—even though it was a decade since it had ended. He told me that the rusty tractors we played on in the fields had once worked, but now there were no parts to repair them. The pairs of bullocks I saw plowing and pulling loads were something that had been used *before* the tractors, and they had to be brought back again, because of the war. The war that wasn't there anymore. I didn't understand.

I liked my uncle, and I liked his car. But I didn't want to go away. My papa might come back.

Nonno said Papa was a soldier in the war for six years, three of them as a prisoner. When Papa returned to Collemare he began courting my mother and building our house. In 1950 they married. A year later I was born and when I was still very little he had to go away again because there were no jobs in Italy. Now he has gone to work in the country he was fighting against—Germany!—but I'm sure soon he will come home. I didn't want to be away when my papa came back. And I didn't want to leave my friends, or my house, or my mother, or my brothers, or my *nonno*, or my cats—or my papa, when he came back.

My mother wouldn't listen. I was told life would be better with my uncle, that I'd have *real* soccer balls, *real* shoes and *real* soap. I told my mother I didn't want real ones: I liked the balls my brother and I made from paper and rope, and I liked the gray ash we used for soap, and my *ciocie*—the soft shoes she stitched together from rags. My mother said I *had* to accept my uncle's kind offer of all these wonderful things. I told her to tell my uncle he could send them to me and I would stay at home in the village with my brothers.

My feet slid along on the white gravel as my mother gripped my arm firmly and pulled me toward my uncle's car. She opened the door, dusted off my pinafore and handed me another biscotto. Her eyes looked wet. She kissed me and said that if I learned well I would soon be back to live with her and my brothers.

I knew I wasn't coming back.

My uncle was kind, and my mother meant well, but I knew I wasn't coming back. My two-year-old brother seemed to know it too. I remember glancing back to where Luigi stood in the doorway holding the hand of my *nonna*: I saw the shock and silent tears on his face. Something big was being taken from him. There would no longer be an older brother to follow around or run to. *He* was now the eldest in the house.

A distant noise startles me, bringing me back to my room, my warm, cozy bed. I look to the window.

Oh . . . the snow! I can play with my friends only if the snow is no higher than my knees. I know that if it's above the third stone on the wall below my bedroom window then it's above my knees. Standing on the bed and stretching up over the sill, I peer through the uppermost corner of the glass, straining to look out and down . . . it's too hard. I stretch my neck even farther—can't quite see . . . I have to open the window.

19

But my aunt will *kill* me if I open the window in the middle of winter after she has spent every one of her waking hours heating the house . . . but how does she *know* when I've opened it? Each time I twist the latch so quietly there is *no way* she could hear it in the next room, yet seconds later she throws open my door, yelling at me as if she knows by magic!

I listen: no one seems to be in the next room. This means my aunt is two shut doors and a hallway away, resting on her bed. I twist the handle on the casement ever so slowly, gently. There is *absolutely* no sound. Forcing the window out, I turn in the same movement and notice my bedroom door suck inward and back with a thud, and watch as a feather from my *trapunta* races across the floor, under the door and out to the hallway in a stream of chill air. Perhaps *that's* how she—

"*Mario!*"

I slam the window shut and jump onto my chair, almost tipping it over. I slap open the book. I can hear my aunt thudding down the hall, muttering under her breath. My uncle says (at breakfast, when he wants more toasted *polenta*) that she's the most pious woman in the village, which makes her smile and ask him to say it again, but when he isn't here she curses sometimes when she's chasing me. In fact, *only* when she's chasing me.

"*Mannaggia la miseria!* Shut that window, *scostumato!*" she yells as my bedroom door flies open under the force of her hand. "Watch out if you touch it again! *All my good work!*" she wails, cupping her hands and looking back in the direction of the kitchen stove that struggles throughout the day to heat the house. It occurs to me that if she shut my bedroom door instead of standing there with it wide open, the cold air in my room wouldn't go anywhere else. But I don't think I should say that right now.

She starts using the finger. "It's a shame you're not old enough to chop wood. I'd send you out to split the dozen *pezzi di legna* you just wasted, the dozen pieces of firewood we'll need to get the house warm again—that would teach you!"

My aunt goes quiet. I keep my eyes down, trying to look repentant. It doesn't work.

"Instead you can stay in this afternoon and help me with the *pane.*"

Not seeing my friends *and* kitchen chores with my aunt... "But Uncle said I could go to Guido's to play cards... *scopa*..."

"*I don't care.* You can help with the bread and husk *castagne* ready for Adolfo's oven tomorrow. At least that will make up for my extra work fueling the stove."

She turns, but her eyes are caught by something on my shelf: her sharp eyes that detect anything out of order, anything *broken.*

"Soon I'll throw out that bus," she says, and then shuts the door behind her.

She won't. If she did, my uncle would have something to say. Then again, maybe he would think it was another wondrous lesson in *not* coveting! Have to hide the bus.

Anyway she's not my real aunt. My uncle explained to me that she is a *perpetua*—a relative who lives in as the priest's housekeeper—and he drew me a picture to show me where my "aunt" fits into our family: she is the sister of the wife of my mother's brother. It took me a while to realize that she is not even related to my uncle! *I am.* This made me happy.

I learned the full story of my aunt's situation not long after I came to live with them, when I asked my uncle if he and my aunt were going to have a baby (I didn't want one because my friend Luciano had just got one that grunted stuff into his diaper that you could smell three houses away). I found out then that priests can't marry and was told that, regardless, my aunt is part of our "family" and has to be treated with love and respect.

I don't know how I'm supposed to love a tank. That's what my aunt reminds me of—a baby tank like the ones I've seen in war pictures—when she barges toward me with her elbows flying. She's almost as broad as she is tall (which isn't very, I'm taller than her!), and someone said that with her short stature, olive skin and dark eyes, she was a "true southern Italian." This confused me because my mother is from the south and yet she has yellow hair and fair skin . . . anyway, my mother is *beautiful*. Uncle says my aunt has a "handsome face," but I can't see it. And she's so fussy about her appearance: her skirt, sweaters, shoes and stockings are always of good quality and *neat*, with never a mark or fold out of line. The only thing that's not flat and straight is the small lace handkerchief that peeks out from the cuff of her left sleeve. Even when she cleans the church with the other women, they turn up in their old clothes and Aunt with her apron on; after an hour of dusting, sweeping and mopping, Aunt whips off her apron to reveal a pristine outfit with not a crease in sight. Aunt says she is proud of her *"bella figura."* Trouble is, she's fussy about *our* appearance too: my uncle and I. Whatever I have on is always spit-cleaned, brushed, pulled, picked and rubbed before I can get out the door. And she's continually tugging at buttons to see if they are loose: she even yells at me if a button has begun unthreading—as if I did it!

But the worst of it is that Aunt is also in charge of disciplining me when my uncle isn't here. And she disciplines me a lot, but when my uncle is in hearing distance she is careful not to do, or say, anything harsh.

Trouble is, my uncle doesn't know what she says to me when he's not here. My aunt reminds me daily that she no longer has the peaceful life she enjoyed as Uncle's *perpetua* before I came. Her nickname for me is *scostumato*, which means "insolent and unruly"; she says it is a pity she can't find one word that also includes "lazy." She told me I would be the cause of her first heart attack, and then clipped my ears when I asked who was giving her the second (I thought you died from a heart attack and I didn't know you could have more than one).

My aunt says lots of things, but only four words hurt. Sometimes, after scolding me for something that has particularly annoyed her, she will pause and say, "No *wonder* your mother..." and walk off. That's all she says: she never finishes the sentence.

Anyway, my mother said that if I learn well I can come back to live with her and my brothers. I don't think it's true. But it might be. So I'm learning things. My uncle said that, outside of school, I should be learning from the adults around me: apart from my mother, that means my uncle—and my aunt.

My aunt is the hardest. But now I'm tidy. Well, sort of. She likes everything tidy, but *especially* our clothes. Everything has to be neat and clean and new (or at least *look* new) before we leave the house. Guido told me that his mother says my aunt just wants to show off that our family has money and the other people in the village don't. One day when my aunt told me that cleanliness was next to godliness—*again*—I asked her if Jesus had to brush his teeth. She told me not to be stupid and to put on my shoes and socks as we had visitors coming (it was summer!). When I said it was too hot, she said that God-fearing people always dressed well and had their feet fully covered in company. Jesus mustn't have feared his father then, because he always wore sandals or bare feet. I told my aunt this just as the visitors were arriving, and I didn't get *polenta* for two days.

Anyway, I don't think my aunt is good like Jesus meant. She thinks she is, but I've heard my frustrated uncle tell her—after she has asked for her *third* confession from him in one day—"Please,

please, Ercolina! You don't need this many confessions!" My uncle is more like Jesus: he *helps* people. He even helps people write and read their letters when they don't know how, and some of the women keep coming back. It makes me sad when the women keep coming back to get him to write letters to their husbands, or write letters *asking* about their husbands—husbands who have been missing since the war, which ended fourteen long years ago. "Be at peace, be at peace, sister, *please*," my uncle says to them. "Be at peace. He is dead, he is not coming back..."

So I think my uncle is good and I try to listen to him. He says the best lessons are in the Bible, "the book," so I'm trying that. He says *all* good things are in "the book." I don't know where. The things I like aren't in it.

My favorite things are fried *polenta*, bruschetta, pocket knives, chewing gum and cigarettes (we had one of Guido's father's out the back), but they aren't in the Bible. I like stories about Hannibal and medieval knights, sea voyages and brave hunters, but they're not in there either. The only good thing is the Roman soldiers, and even then my aunt said they were bad because they killed Jesus. But how can they be bad when they're Italian—they're *us*? That ruined the only good bit. The Bible is full of people having babies, traveling the desert and Jesus (in sandals) stories: what am I supposed to learn from that? My uncle says not to worry if I get bored because the end of the book is a lot more exciting, so I'm waiting...

My mother wants me to learn, but she didn't mention books and clothes. She said she wanted me to *be like my uncle*. So I try. I assist with communion, I've learned to sing in church with my gum stuck to a back tooth, and I get more collection money for my uncle by stopping for a while in front of the people who can't find their pockets. But the best part is in the evening when I am alone in the empty church with my uncle, a recent privilege after he decided I am now old enough to stay back late and help him lock up. This must mean I'm grown up. So, to speed things along, I've learned to spit out the large back row candles while I put out the front ones with the snuffer, sweep the dust from the main gallery behind the apostles, and pocket any coins from the floor (the *borsa* has been put away and I don't want my uncle to have to count it all again), and then help him lock the great church door. My uncle says I am a good helper.

And if I'm *really* well behaved I get to read one of his books. Not the Bible, one of the *other* books. Genghis Khan, the wild sea voyages of Conrad, the cries of great warriors with bloodied spears, ferocious beasts, and knights jousting to the death have all crept out from a particular corner of my uncle's study—the corner holding the books that have nothing to do with the church. I *love* that corner.

I shiver. The room is a lot colder since I opened that window. I look down at the missal in front of me. Saint Peter's face looks funny as I bend it with the flicking of the cover. No playing with my friends today, tomorrow at the oven with my aunt, and afterward helping my uncle with mass. But next week I will be free! Next week, for the very first time, I will be allowed to play with my friends outside of calling distance, away from the eyes and ears of my aunt. My uncle said I'm old enough. This means that I will be able to explore and do wonderful things away from our house. But I can't go too far—my aunt said no farther than our street.

I don't think she'll miss me if I go to the castle ruins up on the hill. I have to. Hannibal is up there waiting with his elephants, and my friends and I have been called on to lead the entire Roman legion into battle against him. But before we go I will have to sneak *pane* and almonds from my aunt's kitchen, Guido has to get another cigarette from his father's case, and along the way Renzo will have to feed his pigs.

Hoo-oo-oo-oo . . . A howl from far, far in the distance. Suddenly dogs begin to bark all around the village.

Hooo-ooo . . . There it is again, rising above the noise of the dogs: a strange howl that sends a shiver down my spine. I peer out through the condensation on the window glass, past the silent white, and I begin to think twice about our journey up the hill . . .

Il Lupo **THE WOLF**

2

Crunch of snow: crackling, white and crusty. The smell of baking bread and dry flour on searing stone. My aunt's apron flickers and catches my face. In the cold it stings. We tread carefully, and slide, down the iced surface under the *tettoia*—the covered walkway— between the church and our house toward the communal oven. Adolfo, the oven tender, has my aunt's loaves from yesterday, which she brought down soft, warm and yeasty. He turns these mounds of acrid-smelling pastiness to golden crisps, the centers soft, feathery, dissolving on the tongue.

We reach the oven: dome-topped, its stones changing color with the varying intensity of the heat, it stands beneath an ancient wooden shelter. No need for Adolfo to wear his warmest *vestiti*: the heat of the oven keeps him in a continual sweat even now, on the shortest, coldest days of the Appennini winter. I watch as his strong arms, hairless from years of singeing, push the wooden *pala* in and out of the oven, shuffling the loaves to ensure they cook evenly.

My aunt greets two women who are just leaving with their baskets full of baked goods. I sniff, and spy cooked chestnuts in the basket of the younger woman. She notices my gaze, and looks away—no hope of a treat there.

Adolfo calls: "*Quadra!*—Boy!" and tosses me a chestnut. I see he has a small pile in front of him, and he munches away as he works; they are part payment from the woman for his baking duties. It reminds me of the *castagne* I had to peel for my aunt just yesterday, using my shoes to rub them open—keeping my fingers away from their stinging, spiky husks.

Adolfo smiles at me, a broad, broken-toothed smile, ground chestnut on his teeth and lips. I notice he makes no effort to close his mouth as he eats. I like him. He winks and jerks his head toward the oven. I look over to that greatest of all treats, *crosta*—the strip of dough that is pasted around the oven door as a seal: a strip of impasto that cooks to a delectable brown crisp over the hours. The oven tender snaps off a piece of the *crosta* and holds it out to me; initially it's bitter on my tongue, I crunch and it dissolves to a milky soft nuttiness in my mouth. I crunch again.

Adolfo returns to his work, the women talk of husbands, and ailments, and . . . Their voices become a distant murmur as my eyes wander, searching the snow: a new fall overnight and the excitement of animal tracks—animals never seen near the village during warmer times come in foraging, desperate for food scraps, anything, in the freezing, unforgiving midwinter. From the cover of the shelter and the warmth of the fire, I crunch the last of my *crosta* and hunt for tracks: a rabbit, a fox. If I'm lucky, perhaps a deer.

I know most of the animal tracks. Nonno taught me back in Collemare, and my friend Renzo and I now hunt at the end of his paddock, where the wild shrubs meet the farmed land, using slingshots. The older boys make fun of us, but we are very accurate with our *fionde*, stunning birds, lizards and, once, a rabbit, from a distance. One day I will have a knife and be a *real* hunter. In a few years, my *nonno* said. The knife I want sits on the mantelpiece in an oak box—stainless steel and brass with an ebony handle. It is the most beautiful hunting knife I have seen. It was my grandfather's, and one day it will be mine. I want it now, but I have to wait. "When you are a man," says Nonno.

Something unusual catches my eye in the snow. Large footprints: dog footprints? *But what a dog!* I leave the shelter and scramble several yards down the hill to take a closer look at the deep, frozen recesses. I place my left hand in one. The footprint is twice the size of my hand! It must be a *maremmano*, the famed white mountain sheepdog the size of a small pony. The Calvari family has one, but they live at the other end of the village: what would their dog be doing here, near the oven?

I reach over and shove my right hand into the next footprint. *Madonna!* I am amazed at the *size* of this beast. The footprints are deep and the stride more than I can reach by keeping one hand in place and leaning way, way forward and—something isn't right. This doesn't seem like the pace of a large, lumbering sheepdog. I place my hand inside another footprint, my palm now completely numb; this print is so deep that the sides have cracked and caved in. I am half squatting, half kneeling, my left knee cold and soaking into the snow, but I don't really notice. I am mesmerized. What could have made such a print? What could force itself into the Abruzzo ice like this? I suddenly tense. Whatever it is has to be big, and powerful, and—

"A wolf." A male voice behind me.

CHEWING GUM IN HOLY WATER

I withdraw my hands as if electrocuted. After a second I shiver, and then become tense again, trying not to show my fear.

"By the look of those tracks, a big one." Adolfo places his hand on my shoulder.

As I turn to look at him I start to breathe again. Without a word, I stand and grab his hand, my panicked scrambling keeping pace with his stride as we head back to the shelter. The oven tender calmly returns to his baking, and my aunt looks surprised at my reappearance—she didn't notice my absence, but feels the need to cast a quick, disapproving look over me before resuming her conversation.

I stand close to the oven between Adolfo and the chattering women and stare through the timber slats at the footprints in the snow. The oven bricks radiate heat to warm my frozen hands; I move my body closer, the fire drying my wet knees, my snow-soaked sleeves. I tell myself this is why I am so close, almost on top of the oven, my face burning, my nostrils filled with the searing heat. But there is another reason I am drawn to the fire: it feels safer somehow . . . *Il lupo*—the wolf. Dripping fangs, piercing eyes, blood on the snow . . .

I am trembling despite the heat as I battle with frightening images of ripping and tearing teeth. The women are talking in high-pitched voices now that Adolfo has pointed out the footprints.

"I *knew* it," says my aunt excitedly. "This explains a lot of things!"

"Well, it explains the chickens taken from Faustina's," says Adolfo.

Chickens. Thank God! The wolf goes for small prey. I could easily defend myself because I'm a *lot* bigger than a chick—

"And the calf at Alberto's. He's come in hunting beyond the fringe paddocks."

A *calf!* What hope do I have?

My aunt leans forward, her eyes wide and bright: "Maria Stalonti says that a she-wolf once came in and took the bones from her soup pot while she hung out the washing."

"And my husband wouldn't believe me when I told him that two cheeses and a *pancetta* went missing from my *cantina*," says the younger woman.

The older woman of the three offers some serious advice: "You need to keep *all* the doors locked midwinter. My *nipote*—my daughter's little ones—sleep in the attic when they stay...just in case," she says.

Heads nod and there are murmurs of agreement.

Adolfo cuts in, addressing the young woman: "I'd say the only fangs your cheeses and *pancetta* are in are those of the Monetti boys. They're better at opening *cantina* doors than any wolf."

I don't hear him: I only hear the women, the fear. Soup pots, *cantine, attics*? So I was right! All those terror-filled nights when I was sure something prowled my room, when shadows jumped, when I could hear footsteps in the kitchen, when I was shaken, crying, afraid—when I was told emphatically by my aunt not to act the *bambino*, that I was perfectly safe...

"Then there was that soldier—" my aunt again—"the one lost in the woods near here."

I feel the tension rise in the group.

"They *told him* to take the long way round, not to go through the woods, but he ignored them. He was young, had a gun and sword, thought himself invincible. He never arrived at the other end."

Silence.

After a moment my aunt continues: "They found his boots and the metal horseshoes. That's *all* they found."

My mind races. I remember the older men telling me that the wolves circle you from a distance, waiting, watching, following you for hours, not wasting any precious energy. Waiting for *you* to tire. Watching, watching. You—the prey—seeing only a flash of gray through the trees every now and then: just enough to drive you mad. Prowling, circling, taunting. The entire pack silently pacing, waiting for you to weaken, fall, make a mistake. *And then!* Green eyes and great teeth: snarling, ripping, and tearing. *Oh!*

"That soldier disappeared just after the war. The *first* war," says Adolfo to my aunt. "I hardly think whatever took him is still alive. Anyway, Italo will be cleaning his gun by noon, ready for the *posta* tonight. Our beast won't be breathing by morning," the oven tender reassures them, giving me a wink before he returns to his work.

Good. Shoot them, kill them, *kill them all!* I put my hand on my *fionda*, always in my pocket, ready, prepared, making me feel secure. Until I get my hunting knife, my slingshot is my only protection. One day I will hunt the wolf! Heroes hunt wolves. I've read my uncle's books and I know that Africa has its lion, India its tiger— Italy the wolf.

"Can you kill a wolf with a slingshot?" I ask Adolfo. He smiles; my aunt glares.

"Don't be so ignorant, Mario. Get my bread, will you," she says, handing me her basket.

On cue, Adolfo slides out our loaves, tosses them in flour and pushes them to one side on the stone benchtop to cool. He busily removes all the bread from the oven and shuffles in almond pies and *confetti*, for the oven heat is now right for such delicacies. I have learned the order of baking—my friends and I find it useful for timing our visits to the oven—first pizzas, then bread, then cakes and pastries, and lastly fruit. The oven, stoked to full heat at the onset, gradually cools over the hours, its temperature dictating what victuals slide in through the small iron door. There is no need of a thermometer, no need to check the fire. A master oven tender like

Adolfo reads the color of the oven stones to within a few degrees: from black, to ocher, to red, to muted white, the color and searing odor telling all.

But food is the furthest thing from my mind now. Benumbed, I stare out at the snow, at the footprints, my eyes following their line along the embankment, down the crest of the hill to the valley. I feel the weight of the basket on my arm as Adolfo loads the bread, but I only have eyes for the dense, snow-crusted pines on the mountain across from us—was *this* the forest? Are the soldier's boots still there? Again, I shiver.

Incense and warm air meet a blast of icy chill: my face instantly numbs, nostrils stinging and burning with each intake of breath as I exit the church. My body shakes involuntarily, trying to adjust to the drop in temperature as I stand on the smooth stone steps awaiting my uncle. I bend and pull knee-high socks to my thighs, then pocket my hands and shuffle, stamping my feet.

It is six p.m., the end of the *Rosario*, and I am helping my uncle, the priest, to lock up. I stand at the doorway while my uncle straps books together, flicks switches, fiddles with the locks on the church's great iron doors, which are parted in front of me. I am on the edge of two worlds. Inside: warmth, golden light, stained glass, Madonnas— the scent of just-snuffed candles. My favorite of smells! Those sweet, waxy wisps that follow you around the room, enticing you to breathe them in.

My uncle flicks the last switch: blackness. The church interior no longer exists. Only the stained glass window at the far end, above the altar, can be made out—a lonely street lamp reflecting off the snow and lighting it from the outside. What, only a short while before, had been alive with chattering, laughing, condolences and fervid gossip is now dark, abandoned, curtailed. The blackness forces my eyes outside.

Clang! The great doors are pulled to. I watch as my uncle inserts the huge key into the lock. I am in awe of this implement, and my treat is to carry it home. The ancient key is almost as long as my uncle's forearm, and weighs several pounds. It is large, black, majestic. I sometimes wonder how many hands have held it, how many hands have turned it in its great lock, since it was created. Is it as old as the church? Do I have in my hands something once held by a knight, a prince, a crusader? I close my eyes and see a crusader dismounting from his foam-lathered steed in front of me; it is late at night and he is seeking rest in this house of worship . . . the priest handing him the key in honor of his pilgrimage . . . he turns the key, the metal of his sword and chain mail glinting in the flaming torchlight, the red cross on the white background of his standard flickering in the wind behind him . . .

The crunch of grinding metal brings me back to the present: the turning of the lock. I look at the profile of my uncle: large-brimmed hat, books and staff at his feet, and that long dark cloak that drapes weightily over his body from neck to boots; the cloak of a thousand buttons. It seems to give him more height. My uncle is not much taller than me, but slim and muscly—someone called him "wiry" and when he explained the word to me I realized that I'm wiry too because I'm slim and . . . I'm sure soon I'll have muscles. Uncle has a round face that is mostly serious but breaks quickly into a gentle smile, and his eyes are always alert, bright and . . . kind. Small, round spectacles sit atop his nose, and he has a habit of regularly cleaning them, especially when he's concentrating or annoyed. Unlike my father, who has the dark, leathery skin of a farmer, my uncle is fair, and always clean-shaven and elegantly dressed (my aunty makes sure of that). He's good with his hands—he can peel the full skin off an apple in seconds without breaking the coil!—and mostly good-natured...unless I've done something that starts him vigorously rubbing his spectacles.

I watch now as my uncle uses both hands to rotate the great key in its lock: twisting, turning, grinding. Tonight, the freezing cold makes the task even more difficult; the mechanisms of the lock are stiff. It takes three effortful, screeching turns to secure God's house.

I wait. He pushes at the door to check that it is locked and then hands me the great key: it is ice cold and heavy. I study it for a moment, then put the hollow end of the metal pipe to my mouth, purse my lips and blow. I expect the usual shrill whistle, but tonight there is no sound. It is so cold there is no reverberation in the metal. Suddenly, I get a sound. Low, haunting, it floats across the silence. I shiver—it is as if it calls the dead.

My uncle picks up his strapped books and takes up the staff that is resting against the door. Smooth timber, with a sharp metal spike at its finish, the staff serves him to stab the slippery ice and prevent a fall. He clops down the steps and I follow.

We are on the peak of the hill, the highest point of the village of Vastogirardi. No less a position for the most consecrated of buildings. The road ends at the church and spirals downward, twirling around the mountaintop in ever-widening circles. The shortest way to the manse, our house, is via a narrow path that goes directly down the hill, creeping between buildings and intersecting with the road at each of its loops around the peak.

It is dark, silent. There has been a thick fall of snow and it is the time of the evening meal, so no one is about. We are alone. The dim, struggling street lamps—peeking intermittently between buildings and attempting to illuminate the snow—seem our only friends. The fall has been so heavy that, after the road is cleared off, mounds of snow taller than a man have been left at each side.

It is like walking down a walled street, lined with quiet white. We cannot see either side of us, only down, down to the village.

We don't talk in the chill night air. I know the ritual because this is a journey I have made many times with my uncle. I amble along behind him, my eyes focused on the key in my hands, my feet on automatic, following their familiar path. All my attention is on the key. My key. With an air of importance, I swing it by my side, dreaming, pretending to be the keeper of a castle, a fortress—

My uncle has stopped. Suddenly.

I too stop abruptly and look up to see his arm extended toward me—tense, warning. He is a yard or two in front of me: rigid, immobile—looking ahead but with his arm pointing back at me. I know not to move.

I gently raise my eyes, following my uncle's gaze, and I cannot believe what I see. *Il lupo*—the wolf.

The road curves to the left just ahead, and right at this bend, on a six-foot-high snow mound above us, facing us, stands a magnificent wolf. In the strangeness of that moment, my senses acute, I see sharp green eyes, clear, but not unfriendly; a soft black snout on the end of a long nose; whiskers; soft gray and white fur, gangling long legs that look strong, but out of proportion to the body. I am awestruck, but oddly not afraid. He is beautiful, and I am spellbound. I search my emotions for feelings of terror or fear, but they are not there. Only awe. Perhaps this is how it feels just before everything ends.

My uncle takes action, raising the stick in his hand slowly, ever so slowly, his arm remaining rigid and outstretched throughout. He raises it silently until it is pointing directly at the wolf. What is he doing—copying the movement of a hunter with his rifle? Or trying to defend us with the point of the staff should the wolf jump?

36

Now there is no movement at all, from man or beast. Time is as frozen as the snow around me while the wolf and my uncle silently face each other. Who will give in? Win? My uncle is strong-willed, the wolf... *wild*. I try to tell myself that I might die, but no feeling accompanies the thought; it is as if I am somewhere else, watching. In the long distorted seconds, I look at *il lupo*, at his fierceness and beauty, and wonder what he is thinking. Is he deciding whether we live or die? Suddenly, a panicked thought: did my whistle call him? Or is this simple coincidence, my uncle and I blocking his journey home? I hope he *is* on his way home—and not still ravenous, out on the hunt—

Suddenly, silently, *il lupo* leaps. Recoiling on his haunches, he springs forward and upward with no sound, no warning. Over me... his great movement arcing over my head. My head tilts backward, following his path, and I take in the soft underbelly, whispery fur, grayness, and large paws.

I spin around. *Il lupo's* aim was the snow mound on the other side of the road, behind me. He hits the ground, soundlessly once more. I see him turn back to look at us for a split second. Our eyes meet, and then he is gone.

The crackle of the fire, the morning bustle of the kitchen and the smell of frying *pancetta* seep under my bedroom door. And there is something else... the smell of something else that excites my senses. I am hungry, for I have had a busy night, tossing and turning. The nights since my encounter with the beast I have spent half dreaming, half awake: images of wolves, gun shots, chases, hunters and the hunted, hearing the dull, resonating call of the hunter's horn, seeing again and again the clear green eyes of the wolf; not realizing that this was only the beginning of my connection with a four-footed soul that had spared my life—

"*Mario!*" my aunt yells from the next room.

Leaping out of bed, I hurriedly pull up the bedcovers, kick my *pantofole* under the bed and head for the washbasin in the corner of my room. A porcelain bowl on a black iron stand with a jug of water underneath. The jug is creamy yellow, with fine surface cracks and olive branches decorating its interior. I tip the water into the bowl and splash my face. Oh, the iciness! No need to be told to wash quickly. Besides, I'm hungry and restless as a wolf...

In the kitchen my uncle is seated at the long slab table, reading a sacrament as my aunt cooks. *Pancetta* and eggs sizzle in their pans, espresso bubbles on the stovetop, and ah—there's the smell that drew me out: toasted *polenta*! Squares of flat *polenta* soaked in olive oil and garlic—leftovers from the night before—toasted in a wire trap over the fire. The taste: crisp corn, with tomato, garlic and oil oozing as I bite. Such delight!

My uncle addresses me as I sit: "Mario, your aunt says the prosciutto bones are missing from our scrap bins. She is frightened the wolves have come in close." He raises his eyebrows at me.

I hesitate, and then turn to the food on my plate.

My uncle leans into me, as he begins slicing his *pancetta*: "*This* wolf managed to put the lid back on the bin," he says quietly.

Our eyes meet, my face puckering, trying to hold back a smile. It is the way he said it. My aunt cuts in between us, sliding eggs covered in glistening olive oil from the heavy black pan onto our plates.

As she walks off, my uncle whispers: "Throw the bones well away from the perimeter fence, *never* go alone, and *never* after dusk." And then more loudly: "Delicious *polenta*, Ercolina. You're still the *best* cook in the village. And don't worry about the bones, I'll get Mario to take them well away to the Calvaris' and clean near the bins so there's no scent around the house. You'll be safe."

A "humpf!" from my aunt.

At this very moment a handbell is rung, loud and shrill. And a hunting horn blares out, mixing with the sound of excited voices. So, it wasn't a dream! One of the men from the *posta* that has been out each night this week comes into view through the window—crumpled, unwashed, unshaven—leading two mules. On one mule a rifle, provisions, and on the other—

My uncle rushes to the door, and I follow.

"Your food!" screeches my aunt.

Outside, people mill around the man and his mules, offering him rewards of cheese, bread and other gifts. He is dressed in thick *fustagno* pants, a felt *basco* cap, his short sturdy boots overlaid with a *gambale*—leather gaiters that reach from his ankles to his knees, looking like long boots. The hunter's dirty brown jacket partially obscures a thick leather strap that crosses his chest diagonally: it holds a row of bullets (like those worn by the cowboys I've seen in movies) for the double-barreled shotgun that is strapped securely to the side of his mule.

Behind him, slung over the second mule, is a wolf—limp, lifeless, its paws almost touching the ground on either side of the short, stocky mule, its body extended, lean and graceful even in death. The men prod and gasp in awe—it's a big one—then move aside to smoke and tell their hunting stories; the women and children stand back to begin with, afraid, keeping away from the fangs, the long snout. The hunter will parade his kill from village to village for days, receiving food and gifts: he will parade the beast until it begins to rot and smell. Then his triumph will be over. But for now he is smiling, proud—there is much fuss and acclamation, for the people were fearful and he has made them feel safe. He has rid the village of the beast.

The beast.

I walk over to the wolf, my heart sinking, fighting back emotion. I stroke his long gray snout and murmur gentle words to him. Several children come closer, following my lead. A little boy stands just behind me, waiting for me to start prodding, punching *il lupo* in the face, the body, as we children usually do. I can only touch him tentatively, gently.

Thump! The little boy's hand slaps down on the wolf's flank; he then looks back at his audience. He hits again, harder and harder, laughing and becoming braver as he is encouraged by the other children. I grab his hand mid swing. I don't even look at him. He stops. I realize the other children are silent, watching me.

My uncle appears at my side. "This isn't ours, Mario—our friend was paler." He places his hand gently on my shoulder. I love him all the more, for I know it is a lie.

I taste salt: my own tears. Unashamedly, I turn to face my uncle and the others. The men still talk, the hunter laughs, a group of women chatter excitedly and my aunt is at the window—hand clasped to her throat. She will not step outside. There is movement among the children around me: several have taken a step back, afraid of my tears. They are watching me closely. I quickly stroke the wolf and then move through them, back toward the house. I won't stay here. When there are no grownups around, I will tell them of the beast that *I* know.

Close to the house I stop and look toward the mountains, to the craggy peaks and the clusters of snow-draped pines. Between the trees I imagine I see a flash of gray, hear a low, sorrowful howl—and my heart goes there.

The marble benchtop is cool as I lean on it, the underneath of my arms icy: it feels *so* nice. Sliding forward, I am about to place my cheek down against the smooth marble . . .

Ouch!

A jab in the ribs from my aunt: "Stand up straight, *scostumato!*" She hisses.

I slide up to a standing position, surprised that my aunt noticed me; she was so busy fighting with the butcher. Aunt has returned to her battle, so I shuffle behind her and lean over to study the weird-looking head in the window more closely; it *does* seem long . . . or is it my imagination?

"Don't show me that cut, it's rubbish, rubbish, *rubbish!*" says my aunt. "All fat and sinew—I can see it from here! I'm surprised you're allowed to sell such meat! Show me those sausages—no, *there!*" she says, indicating to the butcher the exact bundle. The patient butcher places the sausages on a sheet of paper and raises them to my aunt. She sniffs them long and hard.

"Not fresh," she says, wrinkling her nose.

It's not true. The meat *is* fresh, but my aunt just likes to say it's not. This happens every time we come to the butcher: my aunt complains and complains and wants the best of everything, and makes the poor butcher fuss around her for ages, even when there are people waiting. The butcher doesn't say anything because my aunt buys a lot; my uncle can afford to buy meat regularly and we eat especially well on religious occasions, so the butcher keeps his mouth shut. But I see the face he pulls through the shop window as we approach and he spies my aunt. I think he does it for me to see, so I smile back.

And I *know* the meat is fresh because I heard my uncle tell my aunt that the butcher can't keep it for more than a few days, and that's why each time he sells all his produce the shop stays shut until a new dead sheep or cow is received from the shepherd or farmer. Then the *banditore*—the town crier—tells everyone it's there. He walks around the village blowing on his trumpet and making announcements: "The priest says mass will be at ten a.m. this coming Sunday . . . the butcher has just received two fresh lambs and will be open at eleven o'clock!" The butcher stores the meat underground in the cool of his *cantina* to stop it rotting, and I watch as my aunt sends him downstairs to cut a new piece—nothing in the shop is good enough.

"I want a lovely, tender section of veal, seven pounds at least, large enough to chop into a dozen thick steaks! Your *best*!" she yells after him as he clumps down the steps that lead from a hole in the floor at the back of the shop.

I look around at the hanging sausages, the sheep and cow carcasses on the hooks with their yellowy skin and popping eyes, at the large wooden chopping board on the bench behind where the butcher stands: from here I can see how it dips in the middle, worn down from years of chopping meat and full of millions of cuts and gashes. It looks greasy, with dark stains and little bits of white fat stuck all over it. Bet it stinks.

I look back at the weird head in the shop window. There are several in a row: two pigs' heads, a cow's head, and the other is a goat's head . . . I *think*. The prickly grey-white hair is still on it: my uncle told me that it's easy to get the skin off sheep and pigs but harder with cows and goats—that's why their heads are left hairy. But *is* that a goat? Its ears are flattened so I can't see if they're big and pointy, and a clump of rosemary is covering its nose . . . its nose looks long: too long. *Could it be?* The hair is gray and its mouth is closed so I can't see if the teeth are big . . . I wonder what the hunters do with the wolves after they kill them. I don't ever, ever, *ever* want to eat wolf.

The butcher reappears and thumps a large slab of meat down on the bench. It is huge: a great, solid, bloody mass with thin white skin that is soft and dimples when he prods it for my aunt. She seems pleased that it is soft; I don't know why. It is a bigger chunk of meat than we would normally buy—my aunt is making a special purchase for our Sunday lunch because the bishop is visiting for the first time and we will have a lot of important guests. I usually carry the shopping, but I hope I don't have to carry this—it must weigh a ton!

Thumping the sausages, chops, pigs' trotters and the large chunk of veal into her basket, my aunt slides it along the bench to me. I try to lift it, but can't.

"Why don't you just carry the veal, Mario, you're strong enough," pipes up the butcher. "I'm sure your aunt is young and fit enough to carry the rest," he says, smiling sweetly at her.

With a huff she hands me the large chunk of meat, lifts the much lighter basket and sweeps out the door. I try to get a handle on the package in my arms; it is heavy, cold and . . . sticky! Argh! There is blood seeping through the paper. As I fumble to avoid the blood, the bundle slips through my arms and hits the floor with a rubbery thud. I look at the butcher, panicked: this is expensive meat!

The butcher sweeps around the counter, scoops it up, quickly wraps the chunk in fresh paper and hands it back to me with a smile. "Tell your aunt I won't charge her for the sawdust," he says with a wink as he holds open the squeaky wooden door for me and I exit out into the narrow, cobbled street.

"*I'll do that!* I told you to go get the wood!" says my aunt, pushing me toward our back door.

My aunt bosses me around but she should be *glad* I'm here. One of my friends told me that. He said he heard his mother say that my aunt could not stay living with my uncle, the priest, as *perpetua*, and acting as if she was his partner, if I hadn't come along: a child for her to *pretend* she is mothering. His mother said taking care of me made my aunt look useful and no doubt was a cover for "grave things" going on behind closed doors. I don't know what my friend's mother meant by "grave," but I do know my aunt loves to kill animals—mice, rats, she even tried to kill a stray dog once—so maybe she's known for making graves.

Anyway, she should be glad I'm here, even if I *did* give her her first heart attack. It was when I jumped off the cliff. I didn't mean to. We had all gone out on a mountain picnic, my aunty, uncle, several neighbors and their children. We had settled on a lovely outcrop overlooking a deep, deep valley. No one had been to this spot before. While the others were arranging the picnic I rushed toward the edge to look. As I got closer I could see there was another ledge just below that wasn't visible from our picnic spot, so I sped up, yelled, "Aaah!" and jumped. From my position on the ledge I heard a lot of screaming coming from above me: *loud* screaming and yelling, from the adults! Wondering what was happening, I peeked over the top and saw my aunty on the ground. People were splashing water on her, scrambling about for things or looking aghast toward the cliff—until a woman spotted me. She just pointed and kept screaming. It was then I realized that they thought I had fallen down to the valley! I ended up in *big* trouble and I hadn't even done anything!

"Get out there!" my aunt says, pushing me to the kitchen door.

She turns her eyes back to her prize. On the table the bloodied paper is flayed open, exposing the bundles of meat. My aunt looks at them proudly for a moment: we are one of the few families in the village who can afford to buy such meat and my aunt enjoys people knowing it. Today she gloats a little more than usual, for the centerpiece of the table—the great chunk of expensive veal—is a rare purchase, even for us.

"Elsa Balboni pulled Mario aside and asked him what he was carrying," my aunt calls through to my uncle in the next room. "I yelled to her, in front of all the others in the piazza, that it was for our important meal with the bishop and, yes, it is one *whole* piece of fine veal!"

"Let us be grateful then," calls my uncle, and I hear him quietly click his door shut. This is his way of telling my aunt not to show off, without upsetting her.

My aunt begins scooping up the meat that is to be stored downstairs in the *cantina*. She leaves the large chunk of veal sitting on its paper on the table: it is to be cut and prepared and some of it cooked— this is why I am getting the wood. She thumps down the stairs leading to the cool, underground *cantina* as I exit the back door and go down the outside steps to the woodpile.

I take one look at the woodpile and then at the snow enveloping the yard. A new fall! I wonder if there are any tracks? My aunt will be some time in the *cantina*, fiddling with the jars and sacks: she never just stores things when she goes down, she has to shift and rearrange.

I walk down to the back wall, all the while looking for tracks in the snow on the slope leading up to the mountain peaks. I can make out small tracks, maybe a rabbit's. *Oh!* There's a trail of cat pawprints spinning and twisting in a line with a bird's prints dancing around them—the bird prints disappear a little farther on—he got away! Or perhaps... Nothing much here: nothing big. I climb up onto the wall. Some trees are speckled with blossoms because it is early spring. It looks beautiful: dots of pink and red among the white. We still get snowfalls in the spring because we're so high up in the mountains. It is quiet here with all the white, *so* quiet, and so peaceful: I am always amazed how the snow muffles all sound, as though God has thrown a big soft quilt over the world. I look up towards the peaks and wonder if—

"*Argh!*" comes a scream from the house: my aunt!

I leap from the wall and run toward the woodpile—surely I wasn't *that* long!

There is another scream, loud and uncontrolled, and then wailing. I can hear my uncle's voice trying to calm her. This isn't about wood—something is *seriously* wrong! I bolt past the wood and fly up the stairs.

"Mario, come with me!" yells my uncle as I enter the kitchen. He heads off into the corridor.

I stop for a minute to take it all in. My aunt has her hands to her head, wailing, and I follow her eyes to the table. The large chunk of precious, expensive meat is no longer there. Nor is the paper it sat on. What *is* on the table is a long, thin streak of blood that leads to the far end. I look around at the floor under this end: there is the paper, but still no meat. My eyes follow the bloodied, brown streak that leads from the paper across my aunt's spotless kitchen floor, out the door and into the room my uncle just entered. I race after him.

"Get the flashlight, Mario!" he calls to me.

"I *told* you . . . I told you to shut it!" wails my aunt.

She's referring to the trapdoor to the roof. My uncle now stands at the base of the narrow, rickety steps that lead up to the trapdoor, to the area between the ceiling and the roof that we call our attic. It is not a room, but simply a space between the highest, peaked part of the roof—where you can just stand—to the lowest point where the ceiling meets the roof. With no lights, it is like being in a low, dark pyramid with a roof that slopes down into nothing. It's great for hiding things. First of all, my aunt *never* comes to the attic—there might be mice—and secondly, it is so dark that even with a flashlight it is hard to find things in among the dust, the spider's webs, the timber struts, and the hard-to-reach sloping edges. Even the smallest person can't get in closer than twelve feet from this edge, so it is great to shove stuff in there with a stick. Though sometimes hard to get that stuff back out.

"You should have shut it!" wails my aunt again, slapping her cheeks with her hands.

I look at my uncle and then at the steps in front of him. The trail of blood slaps and splatters its way up each rise. Who, what . . . ? *Rusciu!*

"Get it! *Get it!*" screams my aunt, pointing up the steps.

Rusciu is the cat my uncle got: a big, fat ginger cat that is as tough as any village dog and not much smaller in size. His stomach is so big he waddles when he walks, he's so strong he knocks you off balance when he brushes your leg hard, and he is so tall his head reaches my knee: yet, despite his size, he moves like a rocket when chasing things—especially mice. And this was why my uncle got him—to kill mice: the mice that were in our garden, in the *cantina*, throughout the house, and especially the mice breeding in the attic. This was why the trapdoor to the attic had been left open these past few days, so the cat could do his job: get in there, into the dark corners, and kill the mice. My aunt didn't want the door left open, she wanted us to lock the cat in—permanently—with the mice. My uncle refused.

I named this big, fat, cuddly cat Rusciu, which is Abruzzo for "red." I love to play with him, my uncle loves to train him for the hunt, and my aunt loves to hate him. And right now she might have good reason. It seems Rusciu has gone too far as a hunter, stalking and killing my aunt's fine chunk of veal.

"Move, Don Ruggero!" screams my aunt, prodding my uncle in the back. She must be upset to do this; she is usually respectful to my uncle.

I hand him the flashlight, and he signals for me to follow him up the stairs.

It's dark. So dark that for a moment we can't see anything in the attic, then slowly things start to take shape. My uncle flashes the light around. I can hear something behind us in a far corner, and can just make out something shifting . . . as I stare, two silvery orbs appear in the blackness, looking straight at me. Eyes!

"Uncle, *there*!" I say, pulling at his sleeve.

He flashes the torch around and there, crouched half on top of the slab of meat, claws dug in deep and hissing at us, eyes glittering and flashing in the light, is the great ginger cat. He is clever: he has positioned himself way, way down at the low, narrow edge of the roof and will be hard to reach.

"Get the *stanga*!" my uncle yells down to my aunt. This is the long carved branch we keep by the back door to use for whacking chestnuts out of the tree.

She runs off and returns, clumping up the stairs. "Where is it?" she asks in a fierce whisper after handing my uncle the stick. She peers into the attic but does not come up past shoulder height. I am holding on to the flashlight and trying to follow my uncle's movements with the *stanga*.

My uncle shoves the pole at the cat; it howls and drags the meat to the left. My uncle moves the pole to the left and tries to scoop the meat forward: the cat sits right on top of the meat, hanging on for grim death. My uncle tries to move in from the right, whacking the stick down behind the meat and trying to maneuver it toward us. The cat hisses loudly, and drags the meat farther back. My uncle gets the stick behind the meat and . . . yes! He pulls it forward, but the cat again pounces, locks its claws in, and yanks it back. It is amazing that he made it up the steep stairs with such a heavy load, so I figure he is not going to give in easily! My uncle sweeps with the stick again, *thwack!*

"Wait... something's coming, something's coming..." says my uncle excitedly, dragging a weight toward him across the dark floor. There is a flapping noise and several papery items fly into view.

"Comics!" my uncle says, surprised, and then quickly tries to push the bulk of the stack back into the dark before my aunt sees.

"*What?*" yells my aunt, who is agitated enough. She looks at me: "Where did you get those comics from, you *scostumato*! I'll burn them when I get my hands on them!"

My uncle looks taken aback; she doesn't normally call me names in front of him. I'm glad he heard. My aunt calls me lots of names when my uncle isn't around: her favorite is Mariolino, which means "little Mario," but that's not why she says it. She uses Mariolino because it's so similar to *mariolo*, which is a nasty word for "prankster": she pretends to make a mistake sometimes and uses the second word. When she's really mad she doesn't try to pretend, and says openly that I am a *mariolo* doing *marachelle*—pranks—which makes me *scostumato*! My aunt thinks comics are "cheap rubbish" and that I should be reading religious books, so I store my comics—all the exciting and hilarious adventures of Cocco Bill, Tin Tin, Tarzan and Ficcanaso—in the attic where I can sit undisturbed, reading them by flashlight while I chew my—

Oh! I wish my uncle wouldn't sweep *over there*. I really wish—

Clunk! He has hit something metal. My uncle's focus is off the cat—which is still emitting a low, rumbling growl—as he concentrates on sliding his new discovery out into the light. But he stops suddenly.

"What is it?" asks my aunt, straining her neck to see around him.

"Nothing, just rubbish. Mario, keep the flashlight on the cat, please," he says.

Phew! It's bad enough that the crinkly pages of my comics make loud flapping noises each time my uncle swings the *stanga*—causing Tarzan to ripple in the breeze right near my aunt's face—I couldn't bear for her to see the contents of my little tin as well!

My uncle leaves the tin and goes back to the cat. He sweeps at the meat again: the cat grabs it. Leaning forward, my uncle digs and rattles the stick further back, stretching himself low, moving over and behind the veal, and managing to pull it forward: the cat digs in and pulls the meat back. Uncle hands me the pole, I lower myself and slide forward, trying to rattle and sweep with the stick. No luck. Each time the cat snatches at the meat and pulls it away. My uncle tries again several times; finally, he gives up.

"He's hungrier than we are," my uncle says gently, and signals for me to go ahead of him to the trapdoor.

My aunt gives a cry and descends the steps muttering under her breath.

Rusciu didn't come out of hiding for ten days. But then, I guess he didn't need to: he was full. And after that he kept out of broom-reaching distance around my aunt. My uncle inspected the contents of my little tin that he brought down from the attic and asked me, well away from my aunt, what the oddly shaped white lumps were. I told him it was my chewing gum—my chewed pieces, ready for reuse. I was surprised he wasn't angry. Gum was disapproved of by grownups, who saw it as rubbishy stuff and *modern*. The American soldiers had brought it with them during the war, but it was a while before it was sold in Italy, so none of the adults here had chewed it when they were young—which is what made it so cool. Nothing infuriated my aunt more than to see me chewing—she hated *everything*

American. I even think she would have been less angry if she'd seen me with one of my uncle's cigarettes that my friends and I choked on behind the barn. Then again, maybe not.

A few days later I found my little tin, its contents intact, back in the attic next to my comics. I love my uncle. But I still knew never to be caught chewing *outside* the attic, and I didn't get away with having the comics, not completely. My aunt didn't get to burn them, but she *insisted* my uncle encourage me to adopt better hobbies; so now I've been told I have to have lessons—lessons *outside* of school—in something.

My uncle won't tell me what. He likes to do this: he will tell me I am going to do something soon but won't tell me what it is, hoping I will ask questions; but I don't fall for that. I only asked him *once* what these lessons were—or maybe twice. And one day I asked him several times whether the lessons were anything to do with comics—I had overheard my aunt telling him to send me to religious lessons, and my uncle replied that if I liked comics I should be encouraged in the things I have a *leaning* toward. I asked again a few days later, but he still wouldn't tell me, so I got my friends to ask when I wasn't there: that didn't work either. So now I'm hoping that I'm going to comic-reading lessons!

Oh! That gave me a fright: Rusciu just brushed up against me in the dark. He has come out of his sleeping corner in the attic, and wants a rub. His purring is loud. I flash the light onto his fat, waddling belly covered in ginger stripes. I love him even more now. We have something in common: neither of us likes my aunt. And Rusciu has forced her to take a different route to the butcher's. My aunt is trying to avoid Elsa Balboni, and has been for weeks. If Elsa's in the street or at the market and I move in her direction, my aunt pulls me back sharply in case I am prompted to answer any questions. I don't know how it got around, but within hours of the incident all the kids in our street knew that my aunt had suffered the humiliation of no meat for the important meal with the bishop—all because of an overtrained cat.

Yes, I *love* Rusciu. And we often sit together in the attic, but I am glad cats don't eat chewing gum: anyway I've got it safely in my tin.

Il Pittore **THE PAINTER**

I watch his gnarled hand gripping the brush as he strokes up and down, up and down, dragging and pulling, dragging and pulling. The blue is bright and luminescent as the moist bristles stroke all the way up Mary's robe until they reach the circle of gold around her neck. He has knobs on his fingers, lumps where the knuckles should be and his hands are all bent and twisted...And he still hasn't looked at me.

I glance upward from the Madonna's faded face to the ceiling of the tiny *cappella*; it looks like a playhouse in which someone has put an altar, and its walls are covered in murals. The chapel was easy to find because it stands alone in a field, but it was a long walk here from the village, so far that I'm sure I'll miss soccer with my friends. The country people use the *cappella* when they can't get to the village church—they come here to remember a death or a saving, a miracle. It is one of several church places that my uncle looks after, and today he has ordered me here to meet this old man.

"Don't know what your uncle wants from me!" the owner of the hand says gruffly without looking away from his work.

I jump as he says this and put the Tarzan comic I was about to proffer back inside my jacket.

I have to learn to paint. *Paint!* That's what the lessons are. I don't want to do it because it has *nothing* to do with comics and, worse still, the teacher is an old, old man, and there are stories that he has a mad son with crazy red eyes who dribbles, mumbles and— when his father isn't looking—chops off and eats one of your fingers. They say he lives in a cave. *What if we have to paint there?*

I clunk my *tazza*—cup—down hard on the wooden surface of the kitchen table; my uncle flashes me a "don't ask again" look as I begin to open my mouth. I shut it, and stare across at him. He looks relaxed as he sits, reading his *messale*. No wonder. He doesn't have to go to a madman's cave.

I tried to get out of it. I told my uncle that I can't paint—he told me it was time to learn; I told my aunt that I would ruin all my good clothes—she told me that I'd be wearing a smock, and then dared me to come home if I *did* get paint on my clothes. And then I heard my uncle tell my aunt that doing this would "*prendere due piccioni con una fava*"—get two pigeons with one broad bean— and now I know I won't get out of the lessons. The old man—Signor Berardo—is a *sacrestano* at my uncle's church and his wife just died (no wonder—she had even more wrinkles than him!) and my uncle says he is lonely and therefore the lessons will be good for both me *and* him.

If he's lonely, why doesn't he live in the cave with his son? That way I'll keep my fingers and be able to go to a real teacher and learn how to make comics. Already I trace the pictures in my comic books and put new words in the *nuvoletta*—the speech bubbles—to tell different stories. I just need to learn how to draw Tarzan's arms and legs so they don't look like sausages when I change their position from the picture underneath: that's all I need to learn. How can an old man who fixes cracked walls and colors in the Madonna's dress teach me that?

And Signor Berardo is not only old, he's unfriendly. At the chapel, where I was told to meet him, he didn't look at me once—just muttered that he used to be a painter, didn't like to teach, didn't know what my uncle wanted, told me to come to his house tomorrow, and then dismissed me with a wave. But I'm sure I saw him look up as I stepped down from the doorway.

On the way home from the chapel I checked the address he had given me: it's in the middle of the village. Nowhere near a cave.

"How long do I have to go for?" I whine to my uncle, who is being poured an espresso by my aunt.

"I've told you: you can decide that with Signor Berardo today. I would think at least an hour or two—no more than three: you'll be back soon enough," says my uncle.

"No, I mean how long do I have to go for—for *all* of them?" I say.

"He means how long does he have to continue taking lessons," snaps my aunt. "*Ungrateful!*" she mouths at me as she passes, heading back to the stove with the *caffettiera* and clanging it down onto the black iron frame.

"You'll go for as long as it takes you to learn, and for as long as Signor Berardo can keep at it, though he's fit and lively enough. He's old but strong as an ox—I've seen how he works in the church," finishes my uncle.

"Mario will shorten his life, don't worry," says my aunt. "More *orzo?*"

* * *

The room smells funny. And it's dark. I'm at Signor Berardo's.

Something is moving in the far corner, by the window. I think it's him: I *hope* it's him. I heard a muffled *"Vieni—vieni!"* when I knocked, but when I do enter I am blinded by the piercing light from the single, thickly glazed window, making it even harder for my eyes to adjust to the dinginess around me.

Slowly, I start to make things out. Shelves, lots of shelves, some of them bent and collapsing and covered in things: in fact, the whole room is full of stuff, every space occupied by books, cans, brushes, stacks of paper, jars, scores of canvases leaning against the walls, and near the window there is a row of mortars and pestles like my aunt uses in the kitchen. Maybe he likes cooking, but there doesn't seem to be a kitchen...Oh! There's a tap over there, and some dishes, an iron pot, and what looks like a stove, but this too is covered in jars and brushes and...what's that smell? The place looks like it should smell dirty—it's dark and dusty and grimy—and there's a strong smell, but it's a *clean* smell. And there's something else: a nice greasy smell like the oil in my uncle's car. I like it. But what's that *clean* smell? It makes me want to suck it up, so I sniff again: out loud.

"Turpentine," says the figure by the window.

Oh, *turpentine*! What's that?

"Turpentine is the resin from pine trees," the figure says, as if reading my mind! "It dissolves anything oil-based, like paints."

"Oh," I say.

"And how long do you intend standing there?" I am asked curtly.

I approach the table. The old man I met in the chapel is bent over it, mixing something in a small white bowl. He's not looking at me, so I can take in the things around him as I get closer. The mortars are full of colors: beautiful bright colors! Several contain a glossy, pasty mixture that offers up a brilliant red, blue, purple or orange: the mortars farther from him are full of little bits of dull brown that look like seeds—

"Pigments," he says, still not looking at me. "So, what do you want?"

Doesn't he *remember*? We only spoke yesterday! Oh, maybe he's mad like his son.

"Well, my uncle wanted—" I begin.

"I know what your uncle wants!" he spits. "I'm asking what *you* want."

Is he asking what I want to *do*? Don't think I should mention comics. I look around for something.

"Could we do a picture like that...today?" I ask, pointing to a painting on the wall behind him. If we can get this over today, maybe next week we can do comics.

Signor Berardo slowly turns his head. He doesn't say anything for a minute as he stares at the picture, and then: "Caravaggio." He looks directly at me for the first time. "You want to start and finish a Caravaggio—" he strokes his cheek as if he's considering it—"*today?*"

I nod.

The old man's lip begins to curl, and his face squints up as if he's in pain. As he turns from me, I'm sure I catch a smile.

"You're ambitious at least," he says, going back to his mixing.

I think that's good.

"But I can see we're going to be here a hell of a long time."

That doesn't sound so good.

"It doesn't have to be that *big*," I say, looking at the large work behind him.

I don't know what a Caravaggio is, but the people in it look real: so real they're scary. They even have wrinkles, and as I move closer, I see that the foot of one of the men is filthy. Yuck. I don't want to paint dirty toenails. The picture is not on a canvas and looks like it's made from paper: a corner of it is yellowing and ripped.

I must be pulling a face because Signor Berardo, who is watching me, says: "Changed your mind about Caravaggio? He'll turn in his grave." The old man leans towards a pile of books and pulls two out. He hands them to me. "Have a look through these while I finish here. And you can look around the studio but *do not touch*. Understand?"

I nod and look for somewhere to sit. Spotting a chair with a broken wicker back, I shift a stack of papers from its seat, revealing a cushion that is thick with dust and covered in colorful splats of dried paint. I like the bright colors: there are flicks of paint all over the chair. I wish I had a chair like this... I wish I had a room like this! Full of interesting stuff, somewhere you could make things and it wouldn't matter if it all got messy and covered in paint. There's no way my aunt would let me: she'd have one of her pretend heart attacks if she even *looked* inside this room! Wish I could show her.

I slap open the first book: it's about Renaissance and baroque art. I don't know what this means, but it sounds *old*...and boring. I sigh, and begin lazily flicking over one page, and then another, and then—

Bosoms. Big, bulbous bosoms and—oh! There's not even anything covering *down there*. The piece of material over *that* part is sheer and you can see straight through it.

I quickly turn the page, back to Madonnas and angels. But I can't stop thinking about the bosoms. Does Signor Berardo know they're in here? Did he give me the wrong book? I flick through the next few pages. The paintings are like the ones I see in church: disciples, angels, Madonnas...wait! I think the bosom picture had an angel in it: but how can that be? How could a naughty picture have an angel in it? I'd better just go back and check...

Yes, it looks like an angel in the picture! And her bosom is *so* big, but it was the angel I was checking...oh! How could she be sitting naked like that showing off her...and how could this be in a proper book? Perhaps the fabric isn't see-through at all and it is something else I can see underneath. I'll just have a closer look—

"There are other pictures in the book," says Signor Berardo.

I jump and slap the book shut in the same movement. How did he know? He's got his head down and can't see my lap from there; *how did he know?*

"I was, um...looking at the angel," I say. My face feels hot.

"Yes, she's *quite* some angel!" he says, smiling to himself.

I think he's making fun of me. But it's not my fault if he gives me a naughty book. My aunt would have something to say to him if she knew the pictures he was showing me. And then there's his messy room...I think I will enjoy my lessons more than I thought.

My teacher is still busy, so I slide off the chair and go to the canvasses by the wall. One is glistening and looks wet: it must be newly painted. Leaning on its side, I can't quite see what it is, but I like the lumps of glossy paint around the edges—greasy, shiny swirls that look like icing on a cake. It smells nice. I bend to one side to try to make it out. The swirls are so glossy I just want to touch them—but they're wet. Or maybe they're not? Some paint looks wet even when it's dry. I'll just touch one corner lightly with my finger...

It's wet. I jump at the indent I've made.

"Thank you for your signature," says Signor Berardo, who is right behind me this time. "Your first lesson is that *don't touch* actually means *don't touch*. Let's begin before you do any further damage. Pull that chair over here."

I drag my wicker chair to his table. Now I can see that the mixture in the white bowl is runny and gold—it's beautiful! Next to the bowl stands a wooden *putto*—a cherub like the ones you see in church. There are three other similar *putti* in a row on the windowsill, their paint dull and faded. I now realize what the gold mixture is for: they each have a faded gold sash around their middles. It's paint for the *putti*. I have seen murals being repaired, but it never occurred to me that someone had to keep fixing and repainting all the statues and every little figure in all the churches. Signor Berardo is about to make the cherubs beautiful again.

He covers the dish of gold and places it on the sill beside the mortars, and the *putto* gets moved back beside his friends.

"What do you think an artist is, Mario?" he asks.

"Someone who paints pictures."

"Yes, and . . . ?" he asks.

"Someone who draws things?"

"Yes, and before this?"

I look at him blankly.

"I'll tell you a secret." He leans over to me. "A great painter is a great alchemist. He mixes and makes things—like a wizard."

A wizard!

He passes me one of the mortars full of unground bits. "What do you think this is?"

"Food?" I proffer.

"I already told you—pigments!" He says excitedly, "*This* is a beautiful color, waiting to be born!"

I look back at the dull brown bits rattling around in the mortar as he shakes it. "Beautiful . . . *brown?*" I ask.

"Watch." He begins to grind with the pestle. The bits have become a dry, pasty lump of brown. After a moment he picks up a small yellow glass bottle. "Watch," he says again, dropping something from the bottle into the bowl.

Purple! The brown bits have become bright purple! It's incredible, just like, like . . .

"Magic!" the old man says, studying my face. "But it's not really magic. It's all about chemicals and their reactions to one another. If you can learn and understand this you will be a great painter." He continues, sliding the mortar under my nose: "Leonardo da Vinci studied for twelve years in his *bottega*, which was like a school for artists. The first *ten years* were mainly spent learning how to mix and make paints."

"Couldn't he buy them from the store?" I ask.

"The *bottega was* the store. Nowadays you can easily buy your paints from a store," he says, watching me closely, "if you want to be an *average* artist. But if you want to be a *great* artist, *ah!* That's different. Great artists know the secrets of alchemy and create *their own colors.* That is why you will hear people say 'the red of Rembrandt' or 'the pinks of da Vinci'—great artists were known by their particular colors. It was like their trademark, it was part of who they were as artists."

"Oh," I say.

"When Michelangelo painted his great frescoes, he had lots of helpers there mixing the colors. He would walk along each day and test each color and would say, 'No good, start again,' 'Add more blue' or 'Rubbish, throw it out.' Each color had to be *just right:* just the right shade, just the right hue, or it would not be a *Michelangelo* color."

"But isn't red *red?*" I ask.

"Is green green? How many greens do you see when you walk outside in nature, Mario? How many different greens in the grasses, the plants, the leaves, the stems? Besides shape, how do you distinguish the different trees? By their different *shades* of green—there are hundreds of greens."

"*Hundreds!*" I repeat.

"Just as there are hundreds of reds and hundreds—maybe even thousands—of shades of each different color. It all depends on the shape of each individual pigment that makes up the color, and how these pigments are separated from each other or bound together. It is all about pigments, mediums and light—*alchemy*."

"Like mixing things in cooking?" I ask.

He pauses for a moment, then says: "Yes, like a cook, an alchemist uses plants, animals, oils, even eggs."

"Eggs!" I say.

"But enough! We will do more on alchemy *next* lesson. Now to drawing. Any good painting begins with skilled drawing, so that's where we'll start."

"Oh good!" I jump in: "Because I like wizards and mixing stuff, but I don't really need to paint. I just need to draw Tarzan's legs."

There is a silence in the room.

"Let's begin, shall we?" my teacher says, after studying me for a moment. "Now, do you know what perspective is?"

"The legs don't have to be real like yours, with dirty toenails," I say.

"I beg your pardon?"

I point to the painting on the wall behind him: "The legs don't have to look real like the way you draw them."

This time Signor Berardo laughs out loud. "That, my boy, is a *Caravaggio*, as I told you. Don't you know what that means?"

I shake my head.

"Sadly, it is *not* one of my paintings; I only wish it were. Caravaggio was the artist who painted this work. For me he is the greatest artist—the greatest *realist*—who ever lived. He was also a wild boy, Mario, who loved tennis, partying and slaying people with swords—aside from being a genius."

"Oh!" I like the bit about swords!

"He painted at the end of the Renaissance, and was the first artist to paint *real* people—peasants and people in the streets—in their natural state, and if you'd got past page eight— " he points to the book I was looking through and I feel my face burn again— "you would have seen more of his great works."

Signor Berardo seems suddenly irritated by his mixing spatula, which is lying paint-covered on the table: he begins cleaning it with a torn, graying rag he has pulled from a nail on the wall. I get a whiff of that nice turpentine smell again.

"So what drawing have you done, Mario?" he asks, still rubbing.

"I do a lot of tracing. I'm a good tracer," I say. "I trace comics, and I like to rub coins and put the tracings on my wall—"

He interrupts me: "First lesson: no more tracing. Stop tracing and *start drawing*. Start to see things as they really are, then train your brain to connect these images with your hands and you will be a great artist. But it all takes time and *practice*." He looks back at the Caravaggio. "Only a rare few of us are bequeathed that gift of genius where the ability comes almost naturally."

"Does that mean I have to have a lot of lessons?" I ask.

He doesn't answer, just slides a piece of thick, wrinkly paper in front of me, plonking one of the wooden *putti* on a corner.

"Begin by drawing this," he says.

"But . . . it's a cherub."

The old man snatches the pencil I've just picked up from my hand. "What do you want with this?" he says, shaking the pencil at me and then tossing it onto the table. "Throw it away!"

He gets up and walks to the fireplace. "Come here," he says, pulling a piece of charcoal from the coals and handing it to me. "Learn to draw with different things. There are many things in nature, all around you, that will help you become a great artist. That pencil will only limit you. Next lesson I will take you out and show you just what there is around you that you are not yet seeing."

Back at the table, Signor Berardo picks up the *putto* and holds it upside down in front of me. I look from the *putto* to my black-stained hand gripping the charcoal, to the curling yellow paper, and then back to the upside-down cherub.

"Now start drawing," he says.

"I *know* you didn't wipe those dishes," yells my aunt, "because the tea towel is the only thing in the entire kitchen that doesn't have your black handprints on it!"

My aunt is never happy. At least she doesn't have to wash the tea towel. Anyway, artists are messy, and I'm now an artist. Signor Berardo told me so. And they have to look at naughty pictures. Signor Berardo didn't tell me *that*, but he looks at them, and he did say to watch and learn from what he does. My aunt has just arrived home from shopping, and I want to tell her about Caravaggio, and Leonardo and Michelangelo and the Sistine Chapel, but she doesn't like history, so I'll have to wait to tell my uncle.

After I had drawn my cherub, Signor Berardo showed me how to use charcoal on paper to make shadows, and how to rub it with my fingers. He told me that my hands had chemicals that made the charcoal melt, and that this made my hand not just a tool, but part of the mixture on the page. Then he showed me more books about great artists and he asked me what I liked. We talked for a long time and he spoke to me like I was grown up. I liked it. And then, as I was leaving, he said: "Come next week and we will see what we can do with Tarzan, but stop copying and start drawing!"

I watch my aunt as she thumps a slab of prosciutto onto the table and begins slicing it. I bet she doesn't know how old Caravaggio is, or what those pig...pig...those funny little shapes that make up colors are.

"So, *did* you learn anything, or are you simply wasting your uncle's money?"

I want to tell her about the bosoms, but I can't. If I did, I wouldn't be able to go back to my lessons and see more of them.

"Rabbits make glue," I say, wanting to surprise her. "Signor Berardo showed me how to stretch a canvas into its frame and paint it with rabbit's glue."

"Well, that's a great lesson in art!" She pauses for a few seconds. "And just how do these rabbits make their glue?"

I hadn't thought of this. "I guess it must come out of them somewhere," I say, wanting to change the subject. "And next week we're doing Tarzan's legs," I finish.

My aunt stops, places one hand on the prosciutto, the other on her hip: "What *rubbish!*" she spits. "I'm speaking to your uncle when he gets back!"

I don't know what we're doing out here: somewhere in the countryside. My fingers are sticky and the stuff on them smells tangy, and a lot more is oozing down the side of the tree. Yuck. I still don't know what being outside has to do with painting.

"Are you watching here or still looking behind you?" says Signor Berardo.

It's our third lesson and the thing worrying me is the mound of boulders behind us that creates a small rocky hill: as we walk around it I have to keep checking that there are no caves.

"What did I just say?" asks my teacher, who has seen me looking away again.

"That you use this sticky stuff—"

"Resin," he corrects.

"For making paints?" I ask. I hadn't really been listening. "Oh, almonds!" I cry, looking up at the branches of the tree for the first time.

"Yes, almonds. As I was saying, tree resin can be used as a base for making paints. The resin of the almond and cherry trees is a particularly good medium."

He picks a white-petaled flower from near his foot and begins dusting off its yellow center into the resin. He rubs it together until it becomes a thick paste.

"Add oil and you will have here a beautiful, vivid yellow. Nature is the great laboratory of the alchemist!" he says, sweeping his arms around him.

"Signor Berardo?"

"Yes?"

"Do you . . . do you have any *children?*" I ask.

"What has that got to do with resin?" he says. And then, looking at me closely: "Have you heard stories?"

I shake my head vigorously.

"Yes, I have a son. He doesn't live here anymore though. The people here weren't too kind to him. Children in particular can be cruel. My son is an albino."

I think that means he's from another country, so maybe he went back there. I'm just glad he no longer lives *here.*

"Is Albino far away?" I ask.

No answer.

"Does he paint like you?" I ask, feeling happier.

Signor Berardo drops his arms by his sides: his body seems to have sagged. "He never learned to paint. That is one of my great regrets: that I never spent the time with him when he was young,

66

that I never passed on my trade. I would like to teach him to paint one day . . . if we ever meet up again."

I suddenly feel very, very sad. I look at Signor Berardo's worn trousers, his knitted cardigan with holes where the stitches are missing, his old, papery skin, and I wonder where his son is. He is no longer looking at me, but out across the hills, as if he is staring at something far, far away.

It's not true what my aunt said about Signor Berardo when she argued with my uncle after that first lesson: that he is an ignorant old farmer, a countryman who has no education and cannot teach me art. My uncle replied that the old man has his heart and soul in his art and that this is what he will "bequeath to Mario." *Bequeath!* That is the same word my teacher used about that great artist who was "bequeathed" his skills! Maybe I won't keep tracing after all.

"So how does the resin turn into paint?" I ask Signor Berardo, carefully scooping from the resin he has cupped in his hand. It is the first time I have touched the old man—I am leaning my cupped hand against his arm—and he seems gently surprised.

"Can you show me, because I'd like to paint legs like Caravaggio," I say.

You can draw with *bricks*!

The whole afternoon with Signor Berardo has been wonderful: collecting resin from trees, oil from nuts, and crushing rocks and flowers to make beautiful, beautiful colors. He showed me how you can use certain stones, rocks, chalk and bits of red brick, as well as charcoal, to draw. He told me to look, and look and look all around me—at nature: her light, her colors, her elements and all the wondrous things she offers us. He told me that paints *can* be made with bought mixtures and chemicals, but that he likes to make them directly from nature, to go outside and collect natural substances for color—even insects! *Bugs!*

I thought my teacher had *really* gone mad when he picked up some ugly, crawling red insects from a stone wall near the chapel and told me that they made beautiful color. Ugly, stinky, crawling bugs!

I watched with amazement as he crushed some flower petals into his hand, added almond tree resin, and then crushed the beetles into it. As he rubbed his palm with his fingers, the mixture became a solid, rubbery-looking ball, and he said: "Watch what happens now." He dropped in some nut oil and the whole mixture became a *brilliant dark red!* The most beautiful, dark purple-red I have ever seen, richer than the darkest, reddest plum! From *bugs!*

"You see how the oil has separated all the pigments so they each catch the light and give it back to you? This is how you see the color, and how much oil you put in will change that color."

I watched, fascinated, as he added more oil and the shade of red changed. He then spread the red mixture onto the stone wall in front of him, where it stood out bright and glossy, and gestured that it was my turn. I rubbed together petals, resin, squashed in the creepy bugs, and watched in amazement as the vivid red jumped out at me from the wall where I had wiped it. It was beautiful.

My teacher said: "See this color now? See this red? It is *your* particular red, and it will be there forever."

I'm collecting eggs. The cracked ones my aunt can't use. And cockroaches—I think they'll make a nice brown. My aunt tipped out the box of beetles I was breeding under my bed, just because some escaped into the kitchen, so now I have to collect more. She doesn't know anything about being an artist.

"Mario, Mario . . . *porco!*" calls my friend Luciano angrily.

Il Pittore

Enrico has scored a goal because I wasn't watching: we're playing soccer in the piazza and I was busy trying to tell my friends you can make color out of beetles. They wouldn't believe me. The other day I tried to explain to them that Signor Berardo is a nice man and that his son isn't mad; it's just that the kids teased him and he went away to live somewhere else. They wouldn't believe that either, and they still scare each other with stories about the cave. And when I explained pigments to them, they got bored and walked away. I like to show off and use the word "pigment" in front of my friends. I have to—my teacher said that if I don't use it when I talk about color then I'm not an artist.

I'm excited because in my pocket I have chalk and some browny-yellow rock that looks like the stuff Signor Berardo said makes a color called ocher: I found it on my hunt up the hill this morning. I'm not sure if it is but it looks like it, and I know my teacher will be proud of me. Signor Berardo told my uncle that in three short weeks I have learned much, and that I am so keen he is sure I will become a great alchemist, and maybe even a great painter. I'd like to tell my friends that I'll soon be a wizard, but no doubt they wouldn't believe that either.

Kicking the ball out from under Enrico, I race toward our goal by the wall, scooting the ball in front of me, when there's a sudden *Dong! . . . Dong! . . . Dong!*

The church bells! Strange—it is not time for a service, and there is no wedding or church event today. I always know, because my uncle talks of these things at home. It must mean something else . . .

"Mario, Mario! *Here!*" yells Luciano, and I kick the ball to him.

He takes it and kicks it past the goalkeeper and hard against the wall—we scream with joy!

"We win! *We win!* Three-two!" I yell.

Running out of time, we had all decided that the next goal would win the match, and so our motley "team"—Luciano, Renzo and I—are the victors.

"Have to go!" I shout, waving to my friends and heading home. I'm already late for lunch and my aunt and uncle will be waiting.

My aunt is standing out the front of our house. As I get closer, I realize she doesn't look angry. Strange. But something is wrong.

"I'm sorry, Mario," she says as I reach the door, "there's some sad news . . ."

What does she mean? I rush past her, inside; my uncle is not at the table.

"Where's Uncle?" I ask, suddenly panicked.

"He's at Signor Berardo's house," she says.

I look at her face, and it suddenly hits me. The bells ringing at no particular time . . . I remember what that means: a death.

"No!" I say, looking at my aunt and waiting for her to reassure me it's not true.

She doesn't.

"*NO!*" I howl, pushing past her and slumping onto the front step. Several tears stain the stone as I hang my head, and then there's something else, a tiny drop of red. I realize I have squeezed the yellow ocher in my hand so hard that it has pierced my skin.

Signor Berardo would say I have made another beautiful color.

I don't trace anymore. I draw. Tarzan's legs look a bit better, and sometimes I smudge his feet with charcoal so they look dirty. Well, it would be dirty in the jungle.

And I keep mixing things. Colors. My aunt even lets me keep some beetles: in a box that has a tight lid with books on top, so that none escape.

I never learned to paint—Signor Berardo didn't have enough time left in his life to teach me—but one day I will learn, and when I am grown up and can paint properly like Caravaggio, *then* I will make good comics.

And I will mail one to Albino.

The suitcases and chests are out again. Everywhere. This means that soon we will move.

We move every couple of years because my uncle is a traveling priest: I've noticed that some of the cases don't even get unpacked before we move again. I hate suitcases. We always seem to move just as I have gotten used to my school, my village, my places of adventure, and just as I have made good friends.

At least my mother is here, for one more day. She came on the train last week with my brother, Luigino: my uncle and I met them at the station. A few days before we had seen them all in Collemare: we were there to pick up my *nonno* and *nonna* and drive them back here, for my grandparents, too, are staying. They all came to visit us—it is the first time my mother has seen where I live with my uncle—because the new place we are moving to is even farther from my home village than we are now.

I don't want to go. Maybe my mom won't be able to find the new place. Or maybe it is across the sea...

"Is it in Italy?" I ask my aunt.

She scowls at me: "What do you mean *is it in Italy*! We're traveling two hours' south, for heaven's sake! Do you think Italy is the size of a postage stamp?"

She suddenly steps back and looks at me kindly, her words gentle: "Don't worry, Mario, we're not going too far away."

71

My mother has entered the room.

"*Mariolino!*" she says, pinching my cheek affectionately, giving me a *ganascino*, before brushing past to help my aunt at the stove. I wish my mother wouldn't go. She's the boss of my aunt, and it's fun watching my aunt have to be nice to me when my mother's around.

I jump at a clanging pan that my aunt just dropped. She seems nervous. It is breakfast time and soon, once again, all the Valentini clan will be gathered around her table.

"So, have you thought any more about your *fioretto*, Mario?" says my uncle as he sweeps in and pulls out a chair at the table. "If you haven't, I think I've got a good one for you."

Oh, no. I forgot about the *fioretto*! A *fioretto* is a promise, a vow you make to God to change something about the way you behave. My uncle said *fioretto* means "flower" because it is a sweet thing, a small promise of sacrifice that you make that can be as simple as regularly placing a flower on someone's grave. Trouble is, my *fiorettos* are never to do with flowers and the sacrifices don't seem small. I have to promise things like not answering my aunty back and not chewing gum in church *ever*, and when I forget, I have to do some horrible chore for weeks. And I can't pretend to forget what my *fioretto* is now, because my uncle makes me write it down after we have decided what it will be in confessional.

A *fioretto* is a serious thing, and when you make it with the priest—and can't pretend you forgot—you can't break it. Not without being in serious trouble with God and every grown-up around you. I know, because I've broken them before. I've broken all of them, every single *fioretto* I've tried to keep, even though I did try; but *this time* will be different. I'll pick something easy. Still, I wish my uncle had forgotten.

"I could eat less *polenta?*" I suggest, hoping this will seem harsh to my uncle, who knows how much I love it. *Less* only has to mean one less spoonful.

"Let's talk about it after breakfast, shall we?" he says.

That means it's going to be a lot worse than less *polenta*. And I bet it has something to do with my grandmother—my *nonna*. I wish my mother was the boss of *her*, but she's not. It's the other way around: Nonna bullies my mom. Nonna and my aunt are both bullies, but I think Nonna is the worst: at least *sometimes* my aunt is kind to me, like when I am in big trouble with my uncle. I don't think I've seen Nonna be kind to anyone—least of all my mother. I don't like Nonna Custodia.

My uncle said he can see it in my face and that I have to change that. He said that I have to speak more respectfully to my *nonna*, and stop doing anything that might *aggravate* her. He said *aggravate* means grating on someone. I said, like grating cheese? He said *sort of*: that it means things rubbing together and annoying each other. Yuck! I don't want to rub together with my *nonna*. I don't even like to kiss her.

And I'm not the only one. I found out my *aunt* doesn't like her. I heard Aunt say to our neighbor that she had "two weeks of hell" coming up, what with "that pompous, know-it-all Custodia" coming to stay. She didn't dare say it to my uncle because Nonna is his mother, and Nonna Custodia is my papa's mother too—but Nonna is only a distant relative of my aunt. I was told Nonna is my *aunty's* aunt by marriage. Now I'm confused.

I also heard my aunt tell the neighbor that Custodia's name suited her—it means "custodian"—because she is famous for locking things up, important things like food and seeds, and then bullying others in the family, like my mother, into doing what she wants or they don't get what they need from her "family" cupboard. They say she would rather keep food locked up until it rots than hand it out to others; everyone in our family laughs about the time she went to serve a special guest some of her precious coffee—unbolting the two locks on her secret cabinet—only to find the coffee had turned into a decaying, foul-tasting powder.

People live up to their names, my aunt said, but her name is Ercolina, which my uncle told me comes from the hero, Hercules, and my aunt is nothing like *him*. She's small, has no muscles, and certainly isn't a hero, though I can imagine her wrestling a mad bull.

"Move up, Mario, and let your brother in," orders my aunt.

Luigi. I shift my chair to let him in, pulling a quick face in the direction of my aunt. He giggles.

I love Luigi. Shorter and plumper than me, and more serious, he is always gentle-natured and sweet. He told me that I am his hero, because I am bigger, because I travel to all these wonderful places with my uncle, and because I have adventures. He said I'm brave because I face punishment from my uncle and aunt again and again by doing things—again and again—that get me into trouble. I haven't told him that these adventures often don't *begin* as trouble, they just end up that way. I don't tell him because I want him to think I'm brave.

Luigi doesn't get into trouble, not like me. My aunt said, referring to my brother, that it was a shame she couldn't "plant *his* head on *your* shoulders." I told her that would leave Luigi without a head, or if he got mine, would leave my head with a fat body, or Luigi's body with a skinny head . . . at which point she told me to go to my room.

"Breakfast *still* not on the table? At *this* hour?"

Nonna Custodia has entered the room, sweeping in and looking around her for something to criticize. I see my aunt and mother change: standing straighter, and moving faster to prepare and place the food on the table. Everyone stops talking.

My grandfather, Nonno Cesare, is putting wine into bottles in the *cantina*—our homemade "fresh" wine has to be removed from the oak barrel, ready for our move—which means he must have had breakfast early, and now we have Nonna at the table *all by herself*.

"Did you sleep well, Mama?" asks my uncle.

"Yes, but no thanks to the way the bed was made," she says, flashing a glare at my aunt and then looking down to rearrange her skirt as she is seated. "And, Mario, still slouching at the table? Doesn't anyone correct you here?"

Another dig at my aunt, who slips with the plate she is passing to my mother. I almost feel sorry for my aunt. Almost.

I sit up straight, exaggerating the movement as I push my chest out. Luigi smirks after checking that Nonna isn't looking, and Uncle gives me a stern glance and then, ever so slowly, begins shaking his head as if he is thinking as he watches me. Now I *know* my *fioretto* will be about Nonna. Oh no. Once I make this promise to God I won't be able to question her when she says things to me that aren't true, and worst of all, I'll have to pretend that I like her *all the time*. I don't think I would like *liking* Nonna. It's more fun grating.

It was fun the other day when she chased me with the stick. It began when I was showing Luigi how to draw. We were drawing the statue of David. I like it because it's got muscles, it's naughty, and I wanted to show Luigi that *realists* draw people with no clothes on. Everyone else was out and my *nonna* was minding us, so I told her that we would draw in my uncle's study—I didn't want her to see.

When she barged in unexpectedly, she demanded that Luigi put clothes on his nude figure, and I told her that David didn't wear clothes. She ignored me, and ripped the drawing out from under Luigi. I told her that I was trying to teach him—that Uncle had paid for me to become a realist like Caravaggio and that realists had to draw *everything*. She didn't say anything, just glared at me until she spotted the picture I was covering with my elbows. She pulled it out from under me and held it up. Luckily, I had only drawn the *top half* of David.

"Madonna, what's *next?*" she asked, shaking her head in disgust.

I looked at where my pencil line ended just below David's waist. "His *sausage!*" I whispered to Luigi, laughter blasting out from my nose. Luigi, too, gave a loud snort, and Nonna went for the broom.

Luigi was in stitches. *Afterward.* When it happened he was laughing *and* crying as Nonna raced into the kitchen, snatched the *scopa*— a broom that looks like the one witches ride—and began the chase. She chased me from the study, back into the kitchen, up the hallway and then into my room, clutching the broomstick. Luigi swears he saw her riding it. She uses the broomstick to try to poke me out from my hiding place under the bed. I wriggled and squirmed, screamed and laughed as I flattened myself against the wall to dodge the stick swinging back and forth around me. Nonna can't bend, so I watched her thick ankles moving around as she shoved, rattled and thrust blindly with the stick. I could also see Luigi's legs jumping around near the door: excited but ready to run in case she turned.

Nonna eventually gave up after assuring me she would tell my uncle and my mother. I was put in my room for two days, but Luigi and I laughed about it for the rest of the week, each time almost wetting ourselves. Nonna chases me with the broomstick nearly every time she comes to stay, but this was the first time Luigi had seen it. And sometimes, *sometimes* I think Nonna enjoys it.

My aunt shuffles around the table, sliding frittata onto everyone's plates. Luigi's piece is bigger than mine.

"Mama, I don't like—" Luigi begins.

I elbow him and signal for him to pass me his frittata when Aunt turns her back. Luigi is fussy with his food, but he doesn't realize that *here* you are not allowed to decide whether or not you like something.

Someone says the word *portone* loudly at the other end of the table.

"Tell that story again," calls Luigi, now happy with his empty plate.

Any mention of the *portone*—the Valentini ancestral home—is always linked to *that* story: the story about the fire. We've all heard it before but it's exciting and we like to hear it again and again. The fire was a major event in our family—it happened when I was little and before my youngest brother was even born—and *still* no one knows how it began. My uncle said that it is a mystery, and better left that way: no one wants to own up, as it would be a very shaming thing to burn down the ancient home of the Valentini family and several other homes in the village, including another family's *portone*, accidentally or not. My mother says the worst part of it was that my *nonna* had to live with us for a year.

I can remember bits of the fire, like a dream. I remember being pulled out of my bed in the dark night and carried outside by my running mother. She couldn't run too fast because she had me in one arm, my baby brother Luigi in the other, and her belly was big with our youngest brother, Alberto. I was warm because I was bundled in a blanket and I could see Luigi in my mother's other arm swaddled in his *fascie*—a kind of bandage wrapped around from head to toe, as they did with babies then—with only his face poking out.

There was screaming and shouting and people racing everywhere. I could see smoke and flames coming from the *portone* three doors up from our house, and people running back and forth with wooden buckets. Scared, I remember asking my mother what was happening. She told me not to worry, that Aunt Antonina's pig had just run away and everyone was looking for him. But I could see the smoke—and the grown-ups looked frightened.

"Why didn't you call the *pompieri?*" asks Luigi. He *always* asks this question when the story is told, and he *always* gets the same answer. He just likes to hear it.

"Because it would have taken *hours* for the fire truck to arrive from L'Aquila," says my mother. "Even with a phone to call on—and we had *one* in Collemare by the time of the fire—it would still have taken hours for the fire truck to make it up the steep mountain roads, and it might not have had any water anyway."

I was told that the fire trucks often traveled empty so that there was less weight to carry, only to arrive in a place like Collemare and find that there was no good water source. Collemare sat atop a ridge and the closest spring was halfway down one side of this ridge: too far down to connect a hose. There was a small fountain at one end of the village, but this only had water after very recent rain.

"There was no time to get help. The people of the village—and their neighbors—had to do it for themselves," finishes my mother.

Their neighbors. I always felt proud when my mother told me that people from a neighboring village across the valley were there with their water by the time the people of Collemare were all out in the street. Some of these people had not been seen for years. When they were asked what they were doing in Collemare, they replied that they had seen the fire from the neighboring ridge—the smallest flame can be seen for miles in the crisp mountain darkness—and they had quickly got together and trudged over a mile with large *conche*—some already full of water—on their heads or pulled donkeys straddled with heavy, water-filled barrels, to save our village.

"People working together to save the homes," says my mother proudly. Her eyes always look wet when she tells this part.

"And not a great job at that," says my *nonna.*

"What do you mean?" says my mother, looking annoyed. "People risked their lives to save your house, Custodia, people who weren't even family."

"Well, we still lost it, didn't we?" Nonna says.

My mother strikes her fork hard on the table, looking directly at Nonna: "Your own husband risked his life trying to save your house and the homes of others."

Nonno saved our little house that was close to the *portone*, and several other houses. He was a hero during the fire. The houses were all joined to the *portone*—the only gaps between them being a few narrow alleyways that led to the fields behind—and were made of stone, which doesn't burn. The fire was spreading via the roofs and thick timber beams that joined the houses. The men protected the roofs by soaking them with what water they had: the only danger then was from the connecting beams. My *nonno* knew that cutting the beam was the only way to stop the spread of the fire.

The ground floor of our *portone* was alight, so my *nonno* climbed to the roof to enter the second floor of the building through the trapdoor. He was inside for some time, in danger of being overcome by smoke, hacking away with his axe at a beam that was old, hard and as thick as my arm was long. He eventually cut a large section of it away, and even though he didn't save his own home, he stopped the fire from reaching the adjoining houses—one of which was ours. My *nonno* was a hero.

"Certainly people *tried*, but not enough," says Nonna, "and such an inconvenience afterward, having to live *elsewhere*." She glances at my mother as she says this.

"Not as much as for some," says my mother quietly.

"But how did it start?" asks Luigi.

Silence: a stunned silence. This question is *never* asked, and the sudden tension means it should never *be* asked. No one talks about how the fire began, which makes me think there is a secret. I have heard some stories but I don't know which is true. My mother once told me that it started in a *portone* a few doors up from ours, and because all the buildings were joined, it quickly spread. But *some* say that it started in *our portone*. I notice my *nonna* pick up the saltcellar and bounce it in her hand without looking at it. She turns in her chair to gaze behind her at . . . nothing.

"An accident," says my uncle, "let's keep to the story."

My mother continues with her tale, telling everyone how I was passed to her friend Rosa and taken to her house at the far end of the village. I remember being placed in Rosa's arm and there, in her other arm, was her daughter Gabriella. She was the same age as me, and bundled in a gray blanket just as I was. My mother said we looked like twins. I was taken to Rosa's house with Luigi and put into bed with Gabriella. That's how talk of the *portone* began today: with Gabriella. My uncle mentioned that the angel in our village festival this year looked like her.

"I remember those hazel eyes and that lovely round face," says my mother, who liked Gabriella. "You're right, she has the face of an angel."

"What are you talking about—village *angel?*" snaps Nonna.

"The angel in the Festa della Madonna delle Grazie," says my uncle.

The Festa is an annual religious festival that the village of Vastogirardi holds to give thanks to the Madonna, and each year a young girl is picked from the village to be the flying "angel." I thought it was funny when I first saw this girl tied to a wire dangerously high from the ground. She flew from a rooftop down to the church door where a wooden statue of the Madonna was waiting to greet her. The "angel"—dressed in white—flies three times along the wire into the arms of the Madonna, each time bearing a different gift. That night there is a procession and fireworks and the next day the angel's flights are repeated, but this time she's dressed in blue.

Being the angel in the Festa is a real honor. At the beginning of June, families with young girls suddenly give more to the church and visit my uncle with presents and sweet talk to try to get him to pick their daughter. The girls are even nice to *me* at this time of year, and my friends and I get to enjoy cheeses, honey and sweets brought to school by the girls as gifts from their parents. Once I put in an order, but I never got it because my uncle found out.

"Mario's friends looking like *angels*!" spits Nonna. She glares directly at me. "I would hardly connect the word 'angel' with you and your friends. Your uncle *tries*, but the discipline seems all a bit late." She flashes a look at my mother, and then mutters to herself: "Wash the head of the donkey and you're wasting your soap."

Now I *really* don't like my *nonna*.

"And didn't Mario have a little accident during that fire?" begins my aunt.

Oh no, not *this*! Someone laughs.

"I believe you left Rosa's bed—and poor Luigi and Gabriella— quite wet that night," my aunt says, suddenly wanting to outdo my *nonna* in nastiness: "Perhaps they should have attached the fire hose to you!" she finishes, giving my *nonna* a quick smile. My *nonna* smiles back and then looks at me, victorious.

I feel myself redden. I need to ask that question. I *really* need to ask that question and I have to do it now. If I wait until tomorrow, I will have done my *fioretto*, and I won't be able to say it.

"Nonna, is it true that the *portone* burned down because you left the bedwarmer in too long and the mattress caught fire?" I say.

Nonna drops her fork. Everyone freezes. All eyes are on me.

"And the *portone* was lost because you couldn't get to the key that opened the closet that held the water buckets?" I add.

Nonna is coughing vigorously, as though she has something caught in her throat. My uncle is patting her back to settle her. He turns to me, his voice higher than normal: "Mario, go to your room!"

"Wait," says my mother, who seems the only one not outraged. "Where did you hear this, Mario?" she asks.

My aunt is up from the table and heading for the door: but not in time.

"I heard Aunty telling the neighbors," I say.

The room is quiet: no one looks at anyone else. My aunt stands awkwardly near the door and I can hear her foot tapping. When I look again, she is gone.

My mother stands. "Let's clear the table, then," she says. "And, Mario, please go to your room as your uncle says and do that *fioretto* tomorrow. You need to learn to be more respectful to your elders . . . *tomorrow.*"

My mother quickly brushes my cheek with her hand before pushing me toward the door. When I glance back, she is already stacking plates, and I notice a faint smile curling up one corner of her mouth.

La Moneta **THE COIN**

"**G**et your foot out of my ear—ow...OW! Get off and give me—"
CLINK!

"*Mannaggia!* You made me drop it again when I almost had it—*blast!*"

"Get down. I told you I *know* how to do it," I say, grabbing the pants of my friend Giovanni, and yanking him downward.

"Don't pull...*don't pull*, I'll fall!"

Giovanni's bulk drops onto me and we fall backward, landing spreadeagled on the cold marble floor. There is a gold angel in the tile to the left of me: I hadn't noticed it before. As I struggle to push my friend's ample backside off my chest, I notice that the ceiling above me is vaulted and some of the paintwork is curling off in the corners. I wonder if my uncle knows. As I push up with a last frustrated surge, Giovanni breaks wind—right in my face.

"*Mannaggia*—you deliberately did that! *Porco!*" I say, shoving him off face first into the floor.

"I didn't . . . *I didn't* . . ." says Giovanni, but he is laughing so hard he can barely get the words out.

I burst out laughing too and we roll around on the icy floor, Giovanni yelling, "Stop it!" in between guffaws and clutching his groin.

"Someone's coming!" calls Bruno from the doorway where he has been standing guard.

There is a mad scramble as we attempt to straighten ourselves and stand.

"Put the wire away, *hide it!*" I yell in a hoarse whisper to Giovanni.

Bruno ducks around from the door and stands with us; we all try to look respectful and "normal," for we are in the *navata laterale* of the church: my uncle's church in our new village. San Giovanni Lipioni.

I like it here. It still hurts each time I leave my friends behind when we move, but I've noticed I'm *faster* at making new friends. I now look around as soon as I get to a new class and wonder who— who out of all these faces I will be best friends with. And with more freedom now that I am a little older, I can go out with my friends more often, and to places well away from the prying eyes of my aunt. And neighbors. This means we can more readily enjoy the things we can't do around adults—like chew gum and smoke. Well, we don't really *smoke*, we each have a turn holding the cigarette and taking puffs. I quickly learned not to suck in because I did it once and almost threw up. But it's worth it; smoking is so *cool*. It all began with my uncle. He often smoked a cigarette after dinner, holding it high in his elegant cigarette holder, and he decided recently that I was old enough to buy them for him at the store. He would ask me to buy four or five so, with some of my own pocket money on me, I would ask for an extra one and keep it.

La Moneta

My new friends were impressed that I had cigarettes—in fact *so* impressed that I now have to keep up a supply. Trouble is, it takes more pocket money than I have, so I had to find a way... My first idea was the coin stacks—taking just one coin off the top of each of the money piles when they were lined up ready to be rolled in their papers—but I had to stop doing that after the bank suggested my uncle needed to be just a "little more careful" with his counting. And there was a church collection purse that worked magic for a while: it was a deep open *borsa* with lining that had split and come away. If you held the lining open, you could get people to slip coins in there and then empty the main part of the purse and collect the hidden coins later. But someone stitched up the lining. That left one last option. It was riskier, but worked well if we were careful. The church donation box. That's where we are now, getting our pocket money.

Last week the church was busy with a religious festival so we couldn't do it, and now we're out of money and desperate for a coin. We don't think it's *that* bad, taking a coin or two. The church has lots of money—sometimes the box is filled with *thousands* of coins!— so what would it matter if a couple went missing? And no one could say we didn't earn them. It took a lot of work to get those coins out, and three people: one on guard duty at the door (it could only be done with an empty church, or with one or two older, deafer worshippers, but the *main* person we looked out for was my uncle), one to hoist the "rattler" up on top of the donation box, and the rattler himself.

And just how did we get coins out of a deep wooden donation box that was locked, immovable (built into the wall), and with only a narrow slit the width of two coins? We inserted a long piece of wire with a small dollop of sticky black tar on its end and rattled it back and forth until we managed to "stick" a coin. It took skill to do this. It was not so hard if the box was quite full, but this was rarely the case as the box was quickly emptied after the "busy" donation days. Mostly the box contained a few loose, elusive coins that slid around and around and around, far down at the bottom of the container—if my uncle only knew the swearwords that have been uttered in this corner. The box was emptied this morning, and we are now fighting to get the few coins deposited since...

A shadow moves on the floor. All eyes follow it. The light from outside casts its long reach through the church foyer and up the main aisle, stretching as though it's trying to reach the altar and light one of the candles. On its journey it elongates anything that gets in its way. Right now it frames the person entering, their silhouette on display to all inside. We watch as the shadow gets bigger, bigger, taller, *taller*—the person is huge, their shape now extending up the whole length of the church. Maybe it's my uncle! Maybe he knows... We hold our breath, eyes widening, as the giant finally appears in the doorway: little Nonna Concetta. The smallest, most bent-over of all the *nonnas* in the village, and one of the sweetest. Well, we think she's sweet because she's the only *nonna* in the village who hasn't yelled at one of us—but then she lives on the other side of the village so we rarely see her.

"*Madonna!*" says Giovanni with relief.

I thump him for speaking. Nonna Concetta peers around at us. She has a strange look on her face. I realize we must look funny, three boys standing inside the church doing ... well, nothing really.

"Ciao, Nonna," I say, trying to sound respectful.

She doesn't smile, just blesses herself with the holy water from the font—all the while looking at us—and then continues walking up the aisle into the darkness of the great church. I watch as her shadow on the floor shrinks the closer she gets to the altar, the speckles of dust dancing around in the light that frames her body, as if making fun of her slow movement, her bent little figure.

I turn back to see Giovanni doing a jiggle as he tries to get the sticky wire out from its hiding place in his pants. I grab it from him.

"I'll get it!" I say in a terse whisper, signaling for him to give me a foot back up onto the donation box.

Bruno watches at the door again, checking both outside and in, to make sure Nonna Concetta isn't heading back our way. This is unlikely, as I know the ritual: she will have lit a candle and be praying or saying her *Ave Marias*, and if a priest was present she would also be making confession, so she won't be leaving the church for some time. Besides, we have a huge pillar between her and us.

I almost have it—almost—oh, *came off again*! There it is, the coin... almost sticking... almost... almost—*there*! I have it, and slowly, ever so slowly, I move it up and out through the slot at the top. *Yes!*

A button. There is a *button* stuck to the tar! We look at it, and then at each other. I quickly stick the wire down through the slot again. *Nothing*. That was it. That was the last slippery, tantalizing, elusive "coin."

"Someone stuck a button in, pretending they were giving a coin!" I say, mortified.

"They'll go to hell," says Giovanni.

Bruno slides in from around the door, sees the button, looks at my face and then sags. Giovanni grabs the button from me, and stares at it in disbelief.

I slump against the wall. No money. There will be no money today, and no chance of collecting money over the next two days because Saturday and Sunday are busy days in the church. What now? Do we give up? No, we *can't*, it's just not fair! There must be *something* we can do! But things look hopeless, and there's no one around to make a donation, except for...*no!*

Nonna Concetta would no more make a donation than part with her britches! The old women in this village are so tight, the shopkeeper told my aunt, that after giving them credit he has to perform surgery to open their purses. It was very likely Nonna who put the button in! The only person who could coerce someone like her into giving a *proper* donation would be the priest, in the confessional. The priest could make her say her Hail Marys and make a donation, but she would have to be told in the confessional—

I push past my friends and look up toward the altar. There is no one in the church but the old woman, sitting among a sea of quivering, glowing candles, large statues and carved timberwork. I look over at the confessional boxes. One is close enough for me to enter without her seeing. Oh no, I couldn't do it! This idea is wicked, *so* wicked, maybe *worse* than a mortal sin, how could I even think it? But my friends need this money. I wouldn't be a good friend if I left them without gum or cigarettes: and my uncle says friendship is important. I look at the confessional box, my body tingling. I *could* do it! But what would my uncle do to me? What will the Madonna do to me, if she does catch you up for your sins as they say, or Satana—the devil—for committing such sacrilege in church? I don't even want to think about *that*—I just have to think of the cigarettes and gum.

I tell my friends my idea.

"Take a *confession?*" says Bruno, horrified.

"Do you want cigarettes?" I say.

"Yes, but you *can't*—" He's unable to say it a second time.

Giovanni's eyes are wide as he shakes his head, saying nothing.

"No way!" says Bruno finally. "If you do it, I'm staying on watch outside—I'm not going in *there*," he says, pointing inside the church.

He casts a quick, fearful glance at the statue of Saint Luke and darts outside to the warm, sunlit steps.

I grab Giovanni's shirt, pulling him along with me before he can change his mind. The church seems to have grown darker in the last few minutes and I want someone—*anyone*—with me. He tries to pull away, but I hold on tight.

When we reach the confessional box, I try the door; it's stuck. Giovanni giggles nervously, and I nudge him to stop. I notice that I'm shaking. The seconds drag until, finally, the door slides open with a loud "thwack!" that echoes around the church. I push Giovanni in and follow.

It's squashy with the two of us inside. Peering out of the slats, I see that Nonna Concetta has not moved or turned around. Lucky! I open the little panel that indicates a priest is now in the confessional, but she can't see it because the box is behind her. I cough to get her attention. No response. I cough again, trying to make it sound deep. No response from the old woman. Oh no, what if she's *deaf*?

She's turned! She peers intently in our direction and then slowly gets up. She's coming over to the confessional. I'm seated in the priest's chair and Giovanni is on the floor beside me, our only protection a few crisscrossed timber slats, and I suddenly feel very scared. *What am I doing?* Committing the unholy act of taking a confession from someone, pretending to be a *priest*! Oh Madonna! This is the *worst* thing anyone could do! But it's too late now— she's coming. Giovanni is making a noise between a whimper and a giggle. I give him a push with my knee and I hear him draw in his breath.

The old woman rattles open the confessional door and slides in. She takes a moment to settle her skirts and then sits silently, waiting.

I have to concentrate now and remember what my uncle says in confession. I have heard him do it so many times that I'm sure I know it by heart. But my mind's gone blank, I'm shaking... can't think. Say something, *anything*, make it up. It'll come back to me...

"Hail Mary, Mother of God." My voice sounds squeaky—*have* to make it deeper! The trouble is, I can't remember the next bit—Latin, some Latin will do. I'm sure most of the congregation don't know the meaning of the Latin they hear. "*Pater noster, qui es in caelis; sanctificetur nomen tuum*," I say, hoping she doesn't notice that it's the first line of the Common Prayer.

Nonna's face is just visible on the other side of the screen: she looks somewhat surprised. I hold my breath for a second, waiting. Finally she speaks: "Father, forgive me for I have sinned."

"And how have you sinned, *sorella*?" I say gruffly (my uncle calls the women "sister," so I'll do the same). Giovanni giggles at the word "sister." I cover his mouth, but it only makes things worse and he snorts.

"Father, I have sinned by saying unfair things about my neighbor," says Nonna.

She stops. I wait for her to say something else. Nothing. Is she waiting for me? Has she finished? Do people come to confession just for *that*?

"Then you—" I start.

"And I've used wicked words against my sister-in-law," she interrupts. "I told her the slops we serve our pig look better than what she puts on my brother's table."

I slap my hand over Giovanni's mouth and wait. Nothing more.

"Then you shall say five hundred Hail Marys," I begin.

Oh! Is that right? Nonna Concetta jumped when I said it—she seems shocked. Maybe it should have been fifty. Hang on... that's right, I think the hundreds are for things like murders! Can't go back now.

"Say five hundred Hail Marys, *sorella*—" she's staring at the screen with startled eyes—"and then as a way of absolution, make a contribution to the church donation box. Is there anything else, *sorella?*" I say quickly.

"No, Father, bless you, Father, and thank you, Father," she says.

She doesn't look thankful; she looks upset. The seat creaks and she thumps against the side of the confession box as she gets up to leave.

"*Ego de* um . . . um . . . *absolve*," I mumble. "Oh, and please make the donation first!" Lucky I remembered that! All those Hail Marys will take *ages*.

I breathe out, relieved, as she shuffles her way from the confessional, then jump as she slams the door behind her.

I peer through the slats: she's angry! Fancy being angry with a *priest*!

Eyes look at me from *everywhere*.

Urgh! There they go again, the eyes on that statue: cold, white, "dead" eyes, with a hole in their center—I'm sure they just moved! I shudder, my spine wriggling all the way down. I never noticed before how Saint Peter's marble eyes seem to follow you around the church; perhaps it wasn't like that *before*, perhaps now they're following me because of *what I did*—oh! Can't even *think* that! Oh God, I wish Nonna Concetta would hurry up with her Hail Marys, I just want to get out of here!

She didn't do as I told her—she didn't do as *the priest* told her! Nonna Concetta didn't put the money in the box *before* doing her five hundred Hail Marys, so I've been cramped down on the floor between the last two pews of the church, waiting, and now I need to go to the toilet. If she goes on any longer the *whole village* will be shut before she puts in a coin! And worse than the waiting is being here *alone*: Giovanni ran outside after the "confessional," saying something terrible would happen to us in the church. I called him chicken but wish I hadn't, because now *I* can't go outside.

It's awful in here. I never noticed before how even the cherubs at the end of the pews have strange eyes, or that the church is so *dark* during the day, and the stained glass window above me has a saint who just keeps staring and *staring*. I move again—*see?* His eyes just follow! I don't care what my friends think, I don't care if they think I'm chicken, I've had enough and I'm getting out—

I hear a movement and peek over the pew. Nonna's getting up, rubbing her knees—they must be hurting! I duck below pew level and watch through the wooden paneling as she shuffles down the aisle, her thick nylon stockings more orange than the sash on Saint Peter's robe across from me. I don't dare look higher up the statue: don't want to meet those eyes again.

I move around behind the end of the pew as the old woman passes. My ears strain to pick up her every movement near the doorway, near the donation box. I wait . . . no sound . . . still no sound! Has she forgotten to put in the coin? Have I been sitting here waiting, *waiting*, all this time for nothing?

CLUNK!

A coin! She's dropped in a coin! I hold my breath. I count to twenty, trying to time her struggle down the steps and out of view before I get up. I can't wait any longer and I race to the entrance— slamming straight into Giovanni and Bruno.

"Did she . . . ?" asks Giovanni, his loud voice echoing up the nave. He climbs up onto the box before I can get there to help him and has the wire down, rattling. After a few quick twists of his wrist: "Got it! I was pulling at the tar outside to get it fresh!" he says proudly.

He slowly removes the wire and shows us his prize—a twenty-lire coin. *Twenty lire!*

I snatch it from him. This is enough to buy *two* cigarettes and a large pack of chewing gum! An incredibly generous donation, lucky for us! Why so much? The usual donation is five or ten lire. Maybe I made her feel really guilty about her sins, or maybe it was because she never finished all her *Ave Marias*—but who cares?

Giovani dances a jig on the donation box while Bruno yahoos. I suddenly realize that no one is guarding the door and am about to say, "Watch out," when something makes me look at the coin again . . .

"*Oh no!*" I yell. "It's old currency!"

"What do you mean . . . ?" Bruno ends his question with a groan.

"We can't use it—it's old money," I continue. "It *looks* like the new twenty lire but it's old. I know because my uncle shows me the coins to toss aside, the ones we can't bank."

"*Mannaggia!*" says Bruno, heading for the door.

"It's started," says Giovanni, looking fearfully at the statue of a saint. "We're being punished!" He pushes past Bruno to get out of the church first.

I pick up the coin, exasperated, and follow.

The warmth of the sun strikes me, and I realize how cold I'd become crouching in the dark building. Giovanni is prattling on nervously, the late afternoon light dappling his face, saying what a wicked thing we've done, that we'll be struck down by lightning or God or Lucifer or *something*, and that he, for one, is *never* attending church again because he doesn't want the building to fall in. I told him that was a stupid thing to say, because why would the church fall in during a service when most of the people inside were good? I told him Lucifer would rather get him in the street. Anyway, he doesn't even *go* to church—my aunt said his family are part of some wicked group that doesn't believe in God, and I know Giovanni only ever enters a church on our "pocket-money" days.

"Anyway, *she's* the one who should go to hell," Bruno says.

I slump down next to him on the worn step and gaze at the village below. People meander up and down the cobbled roadway that leads to the lower fields; this roadway dips in the center, and is so narrow in parts that my uncle's small car can't squeeze through. The Sanniti lived here, at the site of this village, a long time ago. My uncle said that they were fiercer warriors than the nearby Etruscans—and that they beat the Romans in one great battle. Maybe the road I am looking at was *their* road, and this was where they had the battle. Perhaps the road sank in the middle when the marching Roman legions came up the hill to fight the Sanniti, who were behind the rocks with their axes, knives and shields at the ready...

Bruno shifts his foot. I look across to a row of cypress trees running down a ridge to the right of us. Windbreaks: that's what my uncle told me they were. He said these trees are like bright green sentinels, soldiers on guard, and I watch as their windswept tips break rank ever so slightly. Then I remember the coin. No chewing gum or cigarettes all week, after all that work.

My eyes are drawn back to the carts, donkeys, delivery men, merchants—all coming and going at the point where the Sanniti road turns left into the main shopping street. I notice the clock on the campanile. Four p.m. *Two hours* I was in the church, cramped and waiting, risking everything by going into the confessional as a priest—for nothing. I'm going to hell—for nothing. It wouldn't be so bad going to hell if I had actually *enjoyed* what I was going to hell for... *porco!*

Bruno is now raving to Giovanni, who doesn't seem to be listening: "It's sort of stealing, isn't it? Because Nonna Concetta's pretending to God that she's giving him money, but it's not real money, so that

94

means she's taking it back—that's stealing! Don't you think? Or maybe it's lying . . . maybe it's lying *and* stealing . . ."

"I wonder if she knew it was me?" I ask, absently.

What does it matter? If my uncle is right and God and his watchers are everywhere, *especially* in church, then I am done for. *And no gum or cigarettes*—that's the worst of it.

I turn the coin over and over in my fingers, ready to toss it. I'd like to see how far downhill I could get it. I raise my arm and am about to throw when something stops me. I look at the coin glinting in the sun, and I turn it over again. I close my eyes and rub it, both sides, and a fantastic idea starts to flicker somewhere in my brain . . .

The smell of candy and old timber, the crackle of paper as *pancetta* bounces on its bed of greaseproof paper on the scales, and something else, something strong: it almost stinks but is softened by the smell of earth . . . *mushrooms!* I spot a large, overflowing sack of mushrooms just by the door.

I knock a packet off a corner shelf and fumble to pick it up. When I step forward, the floorboards creak again. I am trying to get up the courage to do it, hiding behind the row of shelves so that the shopkeeper can't see me from the counter. *So that he can't see me*—that, of course, is stupid!

Oh, why didn't one of my friends come in with me? At least it wouldn't look so strange, me hanging around the shelves, waiting, waiting until everyone else has left the shop. I bend and peer out the large front window, through the green and gold letters on the glass—written backward (how do they do that?)—declaring that Signor Giuliani is a "Merchant of General Produce and Fine Victuals." The letters blur as I try to spot my brave friends, Giovanni and Bruno, who are across the road hiding behind a cart. I can just make out Giovanni's legs. I look back at the curling letters—I don't remember ever eating a victual. And I've decided that Giovanni and Bruno aren't my friends.

You see, I had this great idea about the outdated coin that looked and *felt* like a new twenty-lire piece. Signor Giuliani, the shopkeeper in whose place of business I am rattling around, is fat and friendly. And *blind*. That's why it's stupid for me to hide behind the shelves, and them behind the cart. The shopkeeper can't see us *at all*. He also won't see the coin.

I kept telling Giovanni this as I tried to pull him across the road with me to the shop, but he screamed that the shopkeeper knew his papa and would know him. I told him that the shopkeeper can't *see* anyone, and that if he kept quiet it would be all right. Instead he kept up the screaming, so I told him that Signor Giuliani already knew everything—because blind people have supersonic hearing—and that he was probably writing a note to his papa right now. That shut him up. But it also convinced him not to come. Bruno wouldn't budge because he said he was our "sentinel" (I wish I hadn't told him that word), and said Giovanni wasn't allowed to take his job. I gave up and headed across to the shop.

The floorboards creak again, and I flinch. I'm *so* glad I'm not known here—in fact I've never been inside this shop. My aunt does her purchasing here, so we buy our cigarettes and chewing gum on the *other* side of the village, well away from her prying eyes and talkative friends. I know Signor Giuliani because every Sunday his wife forces him to church—she holds his arm as if to assist him, but my aunt says everyone knows she's dragging him—but I've never been near him because he sits in the very back pew and is always the first out the door.

Signora Rosa has just left. I'll do it *now*—oh no! Someone *else* is coming in. The new customer entering has picked up a copy of

Messaggero and is leaning forward to place money on the counter. He says "*Grazie!*" and leaves.

Now's my chance! The shop is empty: I have to move quickly, before another—*Oh!* I crash into a shelf and yelp as I tread on something soft and squishy: mushrooms! I've knocked the sack and they're all over the floor. I start picking them up and placing them in the sack. Oh no! The coin has fallen in. I pull at the soft, spongy lumps—the sack is deep—and then I find it caught in the cap of an upturned mushroom.

I sigh with relief and look up to see Signora Rosa standing above me. She has returned with empty bottles for the shopkeeper. She moves to the counter and thumps the bottles down, all the while staring at me.

"*Grazie*, Signor Giuliani, *buon pomeriggio*," she says.

She hasn't taken her eyes off me.

"Ciao, *bella* Rosina!" says Signor Giuliani.

Oh! He's calling her *beautiful*, but she's married, and old, and nothing *like* beautiful... I bet she's glad he's blind.

Signora Rosa heads for the door, then stops abruptly and turns to me again. She knows my uncle, has seen me with him, and I know what she is about to do.

"Aren't you—?" she begins.

"*No!*" I yell adamantly.

Without thinking, she takes me at my word and exits.

I rush to the counter, repeating my lines over and over in my head.

"Yes?" says Signor Giuliani.

Oh! How did he know I was here?

"Two Nazionali and a pack of *gomme, grazie*," I say. Good! I did it well, it sounded grown up—I think...

"Fifteen lire," he says. He wants the money first.

This is it. I glance outside, wanting to catch the eye of my friends, but I can't see them. Even the cart is out of view. I'm all alone.

I slide the coin across the counter. It's such a *big* counter, and my arm looks skinny among the boxes of sweets, cigar tins and the stacks of butcher paper. The shopkeeper's arms, hands and body look so large on the other side. Signor Giuliani is not tall but he's big and broad, and he has medals on his shirt. Lots of medals, which must mean he's brave. I suddenly feel very scared, and swallow hard. I must remember he can't *see* me.

He takes the coin.

"It's twenty lire," I say quickly. "That means five lire change," I tell him, just in case he forgets his math.

He feels the coin, sliding his finger and thumb carefully over both sides. *Oh Madonna!* It looks so small now, smaller than it should be, or am I imagining it? He seems to be taking ages, rubbing the coin, turning it over and over...

He pulls back and places the coin in his money drawer.

I start to sigh with relief when I remember he can *hear* me! Instead I grin and clench my fist—so pleased! *I did it!*

I look out the window, hoping my friends can see. I hope they realize how lucky they are to have me. I watch as Signor Giuliani— *lovely* Signor Giuliani—gets two cigarettes from the yellow box on the shelf behind him and places them in a small paper bag; he gently folds over the top of the bag and puts it on the counter. He pulls a pack of gum out of its display box and places it next to the cigarettes. Juicy, pink cubes that you snap off and chew: I can taste it now! *And there's even change!* I watch as he gets it from the drawer.

"Five lire," he says, snapping the coin down on the counter.

I look outside again, savoring the moment. I told my friends to come with me, I bet now they feel stupid...

"Your gum," he says, sliding the pack toward me.

. . . *really* stupid hiding behind a cart . . .

"Your cigarettes," he says, sliding the bag forward, "and your change."

I go to pick up the coin.

THUMP!

The pain! I'm so shocked I don't realize what has happened for a second; then I see. The blind man has my forearm in a viselike grip. I am clamped to the counter, at his mercy. I fight to stay standing, but my legs are like jelly. The circulation is cut off in my arm. I am stuck.

He doesn't say anything. I wish he would. His medals jangle and I can feel the tension in his body. What is he going to *do*? What do blind people do when someone has done something awful to them? I feel sick from fear *and* shame: I have done something terrible—*terrible*—to someone who *can't see*, and I am the priest's nephew! What will he do? I need to know because I am terrified: he is not only blind and very angry—*he is attached to the end of me.*

"*Mario!*" he says.

How does he know my name? He *can't* know me, he *can't* . . .

His grip is tight, bearing down. I look at the packet of gum and the cigarettes on the counter—the cigarettes are half squashed under his arm. I don't want them anymore. My whole body feels limp, like the only thing holding me up is his grip. I don't want to look at his eyes—his *blind* eyes.

"It's a terrible thing to give a false coin to a *blind* man," he continues.

Oh, the sick feeling again! What have I done? What a shameful thing to do, for *anyone* to do, let alone the nephew of the—

"Bring me the right money tomorrow," Signor Giuliani says, "or I will tell your uncle."

Oh Madonna, *he knows my uncle*! In one sense it's good because surely he won't kill the priest's nephew, but then my uncle will kill me anyway if he finds this out—

The shopkeeper suddenly lets go of my arm and I drop to the floor. Standing quickly, I take a step back from the counter. I want to run but, strangely, feel rooted to the spot.

The shopkeeper pushes the cigarettes and gum toward me—he wants me to take them! I don't want them but I had better not disobey. I wait until Signor Giuliani turns away. I snatch the items from the counter, mutter, "*Scusi,*" and run from the shop into the dull evening light.

My life is awful in church. I feel *everyone* is looking at me: Nonna Concetta, Signor Giuliani and his wife, my aunt . . . and then there's the *aspersorio*. I have to jump and duck around it. It's the holy water.

My uncle said in a recent sermon that after you commit a great sin the holy water burns you for a full year. So now my life is awful: in church, and every time I am out with my uncle doing benedictions. Not only am I supposed to cross myself with the holy water from the font (now I have to *pretend* to touch it, and *pretend* to cross myself with it) but the worst is that I always seem to be near my uncle when he shakes the *aspersorio* over the congregation, the person he's blessing, the choir boys, the *chierichetto*, even animals and the rooms of houses when we go visiting! And I have to keep dodging every single drop. I don't want to get burned.

My uncle has asked why I keep jumping around, and my aunt said I was "up to something." I think she knows. Like the whole congregation—staring at me right now—and the whole village, she *knows* just by looking at me that I am the sort of boy who takes money from a blind man.

I gave the money back the next day. I borrowed it from my uncle, pleading desperately with him and promising to do extra chores for weeks to make up for it. I told him I wanted the money for a new book, and then had to borrow one of Renaldo's and pretend it was mine. (*Another* lie! I hope this doesn't add more time to the burning holy water!) But even after paying the money back, I still felt so bad about Signor Giuliani that I started helping my aunt more, doing messages for our neighbors, and reading once a week to old Nonna Lucia, who lives three doors up and is *almost* blind. This was when my aunt became *really* suspicious. But she couldn't help herself, and started telling people that I was being very good: she said she just had to—it was such a novelty.

Then one day she came home from shopping. "Mario," she said, unpacking prosciutto, flour and fruit on the kitchen table (I had come out at the sounds of unwrapping), "do you know Signor Giuliani?"

I wasn't taking much notice: the fruit had my attention.

"You know, where I shop—the blind shopkeeper?" she said.

I froze. "No, *no*," I said, shaking my head.

"He's given you some gum."

"*Oh!*"

"Oh what?" asked my aunt.

"Maybe I do know him."

"You either know him or you don't."

Her eyes bored into me for a moment, and then she looked away as she went on: "Anyway, we were talking, and he seemed impressed that you have been so good lately—I just happened to mention it—and he said to give you this, and to say that the 'dues are paid.'"

She hands me the packet of gum. "What 'dues,' Mario?"

"I don't know...I don't know what it means," I say honestly.

"It means a debt. It means you paid a debt." She looked at me suspiciously. "Do you owe Signor Giuliani something?"

"No," I say. And that's the truth. Signor Giuliani said it was.

I smile at my aunt and snap off a piece of the hard, brittle gum: gum that will melt in my mouth, stick to my teeth and tantalize every tastebud with its exciting, juicy, tingling, pink sweetness.

I am happy. Signor Giuliani said that I am good again, so nobody will stare at me in church now. I will still have to dodge the *aspersorio*, but that's not so bad. And perhaps now those nightmares will end: where Ivanhoe suddenly drops his sword and grabs me; and I wake up gasping, from a shooting pain in my right arm that seems to come from a tight, fierce grip...

I'm going back home: we're on our way to Collemare.

I know this trip well because we do it once a year during the summer holidays, so that I can visit my mother, my brothers and the rest of my family. My aunt says it's a vacation for her and my uncle more than for me, with my aunt going on to her family in a nearby village and my uncle returning to his work and driving back to get us later.

There's that squeaking again, over the back wheel. My uncle cranes his neck to listen for it. Aunt joked that I must be too heavy in the back, but it's on the other side of the car from me: it's over on *my aunt's* side.

"I think it's the suspension...don't usually hear it," says Uncle.

"It doesn't happen when just you and I are in the car," I say to my uncle.

He flashes me a look in the rearview mirror.

My aunt didn't hear. She is rattling around in her bag finding her purse and her list: she is getting ready to buy all the *confetti* in Sulmona.

I look out of the window at the mountains. The journey back to Collemare takes us up and down through the high peaks and valleys, right through the very center of the Abruzzo, from the bottom near Molise, up to the very top near L'Aquila, and then over to my village. My uncle showed me on the map. I also saw that the Abruzzo is *full* of mountains and is in the very middle of Italy from bottom to top *and* from the sides.

I was shown the map after I told Uncle I was worried that we would no longer be going on my favorite road when we traveled back home—the one we're now on—because we had moved to a different place. He told me not to worry, we would still be traveling from the south and that this road is the one route up through the center of the Abruzzo. I love this road.

We're now heading north along a high mountain ridge. We've not long left Castel di Sangro, and this means that soon, *very soon*, we will be on the Cinquemiglia, the "five miles" of straight roadway on the high plain that Hannibal and the crusaders traveled along and where my uncle said lots of soldiers died, marching in the cold. After this, there's the road from Sulmona to Popoli that has even *more* castles, and battlements and *eremi*—hermits' caves. At school they told us that Abruzzo has more than five hundred medieval castles, watchtowers and walls, more than any other part of Italy— I think all of them are on this road! There are so many things to see that I have to decide each time which side to look at, because sometimes there might be just a fleeting glimpse of a valley or a fortress or a cave that I have to be ready for, before the mountains quickly close up and hide it again!

I lurch forward into the back of the seat as my uncle changes gears.

I like being in the car. I like the smell of it: the seats, the roof, the plastic mats, and all the little gadgets: the ashtrays in the doors and the back of the seats, the cute little side windows that pop out, the indicators that flick right out and back in, the way the gears change and the engine revs, and all the dials and buttons on the dashboard.

Except I can't see the dashboard right now, not properly anyway, because my aunt is here. This means I get the back seat. It's much better when I'm alone in the car with my uncle, which is often, because I go with him to visit parishioners who are sick or live too far from church, to see faraway churches that need fixing, or to attend churches without a priest where my uncle does a service once a month. And sometimes I join him on one of his many *pellegrinaggi*—religious pilgrimages to different festivals or shrines in the region—and there is one of these every few weeks. This means I am in the car a lot. This means I travel a lot, and I love it.

"How far now to Collemare?" I ask—again.

"Stop asking! Show some patience, will you?" snaps my aunt.

She doesn't understand that I am *not* impatient to get there. In some ways I don't want the journey to end.

"A few hours yet, Mario. Remember we have to stop for lunch," says my uncle.

The engine of the little VW revs high as it struggles up the steep hill until finally we reach the top—we're on the Cinquemiglia! It's on the highest plateau in the Abruzzo, my uncle said: he said a plateau is like a mountain with its top chopped off.

I wait for my aunty to say it . . .

"Ah, there's Pescocostanzo, the most beautiful village in Europe— much better than anything in France!" she says.

My aunt *always* says this, and she always says Italy is better than France. My uncle said it is true that Pescocostanzo is famous for its beauty, but it *isn't* true that Italy is always better. He said France was the only country Aunt had ever traveled to—she went with my uncle to worship at Lourdes—and that was why she mentioned it all the time. I asked what was so good about this village and he said it was the beautiful medieval and Renaissance buildings: he said it was also famous for its wrought iron and gold.

"Gold! Do they still make the gold?"

My uncle nodded and explained that a lot of the old ways were still practiced in the Abruzzo because of the high mountains all around. The area was hard to get in or out of, he said—in a way the Abruzzo was cut off from the rest of Italy—and therefore had kept a lot of its traditions: its food, way of life, its trades and crafts. Aunt said the Abruzzo lace, tapestries and blankets were the *best in the world*, but I was interested in the gold. Yes, my uncle said, parts of the Abruzzo were still famous for gold crafting, but they didn't *make* the gold: that came from the ground. So I asked him *which* ground, how far you had to dig, and if it was close to where we lived.

We're almost at the end of the Cinquemiglia! The plateau is bare most of the way, with white/gray rock and tufts of grass, and then suddenly comes to life with forests. The branches of great trees that are hundreds of years old hang across the road from each side and join together, making a long tunnel of darkness under the green. It is a magic place! I can't imagine soldiers freezing here, but my uncle says it is very different in winter, with no leaves on the trees, and everything covered with ice and snow. But for now the leaves flicker above me and I know that it will be dark until...*here it comes*—oh, *fantastico*! We dip straight down a steep slope, and out from under the trees. It always makes my stomach go funny as we just drop away, down, down, with all the beautiful wide valley opening up in front of us. The green roof has left us and we are in the wide-open space—the valley below is enormous, with great white-tipped peaks ahead, and the closer peaks of the Majella mountains to our right. It always makes me gasp.

"I hope we don't meet any brigands, Mario!" says my uncle.

I like it when he says this. He always pretends we are going to be attacked like in the old days. He told me that we are on part of the famous Via degli Abruzzi, the route merchants used to travel from Naples to Florence for a thousand years. He said the merchants chose this longer route instead of the coast road to avoid paying tolls—which is money you give to a man on the road. But my uncle said going this way they often had to give more money to other men on the road because there were many attacks and robberies.

"And who had their northernmost front here?" my uncle asks.

"The Normans," I say proudly, hoping to spot a Norman castle soon so I can show him that I remember what he told me: how Norman castles look different from other castles, often larger and plainer, with round towers. The Normans took over the bottom part of Italy and only came up as far as here, the Abruzzo. My uncle said the mountains gave them protection so they used them as their "front." Now I understand why there are so many castles, hamlets and forts here, up on the high crags—so many to look at that sometimes my neck cricks, especially when I am trying to look out the back window.

Today I've decided I'll watch the *right* side of the road, where there are lots of abbeys and monasteries and spooky caves to underground dens where the hermit monks lived. My uncle once took me to the hermit caves at Roccamorice. It had all these steps running up the side of the mountain and holes in the rocks where people lived, and there was a chapel high up on the cliff that looked like it had been carved from the rock. Uncle said the Benedictine monks lived all along here and built these places, and some became hermits, which is like people who live dirty in a cave. I don't know why you would want to live dirty in a cave when you could live in a nice big monastery where the nuns made you cookies.

"Watch out!" yells my aunt.

A truck is coming the opposite way, and we have to quickly pull over to the side. This happens a lot because the roads are often too narrow for vehicles to pass: my uncle has to swing the steering wheel when we turn a blind corner and come across a car—or worse, a truck. It's scary when we have to move too close to the edge of the road—when that edge drops steeply to the valley floor, like now. I look down.

I shouldn't have looked down.

"What's the next castle, Mario?" asks my uncle.

I think he says this to calm me—and my aunty, who is still holding on to the sides of her seat.

"Isn't this one your favorite?" he adds.

I think I said it was, last time, but now I'm not sure. I like every one I pass. And there's so many. I love Ocre castle, high on the ridge, with its walled village and the convent nearby. Then there's the castle at Calascio, and the one at Pacentro, with its moat and three great towers. My other favorite place isn't really a castle but it has a hermitage on the side of the hill where two kings came to tell a monk he was pope and, just below it, on the flat part, the ruins of the Temple of Ercole Curino—the Temple of Hercules!

"Oh, I know! Roccacasale," I say. "That's my favorite!"

I haven't been inside, but Roccacasale castle *sounds* the most exciting. We learned about it at school. You can see it on its high spur just outside Sulmona. Roccacasale was built as a fortress a thousand years ago when the pope asked a duke and some princes to barricade the entrance to the valley and the Cinquemiglia plain against the Arabs and Byzantines who were trying to invade. Then a famous crusader lived there, and then some of the castle fell to bits in an earthquake, and then the French came and took it.

"Why did so many people from other countries come here when they had their own countries?" I ask my uncle.

"Do you mean invaders?" he asks, looking at me in the rearview mirror.

I nod.

"Sometimes it's because there's a war back home, Mario, or a famine, and they need new land to live in. But more often it has to do with power and money—*greed*."

"Is liking money bad?" I ask. I'm thinking of the coins from the donation box.

"Money isn't bad, it's how you get it and how you use it that matters," says my uncle. "It's useful for life's small pleasures."

I won't think about how I *got* my money. At least it sounds like I used it properly: chewing gum is a small pleasure, and I didn't invade a country or anything.

"There's a Norman castle!" I yell, pointing to Pettorano sul Gizio on my left (oh, not supposed to look that side!), and then suddenly—as we swing around—it's on my *right* . . . now it's on my left again . . . I like this part, the hairpin bends.

"Almost there," says my uncle, "and what's that important town *after* Sulmona, Mario?"

"It's that town with the yellow stuff."

"Navelli, and it's *saffron*," says my uncle.

I can never remember the name but you see it growing everywhere near this town: all the purple flowers with the red bits in their centers which are removed, my uncle told me, to make *yellow*: there are thousands and thousands of these purple blooms on the slopes.

"You were talking about gold before," says my uncle. "Do you remember I told you that the most precious gold for some time was this saffron—from flowers?"

That's right! But how could yellow stuff from a flower be more precious than gold like you find in a treasure chest?

"*Zafferano*—saffron—is a seasoning for food and a dye for clothes," continues my uncle, "and it's precious because it takes eighty thousand flowers to make a pound—that's *eighty thousand flowers to make a handful*, Mario!"

Why would you bother squashing that many flowers? I'd rather have gold like the pirates.

We're now down on the lower plateau and I can see the belltowers of Sulmona, home of the poet Ovid, whose statue dominates the piazza.

"Oh look, there are some boys raking," my aunt says deliberately, pointing to some boys working in a field.

I was in big trouble on my last vacation in Collemare when I was caught paying my brothers to do my share of the field work: the raking of the straw into piles. Well, I had to: Luigi whined and cried that he wouldn't do my share, and I wanted to go into the bush to play Tarzan and hunt with my bow and arrow. Everything was all right when I agreed to pay him some of my pocket money. This arrangement went well for two summer vacations, until my younger brother, Alberto, blabbed. He blabbed because I gave him less money than Luigi: but he raked slower.

"Yes, Mario," says my uncle in a stern voice, "make sure you *help out* this time. You're the eldest, and with your father away, you're the example to your brothers."

I'm glad when we begin swerving through the narrow streets of Sulmona because now Uncle has to watch the road and can no longer glare at me in the mirror. We pull up in the piazza near the tall, bronze figure of Ovid.

Sulmona is famous all around the world for its *confetti*—its white, sugar-coated almonds—so every time we return home we stop here to buy gifts. My uncle hands my aunt money and heads for the church, leaving her to make sure that everyone at home—my mother, my brothers, Nonno, Nonna and all my aunt's relatives—gets the same gift each time: *confetti*. Everyone likes sweets, Aunt said.

I always have to help my aunt buy these gifts, and after a while I noticed that even though everyone gets *confetti*, the *confetti* each gets is very different. When she buy *confetti* for *her* family, they are the fantastic, big ones—like the large trees with lots of *confetti* tied to their branches as "fruit"—and when she buys the *confetti* for my mother and family, they are the smaller packets. I tried to get her to buy a big tree for my mother once, and she said no. When I asked why her family got the big ones, she told me to mind my own business.

I push open the squeaky door to the *confetti* shop and the sweet sugary smell mixed with a nutty aroma hits my nostrils. Yum! Sweet *and* nutty: two of my favorite tastes! Looking sideways at the exciting packages, I thump into the back of my aunt, who has stopped suddenly at a table display near the door. She picks up a packet of *confetti*.

"Who's that for?" I ask without thinking.

"Does it matter?" says my aunt, looking annoyed.

Back in the car I am squashed in the back seat with my aunt's packages. She won't put the sweets in the trunk because she says they might get smelly from the fumes, so now I'm pressed up against yummy smells that I can't eat.

We are heading toward Popoli, and will soon see the famous Roman towns in the valleys: Corfinium, where my uncle said the name of Italy came from, and farther along Peltinium. And near Collemare there's Amiternum; its colosseum—which is now in ruins— was used as the model for the one later built in Rome. But I can't look at it this time because it's on the *other* side of the road from where I'm supposed to be looking.

Anyway, I'm not sure if I want to look at any more ruins. My uncle just told me something sad. Some of the things along the road that I *thought* were Roman ruins were actually houses and buildings bombed in the war. My uncle said the bombs killed people and took away their homes, and the armies on the ground also damaged a lot of ancient historical things. He said some monasteries full of rare and very old books, and other important things like castles and Roman buildings, were bombed to bits so no one could ever look at them again. I'm glad they didn't bomb the castles I like. Or maybe they did, and that's what the crumbly parts are.

I don't want to think of the war. It took away my papa.

Just then I lean on one of the packages and it makes a loud crackling noise.

"Mario," says my aunt, irritated, "could you pass me that, please?"

I pick up the large bundle wrapped in yellow paper, but unfortunately I let go before my aunt has taken hold of it and the package slips down in between the front seats, jamming. I quickly pull at it: the package rips in half and packets of *confetti* spill out over the handbrake, between the seats, and onto the back floor at my feet.

"*Scostumato!*" screeches my aunt.

I madly fumble to pick up the packets and hand them to my aunt, who glares and snatches each one, placing it back into the torn paper on her lap. With all the *confetti* rescued, I have in my hand the very last one. I lean forward, holding it up in full view of my uncle: it is the large *confetti* tree.

"Who's this one for?" I ask.

My aunt tries to snatch it, but my uncle has seen.

"Beautiful!" he says. He hasn't observed a large *confetti* tree before because our family never gets them.

"Is this one for my mother?" I ask my aunt.

"Your mother will *love* it, Mario," says my uncle, "I'm sure she will...," he finishes absently, changing gears and checking for cars behind us in his mirror.

My aunt glares at me. "We'll see...I haven't yet decided," she says, taking the tree from me.

"Who's that for?" I ask, pointing to another elaborate packet on her lap.

"Mario," says my aunt, tight-lipped, "your mother has her tree." She slaps a small packet of the sweets into my chest. "Here, eat some *confetti*, and no more chattering."

I take the packet and sit back. Nestling into the seat, I enjoy the rumbling of the car engine as I eat my sweets and look out at the wild Abruzzo countryside: the valley that stretches out wide, sloping up into majestic, ice-tipped peaks on either side; the villages tucked into the crevices of the gray, rocky slopes; the bright yellow gorse peeking from the dark green shards of grass; the forests on the hillsides that are home to wild animals like eagles, bears and wolves; the castles; and the little houses closer to the road that look like they were bombed—no, I don't want to think about that. I'll just pretend they fell down like the Roman ruins, because they were happy that lots of people had lived in them for hundreds and hundreds of years and now they needed a rest.

My sweets finished, the car rocking and humming, I lie down on the seat in among the crinkly packages, and close my eyes. Nothing awful could ever happen in the beautiful Abruzzo...yes, the little stone houses were just tired, and they needed to lie down and rest...

Il Frate e il Gesuita
THE FRIAR AND THE JESUIT

The curtains billow out, their ends flickering as if they're trying to reach our table.

Signora Flavia has the glass doors open with the Persian doors shuttered across the great window—the window with *three* different curtains. The first two heavy layers have been drawn back, leaving just the final, sheer layer, and a breeze has come up, whispering through the louvers and making these curtains misbehave.

I don't want to look up.

Flak! Flak! The curtains flick again. I can see them out of the corner of my eye. I hope she doesn't close the glass doors: it will shut off the outside. I wish I was outside.

The bishop is sitting opposite me, that's why I don't want to look up. And as for beside me... I can't look either way. The one in black is frowning, and the one in brown—I think he's one of the ones who live in a cave.

We're at a church lunch. Something to do with a saint and an anniversary, I don't know exactly, but it must be important because we had a big mass with several priests, and the bishop is here and other church people I haven't seen before. And it's at Signora Flavia's house. Aunty said they have important meals here because she's rich . . .

I love being in Signora's house. She has beautiful things in all the rooms—big vases, curling green plants, grand old paintings and pictures: fantastic pictures of faraway places like Venice that I stare at for a long time, pretending I'm in them. I get plenty of time to stare because I come here often with my uncle: he does her confession, and I sit in the drawing room with the pictures of Venice, a drink and a slice of delicious cake or tart while the confession goes on in another room.

Signora Flavia is gentle and kind to me when we visit, always saying, "*Come sta questo quadrano,*" as I come in the door—her affectionate way of asking how I am. I have learned that people with big houses get their confession at home. Aunt said it's because they put more money toward the church, and I asked if that meant you paid for confession. My aunt said saying things like that would lead me to become a heretic, which I think is something like a hermit, so I won't say it again because I want to live in a house.

I don't remember Signora Flavia's dining table being so long. Its dark wood is shiny with polish and today it's covered with glittering glasses and dishes. Maybe all the stuff on the table makes it *look* bigger. My uncle is at the other end and there are several people between us and he's just . . . *so* far away. Usually I'm seated beside him, but this time he made me sit away from him, with people I don't know. I hope no one talks to me.

We're still praying: *Gloria Patri, et Filio, et Spiritui Sancto . . .* I sneak a quick glance around the table: one, two, three . . . *nine* men.

I *think* they're all church people, but they look so different. Some wear black with fancy red bits, some have caps, some are in plain black, gray or brown, some have fancy rings, some don't ... They all have crucifixes, though, so they *must* be church people, but then my aunty wears a crucifix ... except hers is little and here they all have *big* crucifixes. Even the crucifixes are different: one black, one silver, one with little jewels around the outside of the cross, and the one on the man in brown next to me is ... *wooden.* A crucifix made from *rough wood!*

I take a closer look at him—eyes sideways, keeping my head down. Don't want the bishop to look up and see I'm not praying: he's told me off for that before. When I asked my uncle how the bishop knew I didn't have my eyes closed if he had *his* eyes closed, Uncle said he was closer to God and could see things others couldn't. I have my head down so I hope he can't see through it.

The man with the wooden crucifix is dressed all in brown. His clothes are loose compared to everyone else, and he looks sort of ... *sloppy:* like he has on a big, dark brown sack, with a flap on top with pockets, a hood at the back and a cord around his waist. Nothing else: a brown sack and cord, and the wooden crucifix. He is wide, with thick rolls around his waist, his hair doesn't sit flat, and he has a *beard.* His nails are chipped and the cracks in his hands look sort of ... *dirty.* I'm sure he's one of those hermits. I wonder what they eat in caves.

Our eyes meet. I look away. Prayers haven't finished and he's seen me looking! I hope he doesn't think ... and I hope *the bishop* didn't see ... good: he's talking to the man next to him. I sneak a look back at the man in brown. He's looking at me, smiling and nodding his head as if he knew I was going to turn back to him.

His eyes dart from me to the center of the table. Grabbing the loaf of *pagnotta*, he tears off a chunk with his big hands, stuffs it into his mouth and begins chewing—but not in a way my aunty would like. The other men around the table chat, not touching the bread.

No wonder he's hungry. I bet he's glad to be in a nice house, with nice dishes, and a nice—

"*Excess!*" he leans across and whispers in my ear, and then—*Clink! Clink!*—he taps the beautiful, smoky patterned wineglass in front of me.

"You don't *need* these things," he continues, "you're just led to believe you do."

Oh! He doesn't like the glasses! I hope Signora Flavia can't hear.

"In fact, all of this," he says, indicating the room, "is unnecessary. Beautiful, certainly, but against the teachings: the example given to us by the Son of God and our beloved Saint Francis."

Now I *really* hope Signora can't hear! I think he's saying all her stuff is bad and that God wouldn't like it.

"He's talking about the beloved Assisi," says the man in black on the other side of me. "He means *that* Saint Francis." He smiles at the man in brown and then at me. "You see, we too have our famous Saint Francis."

What does he mean, we *too* have our Saint Francis? I thought the saints were for everyone. But I do know about Saint Francis of Assisi—*everyone* knows him. He loved animals and he even tamed a wolf, and he lived out in the bush, out in the rocks like a—oh! A *hermit!*

The man in brown offers me his rough hand. "Fratello Franco, and you are?"

"Mario," I say.

"You're Don Ruggero's nephew?"

I nod.

"What a lucky boy you are! To be so close to good teachings so young. And as you go through your life, keep things simple, Mario—the simpler the better. The simple life brings you closer to God."

"He means no fine plates or glasses," says the man in black. "In fact no fine *anything*. Nothing except the utmost necessities: basic clothing and food. Admirable, but not for everyone." He looks across at the other man with a smile. "Franciscans do great works through living simply, but the world also needs science and education. Our society focuses on education."

It seems the man in brown is a Franciscan monk—I've heard of them. So who is the man in black?

"Don Giorgio," he says, offering me his hand: it is slender, soft and pale.

"Are you a Franciscan?" I ask.

"*Jesuit!*" says the Franciscan, leaning across and speaking before Don Giorgio can answer. He pretends to whisper: "You see his glasses? That's how you can tell: Jesuits read a lot and wear their eyes out."

The Jesuit laughs.

I study him. He *is* wearing small round spectacles, and he looks smart: his robes are dark and tight fitting around his chest and his crucifix is silver with little sparkling rocks on it—it's beautiful. His hair is short and neat, he has no beard, and he's thin with long arms. I look at his eyes: they're clear. They don't look worn out.

I look back at the Franciscan with his baggy brown robe and messy hair; the two men are *very* different.

"You forgot to mention our warm shoes," says the Jesuit. He indicates the Franciscan's feet with his eyes, wanting me to look.

I glance down and see—sandals and bare feet. *At the table!* I can't imagine what my aunt would say if Uncle invited him home.

The Franciscan notices my surprise and points to his sandals: "Just as the Son of God, Mario, and just as Saint Francis."

117

He leans across and breaks off another two chunks of bread. This time he puts the larger piece in his apron pocket, checking first to see that the Jesuit isn't looking. *But he must know I saw!*

Two large, steaming bowls of fettuccine have just been placed on the table. The Franciscan drops some of the pasta onto his placemat as he quickly ladles it into his dish. He rubs at the spill with his napkin, and now both the placemat and the white linen cloth are streaked with bright orange.

"Tell me, Mario, what do you want to do with your life?" he asks between mouthfuls of pasta. "Any thoughts of *prendere il saio?*"

Taking the robe! "No ... yes ... *non loso* ... I *think* so," I say.

I don't *really* want to be a priest, not unless I go to the jungle, but I've learned to say yes, because if I don't, church people spend the next hour trying to talk me into it.

"And would that be loving *field ministry*," continues the Franciscan, glancing across at the Jesuit, "or keeping your head closed up in books?"

I don't know. If I *had* to be a priest I'd want to be a missionary in Africa because that's where Tarzan is. I'd want to live in the jungle like Tarzan, so I think that must be field ministry. But I like books, and I would want to take some.

"Can you do both?" I ask.

The Jesuit cuts in: "Of course you can, Mario. That's what we Jesuits do: revere books and education as well as preach—*and* we do our manual labor daily."

I'm not sure about the "manual labor": it sounds too much like the raking I have to do at home. And education usually means school, so maybe the Franciscan way is better. Anyway, Tarzan doesn't wear shoes, so he's more like a Franciscan, and I could always take *some* books, though I'm not sure where I'd put them when I'm swinging through the trees.

"If Franciscans don't like books, does that mean they don't go to school?" I ask Fratello Franco, watching him shovel the last of the pasta into his mouth. I hear the Jesuit laugh.

"Books are for monks in monasteries, Mario. We Franciscans are mendicants, friars: we devote our time to preaching, active ministry. We travel a lot. And we don't *dislike* books—some books keep us close to God." He points to the *messale* on the table near the Jesuit. "We just leave their study to others."

I turn to the Jesuit: "Do you live in a monastery?" I'm too scared to ask the Franciscan where *he* lives.

"No. I live in an open community and teach in the seminary. In a way, we Jesuits are in between *friars*, who are always out in the world, and *monks*, who are inside, cut off from the world. We Jesuits have years of study like the monks, but we also mix daily with people outside, teaching and preaching." He dabs his mouth with his napkin, and then glances over at the Franciscan. "You could say we Jesuits have the best of both worlds—the most balanced way of serving God."

"The Son of God didn't carry books," says the friar.

Thump! A bowl of warm ricotta drizzled with honey has been placed in front of me. Oh, delight! The nutty cheese and earthy-sweet honey aromas reach my nostrils mixed with the lovely perfume of Signora Flavia as she leans over me. I realize I have hardly touched my pasta as my plate is removed. The dessert bowl that replaces it is pretty, with gold edges and—oh! I hope the Franciscan doesn't say anything. I hope he doesn't call it that bad thing starting with x.

Signora smiles sweetly at me. I like her. I watch as she moves away to get more dishes from the tray. Even though she's old, Signora Flavia is pretty: she has a lovely face, soft, neat hair, a slim figure, and she dresses in beautiful clothes. And she's *always* smiling and gently spoken.

"That's because she's *noble*," said my aunt when I told her I liked visiting Signora. My aunt always thinks people with big houses are nice.

The friar is next to be served, and I watch as Signora approaches him with the bowl. The Franciscan doesn't see her coming. He snorts loudly and is rubbing his mouth on his sleeve when Signora Flavia taps his arm. He jumps with surprise. Signora places his dessert on the table.

"Thank you," he says gruffly.

He looks at the bowl and I'm waiting, waiting...

"*Bellissima!*" he says, turning to give her a big smile.

Oh good!

I watch as Signora Flavia speaks with him, *as she touches him*, placing her hand gently on the Franciscan's shoulder: she seems to like everyone, even what my aunt would call scruffy people.

"*Pia Signora!*" says the Franciscan to himself as she moves away, "A good, pious woman"; and then, through a mouthful of cheese: "So, Mario, how is your Latin?"

"Good. My uncle is—"

"*Labor omnia vincit*, Mario," says the Franciscan. "Books are one thing, but *labor omnia vincit*. Yes?"

I know the regular prayers and *some* religious words in Latin, but this...I recognized *one* word: *labor*, it means *work*, but as for the other words! I glance at the end of the table, glad that my uncle can't hear. I can't let him down by showing that I don't understand these three simple words—

"*Si*, work is..." I don't know what to say next, and I can feel my face burning.

"Was that first word *labor*, Brother, or *scripta?*" the Jesuit intervenes, and then says to me: "Isn't this ricotta beautiful?" He returns to his bowl: "Mario can give us some Latin another time."

Think I'll be a Jesuit.

"What about animals, Mario?" asks the Franciscan. "Do you like animals? Trees, flowers... nature?"

"Oh, I love going into the mountains with my friends, hunting birds and lizards with my sling—"

"*Don't kill*, respect all life, all animals, all peoples, these are our beliefs. We Franciscans work the land, giving and taking of its rich bounty. We undertake our daily ministry and keep our lives simple," says the friar. "*This* is what being close to God is all about."

He shows me his gnarled hands, turning them over. I can see they are cut, callused and worn from working the land, the same as my *nonno's* hands and the hands of the other farmers back home.

He pulls at the fabric of his simple tunic: "Just as Saint Francis," he says, rubbing the rough cloth.

The Jesuit says something, and as I turn to him the Franciscan grabs my arm. "Do you like donkeys, Mario?" he asks.

"Yes!" I say. I *love* donkeys: they are so cute and quiet and *stubborn*, and they have that sweet face, with big ears and gentle eyes that just *look* at you.

"We have *several* donkeys," says the Franciscan. "We also have apples and raspberries, plums and cherries that we pick straight from our trees. You should come and visit us sometime."

Donkeys *and* cherries, and no school—I think I would have to be a Franciscan! But what about...

"Can you live in a house instead of a cave?" I ask.

The Franciscan laughs. It's the first time I've heard him laugh, and the Jesuit joins in. I feel myself reddening again.

"Oh, Mario, you are thinking of the *hermit* monks!" says the friar. "We're not hermits. We live at the friary surrounded by our *orto*— a walled area with our kitchen garden and orchard—and a small paddock for our donkeys."

That's it. Donkeys, cherries, no school, and bare feet like Tarzan. I want to be a Franciscan. I could sneak the occasional book.

"Tell us, Mario," says the Jesuit, "what do *you* like? We've been talking about what we do; what do *you* like to do?"

"Um..." I'm thinking, thinking, not sure what I should say. I have to be careful when talking to church elders because I am the priest's nephew. My uncle would expect me to say I like religious studies, my aunt *schooling*...

"Come on, Mario, speak up: tell us what you love!" says the Jesuit.

I look from him to the Franciscan.

"Weapons!" I say excitedly.

I notice the friar sit back in his chair.

"I like weapons—like daggers and knives and swords and things!"

The two men are silent for a moment, and then the friar begins: "War is not always a good thing, you know, Mario. Don't glorify war and its weapons *too much*. Remember, killing is against God's law."

"What about the crusaders?" I ask.

I see the Jesuit smile.

"Sometimes Christians feel they *have* to battle to keep their faith," says the Franciscan, "but it's not the Franciscan way..." his voice trails off. And then: "It's best to take up weapons that *build* lives, not destroy them."

"*Build* lives?" I ask.

The Franciscan fumbles in his apron pocket and pulls out a knife. It's big, with a chunky wooden handle. He holds it at the wrong end, covering the blade with his large fingers, and as he slowly moves them away I see that the knife has no tip. It is a large knife with the top of its blade cut off flat.

"Now what is the difference between this knife and *your* knife, Mario?" he asks. "The one you have in your pocket?"

How did he know? I have my penknife in my pocket, but I am not supposed to bring it to church, and I am not supposed to have it at a church lunch. Maybe he's like the bishop and can see through...

I hesitate, but his eyes won't leave me. "Your knife is bigger," I begin.

"And?"

"Yours is funny because it's chopped off at the top. Did you break it?" I ask.

"No. We have knives without tips to show they are *not* weapons. Our knives are for cutting bread, salami, fruit; slicing and chopping so that we may eat and live; they are used to prune plants and to make things—for daily survival."

I don't want a broken knife. I wonder if the Jesuits have broken knives.

The Jesuit turns to me: "So, Mario, what do you like about these weapons of yours?" he asks.

"They give you power! They make you win," I say.

"There are other ways of winning," he says. "Brother Franco said in Latin *labor omnia vincit*—'work always wins'—and I said that the first word could be *scripta*, making it 'writing always wins.' The written word is a powerful, powerful weapon, and can be used to win great battles: we Jesuits have proved it over the centuries."

Words as *weapons*? How can you strike down an ax-wielding barbarian with a *word*?

"Working hard and living by example is a better weapon," cuts in the Franciscan. "Being an example to others: you can win great battles with that."

"But which one is *right?*" I ask, looking from the Jesuit to the friar and back again. "If two people say different weapons, then which one is right?"

"Well, it's not that any particular one is—" begins the Jesuit.

"*Ours!*" yells the friar. "If a weapon has to be a single object, Mario, I will show you the *greatest* weapon of all!" He puts his arms straight out in front of him, his thick hands together, and makes a pulling motion toward his body—a *plowing* motion. "*Il bidente*, Mario, the *hoe!* The hoe that tills the fertile soil, that feeds the masses, that brings rich food and life again and again to all of us. *This* is the most powerful weapon of all!"

The hoe! I never thought of a hoe as—

"Certainly it's a good weapon," says the Jesuit, "and example is a great thing. But living by example does not *always*—"

"Example is powerful!" says the friar. "The Franciscan beliefs of liberty for all—rich *and* poor—and universal brotherhood formed the basis of our Italian government!"

The Franciscan is right. My uncle says we should be fair and look after the poor.

"Yes, but there *are* times when you need to change people's minds much faster than example will allow," says the Jesuit. He turns to me: "And how do you move and inspire *thousands* of people, even in distant places, Mario?"

Signora Flavia interrupts us as she and another woman begin clearing the table, removing the plates and the beautiful glasses. I don't want to go home yet. I don't want to go and leave the friar and the Jesuit because I still haven't decided which one I would be if I *had* to—

"Mario," says the Jesuit, who has turned fully to me, "before we go I want to show you the *most powerful weapon of all*. And I want you to remember."

He slips his hand inside the breast of his cloak and watches my face. I am tense. What is it? A dagger? A sword? A *pistol*?

The Jesuit keeps his hand inside his cloak: "*This* weapon will give you more power than any sword or battle weapon, for *this weapon* can slay a million in one stroke."

Slay a million! In *one* stroke!

He withdraws his hand and lays the weapon on the table in front of me.

I look down at a sleek, black fountain pen.

"The greatest weapon is the pen, through which comes the written word," says the Jesuit. "With this, you can reach millions, and change hearts and minds."

"The *spoken* word is powerful," says the Franciscan quietly. "That is why we go among the people and preach: we pass on the Word of God."

"But not to *millions*, and not for *generations*," says the Jesuit to me. "Isn't it better to have your words pass down to the next generation, and the one after, and the one after that? Wouldn't it be good, Mario, to have your words reach people even when you are no longer alive? Remember: *Verba volant, scripta manent*—'Words fly away, but the writing stays.'"

Oh, I like that! *Words fly away!* I guess they do when you talk. They just fly away and no one remembers them, and he's right: books *do* say your words for you even after you're dead. I never thought of that. And books make you want to *do* things, and *be* things . . .

The Franciscan and the Jesuit turn away from me and begin chatting with others who are leaving: the talk has become loud and excitable, with people shaking hands and standing to say their farewells. With the clatter of dishes and movement, I become invisible. I sit back and imagine the Franciscan, the Jesuit and myself seated side by side with our weapons on the table in front of us: the hoe, the sword and the pen.

The Jesuit has finished his goodbyes and turns back to me. He picks up his pen, smiling, as he stands: "One day you will have to choose," he says, and walks from the room.

"*Argh!*" screams an old woman from the back of the church. "Aye yay-yay-yay-yay!"

I'm saved! My uncle was just about to check under my *chierichetto* smock. He had seen me holding my chest every time I bent to snuff out the mass candles and figured out that I was holding on to something in my top pocket. He thinks it's gum, but it's not—it's my secret weapon. My secret weapon I *don't* want him to see because I borrowed it from him: it's heavy and gold, with a split nib and his initials carved into its side.

"There's something there, it touched my hand!" yells the old woman. "An animal!"

An *animal*? In church? Must have been a mouse.

I feel for my pen. Good, it's upright. I had a bad accident the other day when ink leaked out all over my shirt, which is now hidden in my secret tree until I can throw it away somewhere. Aunty is on the hunt: I told her that I put it where I *always* put my dirty clothes—on my bedroom floor—and I have *no idea* where it went. So now I'm forever checking the pen, and to be honest I'm getting sick of carrying this weapon. My friends asked how you used a pen *in battle* and I told them you write letters to scare your enemy: they didn't look interested. So I said if *that* didn't work you could stab them in the eye with it. They still didn't seem interested: they didn't even ask to hold it.

"*Madonna, Madonna!*" the old woman is muttering. She is near the church entrance, near the font, where people are saying their goodbyes after mass. There is a lot of fuss and chatter. She said it *touched her hand,* which is strange because mice usually scamper off. Still, I am *very* glad for this mouse!

"*Mario,*" whispers my friend Marcello from near the pulpit. He too is a *chierichetto,* and his job today is sweeping the choir stand. "Watch out," he says, pointing down toward my uncle.

"I know, *I know!*" I say, patting my pocket. He must have seen my uncle accost me: my friends know about the "borrowed" pen. "I'm going to put it somewhere," I say, heading for the sacristy where there are plenty of hiding places.

"No, no," says my friend. "Not that!" He points emphatically toward my uncle.

"You've had it!" says another *chierichetto,* who has come up beside me from the font. "She felt something in the holy water."

I freeze.

It's not a mouse that touched the old woman's hand. It was something smaller and lumpier.

But how did it happen? I made sure the gum was stuck up on the side of the font, that it wouldn't fall in. It's not *my* fault. I'd been told the contents of my mouth would be checked—in church— so I had to put it *somewhere.* I was caught popping during mass. With the congregation to the back of us, and me in the row of *chierichetto* boys facing the *back* of my uncle as he performed his ritual at the altar, I would occasionally blow a small bubble of gum. I did it quickly and it was enough to cause a soft giggle down the line. Once in a while the bubble would accidentally pop, but not loudly. Except for last week. That time it made a loud *pop!* and my uncle heard.

Today I forgot the gum was in my mouth. I entered the church and suddenly realized I had to get rid of it before I got up the front, near my uncle and aunt. I'm sure I stuck it hard on the side. *I did.* I stuck it under the lip of the font, squashing it forcefully between the two ridges that circle the bowl above the water. The font is high and you can't see into it easily. You definitely can't see under the lip on the side closest to you as you stand in front of it, which is where I put my gum. I just wanted to keep it there until after mass, so I could enjoy it again. But it must have fallen in.

"*Comunisti!*" cries a woman with disgust as my uncle displays the object he has retrieved from the font.

"Sacrilege! *Sacrilege!*" screams another woman: "*Si, comunisti.*"

That word again. Whenever something *really* bad happens people say the communists are responsible. I've heard my aunt say they burn Bibles, get divorced and worship Satan in shirts that are colored red like the devil—and she had *heard* they ate babies. I wanted to know more, but my uncle wouldn't let her tell me: he said it was bigotry. I like bigotry. I'm not sure what it is, but it always seems so exciting.

My uncle's coming! He seems to have calmed the crowd—everyone is now leaving—but he doesn't look calm. I go back to blowing out the candles. Very fast. I can see Marcello vigorously sweeping to the side of me, and Giovanni dusting the pews: he keeps looking back at my approaching uncle. I wish he wouldn't!

"Into the sacristy, all of you, *now!*" says my uncle, turning a sharp left into the small room without waiting for our response.

I watch my friends slowly drop their cleaning rags and brooms, and head toward the room. I push in before Giovanni: I don't want to be last. There are six of us, all in our lacy white smocks, stuffed into the small room.

My uncle holds up a pale pink, lumpy mass the size of a small walnut. "What is *this?*" he asks. He's usually serene, but right now his face is red and the veins along his neck are bulging out.

Silence.

"Come on, boys, what does it *look* like?" He squeezes the lump tight and then stretches it out so that the gum hangs in a string between his fingers. "It's sticky and it stretches, and...Giovanni? Mario? You don't know what it is?"

"No," we say in unison.

My uncle glares at me so hard I feel as though he is looking through my head to the wall behind me.

"I know *what* it is," I say shakily, "but I don't know..." My voice trails off.

"Where it *was?*" asks my uncle. "Is that what you were going to say?"

I nod meekly.

"For those few, if any, in the room who *don't know*," says my uncle, "this gum was in the font."

I hear a couple of gasps. Marcello glances at me and I try to look shocked.

"Chewing gum in the font," says my uncle as he looks from face to nervous face. He clenches the hand holding the gum: "*Chewing gum in holy water.*"

No one dares speak or move.

"Whose is it?"

No answer.

"Who was doing *chierichetto* down the back of the church today?"

"Mario," says Giovanni.

"*And you*, you were putting out the *messale*!" I say defiantly.

"And I was down the back collecting coins," says Marcello, not understanding my uncle's tack.

"So, nobody knows *anything*." My uncle looks around at us. "I realize it *could* have been someone else, but other children are unlikely to be near the font during service. Did any of you see anything during mass, someone acting strange near the font?" asks my uncle.

"Nonna Grimaldi," says Marcello.

"Yes, and I'm sure old Nonna with her clacking dentures is the owner of this chewing gum," says my uncle.

Giovanni laughs, until he catches my uncle's eye. Then he stops.

"Whether this came to be in the font *accidentally or not*," my uncle says, shaking the gum at us, "it is an outrageous, disrespectful act—a sacrilege against God and his church—that will come back on whoever did it. And I will find out who did it. I will give you all a few days to think about it, and then I want each of you in confession—before Sunday." He turns his back on us and places the gum in a dish. "You can go," he says.

Turning quickly, I almost trip over Marcello, and I push at Giovanni to get past him through the door.

"*Wait*," says my uncle. "You three, stay." He indicates Marcello, Giovanni and me.

We stop, rooted to the floor.

"Until we get to the bottom of this," he continues, "I'd like you three to do a *fioretto* for me, right now. A sworn promise to God. None of you is to buy gum for the next three weeks, and *all* of you—" he looks from Marcello to Giovanni and back to me—"are to throw away the gum you have now. Is that understood?"

We nod and swear our *fioretti* with sighs and looks of dismay.

"Mario, *wake up!*" calls my aunt.

Her voice sounds distant, and I'm suddenly aware of rocking and a strong smell of vinyl—right against my nose. That's right, I'm in the car, on the way to Collemare, sleeping on the back seat. I slowly raise myself, groggy and yawning, to find that we're almost there.

"Straighten yourself up before your mother sees you—you look like a tramp!" my aunt goes on. "And *this time*, help with the bags."

It's a week since that terrible incident with the font and our *fioretti* about the chewing gum: we suffered for *three days* without gum before we worked out that there was a way around the promise. My uncle had said we couldn't buy any gum and that we had to throw away the gum we had. So, it was simple. We gave Giovanni's older brother *our* gum and he went and bought new gum for us.

"Won't we go to hell for breaking our *fioretti?*" Giovanni had asked me as I snapped off a piece and handed it to him.

"We *didn't* break it," I replied.

Giovanni had still looked worried so I went to grab the gum off him, but he snatched it away and popped it in his mouth before I could get it.

My aunt again: "And *this* time, try to be a *good* example to your brothers and don't go killing birds!"

Aunt Ercolina never lets me forget anything I've done—anything *bad*, that is. She refers repeatedly to the bad things I've done, and it's worse in the car where my uncle and I are captive. My uncle said that one day he would like to get a radio for the car. I think I know why.

"Mario's learned from that," he says now.

Aunt doesn't know how bad I felt killing that mother bird. I swore to myself I would never use my *fionda* again! I even told my uncle about it when I got back home from my holidays and asked him if I could do a *fioretto* that I would never hunt again, to make it a promise to God, but luckily he talked me out of it. What happened was that I had been out hunting with my brother Luigi and some friends, and my beloved slingshot, with which I'd had many great kills and exciting hunting adventures. It was made from a forked branch of an ash tree, with rubber from a bicycle tire stretched between the two forks and a small piece of leather in the center to hold the rock. It was easier to use than the old-style *fionde* that my *nonno* had shown me how to make: the old one had a leather pouch that you swung around with the rock in it … and then let the rock go. Too many of my friends (and once my brother!) standing too near me ended up with bruises or cuts on their face, so I was told to give it up. And then I made my new one.

I was skilled with my new *fionda* and had killed lots of things with it, from lizards to frogs and once, almost, a rabbit. We would skewer our kill onto a pole that we would carry between us on our shoulders, with rows of frogs' legs and lizards' tails dangling and bouncing along as we walked—like real hunters! And then one day I got *too good* with the slingshot. I was mucking around, aiming at a mother bird and her two babies high up in a nest, when I let go. I hit the mother bird full on and she dropped from the nest right at my feet. All I could hear was the squawking babies crying out for their mother. Horrified, I climbed up and got the two chicks and took them home. I nestled them into a box under my bed, keeping them warm and feeding them *polenta* and any other mush I could sneak from my mother's kitchen all through the day and night. I didn't leave the house for three days. They died. That was when I swore to myself that I would never use my *fionda* to kill again.

Right now we're about to drop into the great valley around L'Aquila—the capital city of the Abruzzo—with its enormous castle, its great piazza and magnificent fountain with ninety-nine spouts. My uncle said there's a pope buried here, the only one buried outside the Vatican. After this we pass the ruins of the Roman town of Amiternum, and soon I will be somewhere that isn't famous or busy, that doesn't have big buildings and isn't historic in an *important* way, that doesn't have a castle, a *palazzo* or even a *church*, but it's the place I love more than anywhere—my home village of Collemare!

"And *this* time, Mario—" begins my aunt (oh no, I thought she'd finished—I get sick of all her "*this* times" just before we get to Collemare)—"*don't go jumping on any sheep!*" she finishes with a cackle.

This is too cruel. I *hate* it when she mentions this, something that happened *three trips* ago, something I know she will never forget! She won't forget it because it was the most embarrassing, most *humiliating* thing that has ever happened to me. I was shamed in front of almost everyone in my home village, and whoever *wasn't* there soon knew about it. For three years the adults in Collemare laughed when they saw me and reminded me of the "sheep incident," and it took a lot of work to become the hero of the local kids again.

It happened the very moment we arrived in my home village that year. My uncle's shiny car was forced to stop in front of the schoolhouse, waiting for a flock of sheep to move off the road, just when school finished for the day. Not wanting to miss a chance to show off—I had *all* the village children, their teachers, the shepherds and some townsfolk nearby as my audience—I jumped out of the car and strutted around to the front of it.

I needed to show off because, through none of my own doing, I had become a hero to the other kids in Collemare and I wanted to keep them believing it. Even the boys who *weren't* friends—and some of the girls—had begun to watch me carefully whenever I came back. They all think I'm rich and lucky to be traveling with my wealthy priest uncle. They say I look and speak like a "city boy," and they're always eager to know about the things I have, the things I do, the places I go. When I run out of really exciting things to tell them, I make some up.

And as for us having *a car*! Cars are rare and a great luxury, and even though my uncle's at the time was not large, and had a crank, it was still a *car*. No one else in Collemare owned one, so I knew this was the *perfect* opportunity to show all the kids how accustomed I was to traveling in one. I also had on some very fine "city" clothes that my aunt had just bought me and made me wear home to show my mother that I was fashionable *and* well cared for.

All was going well until I waded in among the sheep in front of the car. In a split-second decision—with all the adults and kids looking on, some waving and yelling, "Ciao, Mario!"—I decided to jump on a sheep's back. That was my mistake. I had only intended to *sit* on the sheep's back, to be a sort of cowboy, shouting "Giddy-up!" and swinging my arm around like I was holding a lasso. I hadn't intended to *ride* the sheep. But that's what happened.

Shocked at being jumped on, the normally placid, sweet-faced sheep bolted in terror: tearing forward and then stopping abruptly and turning a sharp left. I only just managed to hang on, at first gripping for dear life on to the woolly scruff on the back of its neck and then bending to hug its whole neck with my arms in a desperate bid to stay on. I could hear laughter somewhere as I passed the gathered schoolchildren—*twice*—and then my woolly mount made its final bolt in the direction of the shepherd.

This time the sheep pulled up so violently before turning that I couldn't hold on. I flew over the sheep's head, skidded along the ground for a while, and then landed—head down, knees grazed, and buttocks in the air—at the feet of the shepherd. I was muddy, wet and stuck all over with sheep droppings. The roar of laughter behind me was deafening.

I had to get up and pretend I wasn't hurt, smile, and quickly get back into the car. Except my aunt wouldn't let me in the car. It was the mud and sheep droppings, she said—and the shame. I had to walk the rest of the way to my house in the village—to my waiting mother—covered in dung and mud, with the village kids laughing and jeering behind me. They repeatedly sang *that* song, the song I hate—the one they made up about me and my brothers:

Mario, luzi luzi pella
Luigino zeppetella
E Alberto ridarella

It meant I was very, very skinny, Luigino talked too much, and Alberto laughed all the time. The song made me want to punch whoever sang it, but on this day I suffered it and walked quietly. It took a long time to become their hero again.

The movies won them back, and the stories. They were all fascinated that I saw *movies*. No one saw movies in Collemare, where entertainment was limited to the radio and the mail bus that arrived once a week up the white gravel road. Movies were rare outside the large towns, and the kids in my village wanted me to tell them, over and over again, about the stories I'd seen or heard. It became a ritual for a group of us to meet up in the loft of an abandoned barn the day after I came back home, all of us lying about in the warm, prickly straw as I told my stories. Stories from movies, books and comics, stories about the places I went and the things I did with my uncle.

It became harder when the girls grabbed at me, giggling, and said things like: "Mario, today can you tell us a story about *love?*" I had to tell stories about a topic *they'd* picked, and—not wanting to disappoint them—I made some of it up.

It wasn't until I returned to Collemare for the holidays that I realized just how lucky I was to be with an uncle who not only gave me so much freedom, but who loved to *show* movies. It was unusual, especially for a priest. My uncle thought movies were invigorating and uplifting for people in hard times, and he would regularly order them from Rome and show them in the villages we lived in, or nearby, getting the women to sew sheets together to make a great screen that would be hung up in a hall or against a building in the piazza, and we would all gasp and yell and thrill at films about cowboys and Indians or great epics like *Spartacus, The Ten Commandments* and *Ben-Hur.*

Of course, there were strict rules from the Vatican about what could be shown by a priest, and my uncle often had to splice pieces out of a film. My friends and I would help him by emptying his trash, thereby collecting all the dirty bits and taking them to a quiet place to view them against candlelight. I remember one part was *really* good, but most of the time it was only kissing and stuff that was cut, and we couldn't believe it when some of the village women asked for the movie to be cut *again* after its first showing, just because a man might have *looked* at a woman a certain way! Still, we collected those parts too, and I soon found these scraps of film worked magic with the girls, for these were the parts they liked to hear about *most.* They wanted all the details: "So they kissed?" the girls would ask.

"Yes," I would say.

"And how exactly was he holding her?"

I would demonstrate. "And they *kissed?*" they would ask again, breathlessly.

Once I even managed to smuggle my box of naughty film clips back home to Collemare and, with everyone now convinced I was a movie "director," it repaired my damaged reputation from the sheep ride more than anything. They all knew I helped my uncle load and unload the great reels of film behind rows of seats filled with gasps and gaping mouths, outside in the village streets or in the halls. It was like I was a famous movie star just because I helped *show* them: everyone seemed to be caught by the dreamlike magic of movies. No matter where my uncle showed these films, it was always exciting for me: the darkness, the thrill of loading and unloading film, the flickering light, the fantastic stories playing out larger than life in front of me, and the whirring of the great reel above my head.

Oh, *we're coming up the hill that leads into Collemare!* I am happy for two wonderful reasons: I am almost home, and my aunt won't scold me anymore because we are too close to arriving. Only once did she say something nasty when we were actually in our village— I was still asking what *the bad grass you can never uproot* meant as we got out of the car. My aunt went bright red and told me to be quiet: she knew my *nonno* didn't like any criticism of the family, and my mother, who was not too keen on my aunt although she respected her care of me, would not tolerate such comments for a moment. I noticed everyone was very quiet at lunch that day.

Now we're in the main street...and there's our family *portone* with its great arched entrance, which means that any moment we will be—

"Mario! *Mario!*" yells Claudio, my next-door neighbor and best friend, as he runs alongside the car. "Do you have comics?" he whispers excitedly through the car window.

As our car pulls up I signal for Claudio not to mention comics in front of my aunt and uncle. I have a stash in my bag that I was not supposed to bring.

Claudio and I have been best friends forever: although I'm a little older than him, he likes adventures like me, he likes to read and know things like me, and he lives right next door to me. In fact, he lives *too* close sometimes. The houses in our street are all linked up to each of the large communal family houses, or *portone*, the little *casas* being built up against the big ones until the whole main street of Collemare became a row of higgledy-piggledy buildings, great and small, leaning into each other. My parents' little house is just down from the Valentini *portone*, and Claudio's small house

adjoins ours—in fact, Claudio is an Antonelli, the family that
originally shared our *portone* (there are very few surnames in our
village). I like having him next door, and you can hear little through
the walls except at the fireplace. Here the wall is thinner and you
can hear everything in the room next door if you press up close;
any *loud* noise next door can be heard *without* being close.

This was never a problem except when Claudio and I had been
up to mischief. We always played together and often we would be
out killing something we shouldn't have been killing, collecting
something we shouldn't have been collecting, coming home really
late, or generally doing something we knew our parents wouldn't
like. Trouble was, I was much better at hiding things than Claudio:
he *always* seemed to get caught out by his mother.

When we got home we would say goodbye at our adjacent doors,
and go inside. I'd give my mother some story about what we'd
done and where we'd been. Within minutes—*minutes*—there would
be a slap and a howl from next door. I'd rush to the fireplace to
hear what was happening: I could hear Claudio's mother prodding,
questioning and scolding and I'd be telling him under my breath
what to say back—but Claudio was always too honest and not quick
enough. I'd sit there cringing, waiting for the next slap. It would
come, along with Claudio's cries, and at this point I'd be hoping
he'd go upstairs to the bedroom, *anywhere* away from the thin
fireplace wall, because by this time my mother would have begun
looking at me.

"What's Claudio in trouble for?" she would ask suspiciously.

"I don't know," I'd shrug.

Another howl from next door.

"You two were out together—what have you been up to?" My
mother would then start moving toward the fireplace.

I'd quickly step in ahead of her and pretend to listen at the thin wall. "Oh, he hasn't done his chores again," I'd say.

My mother would dart me a look and go back to her cooking.

The worst time was when we collected snakes. We caught a snake each and put them in jars. I told Claudio to keep his hidden but he couldn't help himself and showed his little brother, Gabriele, as soon as he got home. The snake escaped. For the next twenty minutes all you could hear from next door was Claudio's mother screaming, Claudio screaming, and walloping going on all over the house. I had to come up with a really important chore that Claudio hadn't done *that* time, but my mother didn't believe me and finally called in next door.

I couldn't go out for two days and lost the snake and lizards that were under my bed, so Claudio and I now have a secret hiding place *outside*: a huge chestnut tree with a cavernous center that can only be entered through a hole in the trunk high above its first branches.

I love to see Claudio because he is *always* my friend. I lose other friends because we move around, but Claudio . . . Claudio is always here, and always the same.

I clamber out of the car and into the small crowd that gathers whenever we arrive: there to greet us and be the first to get any news—family, neighbors, more neighbors, an old man on his way to the bar, even the village dog. I can see Nino, the head of the rival gang from the *northern* part of the village. I'm head of Collemare's *southern* gang, but Nino is still one of my best friends because we both like wild adventures and go on them together. Beside him is Serafino—the strongest boy in Collemare, who we've tried to get to join our gang—and Settimio, who is younger and very, very shy: he quietly follows us around, waiting to be asked to join our quests. We always take him.

Claudio and I grab and slap each other, laughing, and I whisper something in his ear. My uncle interrupts with a quick, "*Mario*," gesturing toward my mother.

"*Ciao, Mama!*" I call, running up and hugging her. She grabs my face in her hands and kisses me on both cheeks, but quickly stands up again, her eyes on my aunt. My mother doesn't relax until she is gone.

Claudio follows me into our house: we leave the adults outside, chatting and smoking. The house looks smaller than I remember. I was born here and know it well, but it seems smaller each time I come back. My brothers, Luigi and Alberto, tear in behind me. Whenever I return they pull at me and want to go everywhere with me until we have our first fight—which is usually after a couple of hours. I give them some chewing gum and tell them I will be out in a minute. I can tell Claudio wants to know something.

"You said you had a *new weapon?*" he says, wide-eyed.

"It's too secret. I'll tell you about it later," I say.

I can smell something—something *strong*—in the air. Claudio notices me sniffing.

"*Pomodori*," he says.

Oh, *tomatoes!*

"We've been bottling," he adds, pointing to the land behind our house: my father's land, a small section of the great Valentini *terra firma* that once stretched into the distance around our family *portone*.

We run out and down the side alley. A large vat has been placed over a fire in the back paddock: there is a shuddering, rattling sound coming from within. I know this ritual, the making of the *sugo*: the cooked tomatoes that are a base for many pasta and other dishes; the tomatoes that cannot be lived without during the freezing winter months when no other fruit is to be had. My *nonno* told me that even during the hardest times there was always a rule that there were to be four hundred bottles of tomatoes a year per family. To not have this was to not survive, he said, and those with extra gave to other families. Every August the *sugo* making begins: neighbors work together until all the tomatoes are picked, pulped and put into jars. These jars are then placed in a large vat full of water—the larger vats hold *hundreds* of jars!—then the vats are covered, and the jars are boiled for several hours over an outside fire. Once cooked, the jars are covered with a sack and left to cool for a day. We are told to keep well away because some of the jars explode. And this is what I can smell now, the strong smell of a just-exploded jar of juicy, ripe tomatoes...

This is home. *This* is my Collemare. From the day I was born—in my mother's bed in our little *casa*—I've watched as our food is sown, grown, picked and then preserved, cooked and eaten. Every animal is lovingly cared for and then killed the proper way and smoked, pickled or dried: every bit tasty, succulent and safe. Very little is bought from the shops here, unlike in the large towns—unlike the way my aunt keeps house. Here, you know where *everything* has come from and, if local, you know it was prepared with love and care, from hundreds and hundreds of years of tradition, hundreds and hundreds of years of practicing the same methods and getting the food so very tasty and so very *right*.

"I've been corking," says Claudio.

Most people can't afford the expensive jars anymore, and wine bottles are now used for the tomatoes. I often had the job Claudio's been doing—punching corks into the just-filled bottles.

"Remember when we did the grapes?" I ask, beginning to feel a bit left out.

The last time I was here the grapes were ready, and Claudio and I got the best job of all: crushing them. It was the first time we had been allowed to do it and we had so much fun jumping and slushing and slipping around inside the great tub filled with the juicy purple orbs, deliberately falling down so that we were covered from head to foot in red juice! I was very proud of being allowed to do the grownups' job of grape crushing and deliberately left my toenails purple for several days.

"*Mario!*" yells my mother from the house.

Back inside, I find her scrubbing the last of the dough off the kitchen table. From the bowl near the fire I see that she has been making gnocchi. Aunt and Uncle are serving liqueur to the guests: there's Claudio's mother, and my cousin Sandra is here! She is like my little sister, always so sweet and fun to play with. Aunt Ercolina *adores* her, and made it very clear that if she'd had a say in who came to live with her and my uncle—*oh*, my cousins Adriana, Marcello and Dario are here! The two boys grin and wave, then come over to hug and slap me on the back. They're both older and so *cool*. I always take note of what they wear, how they walk, everything they do. Clara, Marcello's older sister, isn't here. She is fiery and *so* beautiful. Nonno told me that men come to woo her from villages far, far away. He said she looks like a famous movie star called Sophia somebody. I see Nonno over by the door with his cigar, my brothers are seated halfway up our bedroom steps ripping open *confetti*, and several other neighbors have crowded into our little room, not yet wanting to leave. It's *great* to be home.

"I have a surprise for you," says my mother.

The others are all watching me, so they must know.

"Your father will be home tomorrow," she says quickly, turning back to the stove.

My father! My *father is coming!* He only comes back home from his work in other countries once or twice a year. There's no money for more frequent travel, so my mother rarely sees him. And because I am hardly ever in Collemare, I get to see him even less, often

142

missing his visits. When I do see him, sometimes it's only for a few days, and at one stage I didn't see him at all for *two years!*

"*Papa!*" I yell, and then blush red at sounding babyish in front of all these people. But no one is looking at me: my cousin Clara has just walked in the door...

When my father arrives he lifts me up, swings me around and hugs me tightly to him, *before* he does it to my brothers. He says I've grown *so much*, and look so much a young man, that *next time* we will have to embrace—as the men do.

My father gives off his usual delicious tobacco aroma, from the small *sigaretti* that he smokes whenever he is home. I notice his muscly arms...they *are* dark. I notice this more now that I've been around my fair-skinned uncle. And my father is thinner, with a bigger nose than my uncle, but his dark hair and green eyes are like mine! His clothes are loose and simple; my mother said papa always felt *goffo*—uncomfortable, awkward—whenever he had to wear a suit and tie for a wedding or a funeral. But he is always clean and neat, and I love the smell of his hair, his skin, his strong, wrinkled hands that have worked farms and machines—and held guns. He fought in the war for Italy with Germany and then he fought *against* Germany, and then Germany imprisoned him...and by the time he told me all this I was confused, but I knew that it was sad, that my father had been very sick and thin in prison and that my mother missed him and for a long time thought he had died. He loves my mother. I notice the gentle way he strokes the back of her hair as he talks with her by the fire, the way he demands we speak respectfully to her at all times, the way he helps us boys wash and wipe up the dishes after she has cooked a meal...

The very first thing I say to my father is: "I don't want to go to the sem—"

"I *know*," my father cuts me off: my mother and uncle are watching.

Now ten, I've recently been told I am to go the seminary next year. I will have to live there—spend the rest of my school years there; it's where they make you become a priest. I don't want to go—but my mother and uncle have decided, and there's no way out. Still, I know what my father thinks about the seminary, so I thought I'd tell him that I'm like *him*. But he doesn't say anything out loud. He is always polite and never upsets those around him; I've never heard of my father offending *anyone*. Nonno said that in Collemare my father is known for being strong and quiet, for helping others, and for going about his business without being too outspoken. He said my father has strong opinions that he keeps mostly to himself, only offering them to those who ask. He called my father a "calm and courteous man who keeps out of trouble," adding that I was distinctly *unlike* my father in some ways . . .

As I stare into my father's clear, gray-green eyes—eyes that smile— he finally says: "And since I rarely see you, my eldest son, I have a real treat this time—" he drops me, breathless, to the floor—"you and I are going on a journey!"

My father wakes me when it's still dark—*really* dark—and I am in a warm, deep sleep. I ask him the time. He quickly says, "*Le tre,*" and thumps downstairs to his espresso. *Three!* Who gets up at three? I wish I hadn't said yes to this journey.

My father acts as if it is nothing to get up in the middle of the night, and seems annoyed when he walks back in and sees that I have moved closer to the end of the bed—*under* the covers. The ripping back of the quilt and swift pointing of his finger mean get up *now*: especially since I am beginning to wake my brothers, who are nestled up against me in the same bed—there being only one bedroom in our tiny house. I look across to my mother's bed: she's pretending to sleep but I know she's aware of *everything* going on in the room. I found this out after several smacks for bad talk and disturbing my brothers during the night—and she had *looked* so fast asleep!

The donkeys clop around loudly on the rough cobblestones outside our door; now that I've recovered from being hauled out of my warm bed I'm excited. It's *very* exciting being out in the dark, silent street: everyone I know is asleep. I love being around donkeys and I snuffle my nose into the neck of one, taking in its warm, pungent, animal smell. The donkey shifts away, restless, white steam coming from its nostrils in the cold as my father straps on his saddlebag and the other men tighten theirs. There are four men including my father, four donkeys, and me.

We're going up to the high valley, the valley of Campo Felice, that my father says is the most beautiful, most secret place in the world. It sits high up in the mountains above our village, and I've never been. Nonno told me that our village of Collemare is already very high, sitting 2,600 feet above the sea—half a mile straight up in the sky! From here it just looks like there are tall mountain peaks above us, yet now my father tells me that there are valleys hours and hours farther up—valleys like Campo Felice—that sit at 5,000 feet and higher! It's like there's a whole other world up there that is secret! And that's exactly what my father said this valley is: beautiful *and* secret.

"You can ride, Mario," says my father, pointing to his donkey.

I don't want to. I know that the men walk—they walk the seven long hours up, up, up, following the narrow, winding *mulattiera*— the mule track carved by the grazing animals—and I want to walk like the men. We are going up to the valley to give salt to the cows grazing there; it is a cool, lush place for the cattle in the three hottest summer months, with plenty of water and good feed. Two shepherds care for the cattle there, but my father said there is no salt, so the men have to bring up salt-licks for their own cows. This is why the donkeys now struggle under their loads—saddlebags filled with heavy rock salt—and why the men cannot ride them.

My father gestures again at the donkey's back.

"No," I say emphatically, and my father smiles.

I've only been riding the donkey a *few* hours. Well, it got too steep and I kept tripping. And I trod in cow dung—several times. It's almost ten, and we're almost there. At least I *did* walk a good half-hour of the *very steepest bit* at the beginning.

The sun flees and returns as we walk in and out of gullies and ridges—and it's so *bright*. The first golden light struck the high peaks at dawn and then I watched as it slid down the mountains, the shade beside us running from it, as we walked up to meet the sun halfway, to meet its warm glow. The sun does bring life, as my *nonno* said: I saw the frost slowly melt, and the buds gently open under my . . . well, under the *donkey's* feet.

"Wait!" yells one of the men as he stops to tighten a slipping saddlebag.

I turn to look at the view and it takes my breath away. I can see *everything* . . . lots of valleys and mountains curving into the distance, and there's a large town, way over there: L'Aquila? The valleys dip and rise between it and my home, and it's like looking down on a map, a great, big map, but it's *real*. And Collemare seems *so tiny*! Fancy Nonno, my mother and everyone else there being the size of ants!

I look across at the men: I can't believe they don't look tired. After so many *hours*. The *donkeys* look tired—fidgeting and pulling away every time the men grab at their ropes to restart the walk— but the men *don't*. These men—my *father*—must be so strong!

We take a break at each of the five springs along the way. These old stone fountains were built hundreds of years ago, my father says, and he shows me where the "pipes" have been gouged through the rock into the water source and rough bowls hewn out below the spout. He tells me this after the men laughed when I said it was so *lucky* that there happened to be water rushing out from the rocks at just the right places, spaced out every hour or so. They didn't tell me the joke until we got to the *third* spring: when I saw it was a deep stone bath with straight sides and in a neat "L" shape, I knew it couldn't have been created by nature.

Every time we hear the lovely gushing sound of the spring, we all begin to strip off our boots and socks, ready to plunge our sweaty, aching feet into the cooling water. Well, mine aren't *aching*, but they are hot. I lunged into one fountain up to my thighs after removing my trousers: it was as big as a bath. My father said the troughs were made big enough to allow several cows and horses to drink at the same time, that they weren't built only for men and their *pleasure*—he said this with a pretend scowl as I swished around in my large stone tub. After cooling off we sat beside the fountains and drank the fresh, icy water. The men pulled out salamis, triangles of crumbling cheese, nutty chickpeas, fresh almonds, and shoveled morsels straight into their mouth or slapped the delicious, oily food onto thick chunks of *pane casa*. The food tasted *so* good up here, much better than it did at home, and it wasn't just the taste. I was eating with the men: I was *one* of the men.

"Here it is, Mario," says my father. "Campo Felice—*the valley!*"

I was almost asleep . . . the rocking of the donkey . . . I look up. Oh, *bellissimo . . . fantastico!*

We have just staggered our way up a last steep slope and over the lip of what seems like a large bowl. Stretching out and down before me is a huge flat area: a valley dipped in between the great mountain peaks, just like the craters of volcanoes I have seen pictured in books—except this doesn't consist of ugly gray rocks. This is *green*, so green and beautiful, with trees, flowers and tall grass for as far as the eye can see, and in the center of this great valley is a great still lake.

A *lake!*

Around the sides of this lake and on the floor of the bowl are acres and acres of lush, green grasses and up the slopes, just as the bowl dips upward, the trees begin: the beautiful dark forests that run right up the slopes. I can see that the trees at the lower edges of the forest are the great *faggi*, the huge, gracious old beech trees that lean their boughs outward and over for shade. And it is here, at the beginning of the forest and closest to the lake, that we find the animals, scatterings of cows and horses, grazing peacefully under the shade in this paradise. I can just imagine Indians here, like you see in cowboy movies, with lots of colorful wigwams around the lake . . . it's *bellissimo*. The valley is *so* beautiful, it doesn't look real. I feel like I'm visiting another world! No wonder it's called Campo Felice: "happy field!" And to think that all this time I never knew it was here, this incredible place, way, way above my head when I'm sitting at home in Collemare!

"Down now, Mario," says my father, signaling for me to dismount the donkey that has carried me for the last six hours. "Now you can rest," he adds.

"*Grazie*," I say.

"I was talking to the *donkey*," says my father.

I look across at the lake: it is so *beautiful* I can't stop looking at it. The valley extends for as far as I can see: it is so big that many of the animals under the trees look like specks from where we stand. I wonder where *our* cow is—we only have one—and how far we'll have to walk to find it! I'm tired . . .

Someone approaches us from the near side of the lake. He has a staff and when he gets closer I see that his clothes are dark and grimy and he smells a bit: one of the shepherds. I move away. He chats with the men and then signals to my father roughly where he thinks our cow is, and we begin to walk in that direction.

We seem to walk for *ages*, following the line of the lake, trudging along under the great, cool trees—I have the job of pulling our stubborn donkey around them—but we can't find our cow. She has a tag with our family symbol on her ear but we can't find her anywhere. How are you expected to find a single cow in a place *this* big, with *so many* other cows?

My father stops and begins rummaging in the pack on the donkey's back.

"What are you doing?" I ask as my father places some salt on a nearby rock. "We haven't found our cow!"

"Never mind," he says, crunching more handfuls of salt onto a large, flat boulder.

He's giving *our* salt to *those* cows! Cows that all stopped chewing and looked around the second they heard the rustling of the pack. What *is* my father doing, giving our precious salt to cows when they're not *ours*? I'm certainly not coming all the way back ...

"The shepherd knows we were here," says my father, "he will give someone else's salt to our cow."

That's a relief!

"But how will he know?" I ask. "How will he know that you didn't already give it to your cow, and that maybe you're being sneaky, and now you want him to give someone else's salt to our cow as well?"

"Because I will tell him," says my father.

He passes me a chunk of salt to offer. The cows thump in against me, jostling to get at the salt, their great, rasping tongues dragging at my hand as they lick it. I don't mind: as with the donkeys, I like their closeness—their warm, earthy animal smell.

Looking down toward the lake, I realize this *is* paradise. I have my own secret valley, a place *none* of my friends has seen but where I'll bring them one day: Claudio, Nino and Settimio. I have a tummy full of salami, cheese and almonds and now have the warm animals around me. I am on my first big journey with the men, and the trip back home is *downhill* so I'm sure it will be quicker . . . for the donkey.

Best of all, I have my father: this quiet, brave man I am getting to know.

Il Garibaldino **THE RED SHIRT**

The smell of the vinyl seats is sweet, the rough screech and grind of the gearbox, the warmth of the over-revving engine. My body jolts and jars with the next change of gear, the thrust forward, the pause, the hesitation, the acceleration as we shudder around the next blind bend. I clutch the dashboard, peering keenly over the top for any danger on the road in front of us.

I glance sideways at my uncle and smile: eyes darting quickly back to the white gravel road and my important task. I love these mornings.

I look upward. There it is! Now it's gone. There it is again! *Il campanile*. The tower. The old stone tower of the monastery peeks out triumphantly and then ducks out of sight again as we take the winding bends. I am fascinated that I can see the tower as soon as we start our journey and then it hides and reveals itself, back and forth, as we climb the winding road that travels as much east and west as it does north. For although the village we're headed for is only seven miles away, it will take several hours to negotiate the narrow, snaking road that twists and contorts itself around the steep ravines, dodges creeks and rivulets that flood at will, suffers heavy rock falls, and drags itself to its destination in a forlorn state—for the road is mostly worn down, broken away and treacherous. This is why I have my job at the windshield.

"Stones!" I cry.

My uncle hits the brakes and I lurch forward, my head bumping the dusty glass for the hundredth time. Rocks, large and small, form a mound more than a yard high just in front of us; they have fallen from the mountainside and now block the road. We have seen falls like this all the way up the mountain: most are small, but some, such as this one, are large enough to make the road impassable. I ask my uncle why no one clears them.

"The road to a near-deserted village is of no interest to anyone, least of all the *Regione*. They want the people to move, Mario, to the newer towns, and this leaves no young men in the old villages to clear the roads," says my uncle.

"But what about the monastery up here, Uncle? Doesn't the *Regione* think the monks are *important*?" I ask.

My uncle pulls on the handbrake and smiles at me; he seems to search for an answer. "Come on," he finally says, and opens the car door, inviting me to follow.

The mountain chill rushes me as I step out from the warm interior, and the wind quickly follows: it pulls and flutters at me, pushing me, tempting me to fly. The wind makes me feel alive. I look down into the valley and see the village we have come from on the valley floor; on the slopes near it I see the geometrical patterns of the broad bean crops, and the rows of cherry trees that are heavily laden with soon-to-be-ripe fruit. My uncle told me today that the cherries are already ripe in Rome. Rome. I have never been there, but I know it's where the pope is—the holiest of holies—and I have seen pictures: it is full of hundreds of big buildings. But no mountains. I can't understand why they have cherries before us; cherries belong to June and July.

"It's colder in the mountains," says my uncle. "The cherries here ripen a month later than the trees on the lowlands."

That's it. When I am older I shall spend May in Rome and June and July back here in the Abruzzo. That way I will have *thirty more days each year* of biting into small plump bulbs that squirt sweetness into my mouth, and redness onto my shirt, my pants, my hands. *Heaven!* I look across at the mountain slopes level with me: they look funny because they have patches of dark green grass and shrubs that suddenly butt up against areas of gray, stony ground where nothing grows—it looks like a giant has taken a razor and shaved bald patches on the mountainside. Closer to where I stand, the green patches are dotted with June flowers: I know the purple *lavanda*, the white and pink *valeriana*, and the *camomilla* whose flowers my aunt keeps in her kitchen, but until today I did not know the name of the flower that scatters sparks of bright yellow among the green: my uncle tells me it is *ginestra*. It is the brightest flower of all.

I look straight down and then upward following the line of the slope: it's strange how a mountain can be green and round at the bottom, and sharp and white at the top. And where does the mountain begin? Does it start at that mound next to the village, or is it not a mountain until it gets steep? All I know is that one day I will climb them—I will join the army and become an *alpino*. That way I will learn how to climb them right to the top: all the wild Abruzzo mountains.

"Mario!" calls my uncle.

I turn and crunch on the gravel. White gravel. I love the sound: mile after mile of white, scrunching stones that leave light, winding threads all over the mountains.

"What do you think we should do?" My uncle points at the rocks on the road. I like the way he treats me as a man, and asks my advice on our trips together.

"We need to go around, off the road, Uncle."

"Yes, but where? Now think carefully."

My uncle has taught me the danger of going too close to the loose rocks on the overhang above the road, even though there is a gap there that would just fit our car. I look to the outer part of the road, where it meets the green slope that falls away below us. Driving out onto this part always scares me—I can imagine our little car tipping to one side and tumbling down the steep hill.

"We have to drive on the outer," I say.

"Good boy! Now hop in, and we will stop for something to eat once we get around to the other side," says my uncle.

I glance quickly toward the valley floor before looking back at my uncle.

"Listen," he says, "why don't you walk ahead—you can guide me around. May save us a flat tire."

I run ahead and signal the way, watching as my uncle lurches and lumbers, revving the little car in and out of holes and ditches on the rock-encrusted slope. We are on one of the "shaved" parts: the slope has almost no grass and is covered in thousands of motley gray and white stones. The Abruzzo is famous for its rocks: my grandfather, Nonno Cesare, says, "If you could have a war with stones, the Abruzzo wins."

My dear *nonno*, I miss him a lot. I often look at my uncle and think how strange it is that Nonno is also his father, not just the father of my papa. And I can't believe my uncle was ever a boy, or that he and my papa would have played together. I wonder if they played *zizzola* then, or maybe *bigliardino*? I'm good at *bigliardino*—I bet I could have beaten them, but I can't imagine that they played that game such a long, *long* time ago—

"Mario! *What are you doing?*"

I hear the high-pitched scream of the engine as the little VW becomes stuck, one of its front wheels spinning freely. The left front wheel is in a ditch, and a large Abruzzo rock underneath the vehicle is forcing the right side of the car up into the air.

"You will have to help me push," yells my uncle. "No! Stay at the front, we need to push the car *backward.*"

Il campanile: the old stone belltower of the monastery is in front of me at last. It's smaller than I thought. I wonder how long my uncle will be? I'm hungry. Meals will be with the monks, but I've brought pocket money so perhaps I can buy something.

But where? My heart sank when we first puttered over the cobblestones into the piazza. Well, I think it's a piazza. Piazzas usually have people and children and pigeons and shops—and stands selling crunchy *porchetta*: roast pork. They are surrounded by bars, and are busy with shopkeepers, buyers, *people*. This piazza is covered in a layer of fine brown dust and grit, broken branches and leaves dancing around in the wind. No one sweeps here. The houses around the piazza are mostly shut up and abandoned—there are no shops. I am in the village square *and there are no shops.*

My eyes search frantically for some small sign of activity: a paper seller, a tobacconist, a fruit merchant—nothing. The only living thing that moves is the ear of a donkey tied up in front of one of the houses. It must have been this donkey that dropped the pile of straw-filled dung in the center of the piazza, the only thing decorating it apart from the leaves and dust.

We are here for *three days* and there are no shops—or anything else, by the look of it. My uncle has been sent here by the *Curia* to see whether the church can be repaired back to a useable state: if this is done, he said Rome would send in a resident priest to serve the small congregation.

But what congregation? Besides the monastery and the church, there aren't many buildings; boarded-up shops face the piazza, and behind these are a few houses, mostly with unswept patios and overgrown potted plants—they look deserted. Several sheds and a vegetable garden dot the slope behind the buildings, but that seems to be the whole village. And there is no one about. *No one.* Are the five monks in the monastery the congregation? I'm sure they have to have more people than that to keep a church. I look at the donkey. They could make *him* go: that would be six. They sometimes have animals in churches to bless them, but I don't think it's for their soul, I think it's so they won't die or something.

My stomach rumbles again. I have to wait here, outside, while my uncle meets with the *abate*. I hope the monks can cook. It is two hours since we got out of that hole and had our hillside feast of pecorino—sheep's milk cheese—fresh red wine (fresh water for me), crusty *pane casareccio*, and freshly picked broad beans. I know the broad beans were fresh because I was left rumbling in the idling VW as my uncle plucked them from a field that ran alongside the road when we first left the village. I wondered why it was that my friends and I were committing a sin when we took someone's cherries, yet my uncle could take his lunch from someone's vine and God would not think he was bad. God *couldn't* think he was bad—he's a priest.

"*Un momento*, Mario. I will be out soon!" yells my uncle.

I turn to see him wave from an upstairs window of the monastery before disappearing again. I look at the church buildings that take up two full sides of the piazza on the edge of the village, with the valley falling away behind them. They are large and plain. Church buildings often have murals and pretty stonework, sometimes even columns. These buildings have no decorations, few windows, and the stucco has cracked off, revealing patches of the stonework underneath. I look up. From the front you can't see the belltower: the only things that show this to be a house of God are the small white cross at the tip of the roof and, painted above the door, a faded Bible scene—I turn my head sideways to try and make out what it is. Otherwise, it looks like a big, ugly barn and I half expect a pig to trot out. I snort with laughter at this thought, and the donkey looks at me.

But why am I laughing? I look around at the "village" and remind myself I will be here for the next *three days* with no shops, no children, no fun—just me, my uncle, five monks and a donkey. I think I must be about to have the most *boring* three days of my—

CRASH!

I jump. Something hit the church door behind me with great force, just missing me. It struck so hard that the large door is still rattling! I turn in the direction of the yelling I can hear, but no one is in view. I look around for what hit the door so hard. There it is on the step. A potato. Someone is throwing potatoes. Very hard. *At the church.* There is a dusty brown mark on the door.

The yelling becomes louder, and I turn just in time to avoid another potato that has hit the ground and is bouncing toward me across the piazza. From a side street a figure races into the piazza toward me, half stumbling, yelling something in Latin. He looks like a *fratecercataro*, one of the young monks who beg at houses—and he looks very scared. He trips and then picks himself up again, food spilling from his begging bowl all over the cobblestones. He is tearing toward me, yelling out, "*Open! Open!*" I realize he is heading for the monastery behind me.

The man chasing him comes into view—the man throwing potatoes. He looks fierce and screams out, "*Poltroni!*—Vultures!" As I watch, he raises his arm, another potato in his grip—

I decide to hide behind the car. The young monk rushes past me and reaches the monastery door. He bashes on it, yelling and looking over his shoulder all the while, desperation on his face. Just as his attacker aims another potato at him from across the piazza, the door opens, an arm draped in a monk's robe reaches out and pulls him in, and the door slams shut.

I am left out here. Alone. With this monster. He must be a monster, or crazy, because *no one* attacks a monk or throws things at a holy building—that's like throwing things at God.

The potato-thrower reaches the monastery door and bashes on it fiercely. I crouch down against the car, about three yards from where he stands, hoping he doesn't look my way.

"*Thieves!* Hide, you cowards! You won't get my money for your stinking fascist church. Why don't you go to work, all of you, and *give the money back to the people!*" He gives the door one last pound, spits on the ground and turns to go. "*Scansafatiche!*—Slackers!"— he mutters, as he descends the steps.

He stops.

Oh no, I am still in view—but only if he looks hard to his right. I am trying not to breathe. He pulls out a cigar and lights it. He is older than my uncle: he stands tall and looks quite strong. His arms are tanned and muscly—maybe from potato throwing?

"Don't ever let them brainwash you," he says, studying his cigar.

Who is he talking to? *Himself,* I hope!

"The people are what count, boy, look to the people, not the

158

bloodsucking vultures who seek power, whether church or state," he says, still not turning.

He *is* talking to me! I'm shaking. Should I say something? *Oh, where's my uncle?* Should I come out so that at least I look a little brave, instead of crouching behind the Volkswagon? Slowly I stand up.

He turns to me. "That's better," he says. "Don't ever hide from life. When good men hide, the bastards take over. Here!" He walks over and hands me his last remaining potato. "Put this in your soup."

With that he strides off across the piazza, his goodbye to me a rich puff of his cigar smoke that blasts my nostrils just before he disappears into the street behind the boarded-up shops.

I look down at the potato in my hand.

"The floors and structural beams are sound, and they're the important things," says my uncle. "Like all men, it's redeemable. It needs a fair bit of work, but the church is redeemable."

We are eating lunch with the monks. I look around at them: they're *so* old. Uncle said they're all around eighty but I think they're in their hundreds—there are no calendars or newspapers here so how would they know? I have never seen so many wrinkles. One of the monks is almost blind, another says funny things that don't make sense and then hums to himself as if we aren't here. And Fra Giovanni is so bent over that he only comes up to my shoulders. Can't they bend him straight, I wonder? When he dies (which shouldn't be long) will his coffin have to be curved?

Worse still: they don't eat. Not properly. I look at the table in front of me. Bare timber and plopped in its center is a large wooden bowl full of gray-looking soup that has vegetables floating just below the surface. In front of us we each have a smaller wooden bowl and spoon, beside which sit—on the bare table—a chunk of torn bread and a lump of hard cheese. No plates.

After devouring my soup I wait for the next course. After waiting a long, long time, I realize there *is* no next course. That was it. The meal. But there *has* to be dessert; no meal finishes without something sweet or fruity or...

Five rubbery, yellowing apples are placed in the center of the table. I start to count how many hours we have left here, and how many meals. Can you starve in three days? Maybe that's why the angry monster gave me the potato.

The monster. I was pulled inside just after the potato-throwing incident and introduced to the monks. There was a flurry of activity in one corner where two of the monks were trying to calm the young *fratecercataro*—some of it was in Latin, but I got the gist. They were telling him *not* to go to the house of the potato-thrower: the fierce man had just opened his cask of new wine, and would be *ubriaco* all week. It seemed the young monk was leaving later in the day: he is not at the table, so perhaps he has already gone. I wonder if the potato-thrower made him leave early. And I heard him mention the donkey; it must be his. The donkey will miss his blessing then.

"Padre," the *abate* says, waving away an apple one of the monks has offered him, "we have a lot of work to do in the church, you say. Will the *Curia* assist us in all of this? There is no local funding to speak of."

The *abate* has a gentle voice and is the tallest of the monks. He hands Fra Giuseppe—a fat little monk—the empty plates without looking at him. This fat monk seems to be running around doing everything: he wiped up the mess when the funny monk tipped his soup over—he kept tapping his spoon on the bowl in time to his humming as the fat monk wiped around him.

I quietly asked my uncle if Fra Giuseppe was a servant. "*Only* to God," he answered, and he told me how the monks each take turns to do "the duties." He said humility was of great importance, and this meant no excess in their life. Oh—like the friar! I asked if they were Franciscans. He said no, but that they led a similar simple life, which is why their furniture is basic and their eating simple—including many days of fasting. This was their way of showing humility. I decided I didn't want to be a monk.

"We have limited funds, *abate*—" my uncle again—"the *Curia* only allocates a set amount per diocese. We will have to work out costs. New joists will be relatively expensive, as will the inlays for the altar. Other timber and building materials we can find locally. The big expense will be labor," says my uncle, who is now enjoying a glass of *dolcetto*—a sweet apple liqueur—with the monks.

I asked my uncle if the apple liqueur wasn't one of those "excess" things: the Franciscan had told me "excess" was anything not essential for basic living. My uncle nudged me to be quiet, and said something about a small glass being "good for the soul." So they *do* have an excess thing! Won't God be angry? And why couldn't it have been *tira misu* or *zuppa inglese*, instead of a stupid liqueur? I look at the one sad apple left and slump against the table, bored.

"Will they pay for a builder?" asks Abate Marco.

"Too expensive," says my uncle.

"A carpenter?"

My uncle shakes his head.

"Well, a handyman from Agnone will have to do. The building work is not complex," says the *abate*.

"It will have to be someone local," says my uncle.

The table goes silent. Something has changed in the room. I notice that the hummer has stopped in the middle of a tune and is looking around at the other monks.

"But there is no one here, Padre. There are no fit men, only the elderly . . ."

My uncle remains silent.

The monk continues: "The men here are all past seventy—they can't be climbing ladders. There are some younger women, but, well, this is not women's work."

"It will have to be someone local," says my uncle again. "The cost to bring someone up from the town would be prohibitive. We simply could not do it. The funding will cover materials and a small amount of labor. The work is not hard, just time-consuming. It will have to be someone local."

There is a strange atmosphere in the room. Everyone has stopped what he is doing, and no one will look at my uncle. Except the funny monk: he is back to his rocking and humming, but he is doing it faster, and keeps glancing at my uncle and me as if he doesn't like us being here.

"There is no one else, Padre," says the *abate*.

Fra Giuseppe jumps up, his stomach smashing against the table and upsetting a candle. He grabs the remaining apple and lumbers off, as quickly as his body will carry him, to the kitchen.

"No one else?" asks my uncle. His voice is gentle and he doesn't look at the *abate*. He does this to me when I have done something wrong—something that isn't *too* bad, and he is giving me time to tell the truth about it.

"Well, there is, but we can't—we couldn't possibly . . ." The *abate's* voice trails off.

"We may have to," says my uncle.

"*Eretico! Miscredente! Ateo!* No, no, NO!"

I jump at this outburst from the bent-over monk next to me, who has not said a word except *grazie* until now.

"Lucifer in God's house—*no!*" he finishes.

The funny monk begins chanting: "*Eretico! Ateo! Eretico! Ateo!*" over and over again; he dances his upper body to it, as if to a song. The blind monk beside him is silent.

"He will kill us all in our beds!" This from Fra Giuseppe in the kitchen doorway. He seems too frightened to come out.

The devil in God's house? Heretic? Atheist? Killing them in their beds? I'm no longer bored. *Who* are they talking about? At that moment I catch sight of the funny monk making a movement with his arm as if bowling a...potato.

"Does *he* have a name?" asks my uncle.

The table is silent a moment, and then: "Dante, his name is *Dante*," says the blind monk.

"And this Dante, he is...?" asks my uncle.

"The communist," says another monk.

Oh, a *comunista*! So *that's* what they look like...

"We can't ask him to work with us," says the *abate*.

"Communists have no *anima*!" calls a voice from the kitchen.

"We all have souls," says my uncle quietly. "Tell me, brothers, if I spoke to this man—and he could do the work—do you think you could deal with him on the days I am away?"

I hear a couple of gasps. The monks dart quick looks at each other.

"He is a difficult man," says the blind monk quietly. "He blasphemes, and when he's drunk he bangs on our door and tells us that it is our last day here, that he will come and kill us all in the night."

"He says he will roll all of us into a snowball and then send us down the hill to the valley!" shouts Giuseppe from the kitchen.

The blind monk continues: "He hates anyone who wears the cloth—the townspeople call him *Mangiapreti*—the priest-eater."

The humming monk starts again: "*Mangiapreti! Mangiapreti! Mangiapreti!*"

"*Enough*, Fra Luca!" the *abate* shouts at him.

It is the first time I have heard the humming monk's name. He stops singing, and looks at me with sad eyes. "Mangiapreti," he says quietly.

"We need to work with what we have, brothers," says my uncle. "Without him, there will be no church."

The last two days I have spent sort of . . . hiding. Well, not *really* hiding, I was just being careful not to run into priest-eaters, in case they also eat nephews. This involved sticking inside the walls of the monastery and so close to my uncle that I now know the *via crucis* off by heart. My uncle was pleased to see me taking an interest in the priesthood at last, as I am supposed to enter the seminary soon. I started to tell him that I still wasn't *sure* about that, but he promised me a large box of cherries when we got home. I smiled and said yes to both.

I went everywhere with my uncle except for *there: that* house. The priest-eater's house. Instead, I hid in the monastery with the monks, who seemed even more frightened than me. Abate Marco stayed in his office, Fra Luca and Fra Luigi spent the hour my uncle was away in front of the Madonna, and Fra Giuseppe hid in the confessional—I know because I was in the next cubicle.

My uncle returned and said, yes, it had been difficult, but Dante had finally agreed to do the work for wine and money. He also reluctantly agreed not to drink on the job, to take instructions from the *abate* if my uncle wasn't there, and not to blaspheme in the church. I was shocked to learn he wouldn't let my uncle in. He did not want "the priest's finger"—the act of benediction—in his house, and my uncle had been forced to discuss things on his porch. *My uncle not let inside a house!* Then I realized it was lucky for my uncle that he *didn't* go inside, because maybe there was a pot ready on the stove . . .

I'm *so* glad we're leaving. But the monks don't look happy. Even though their church is going to be fixed, they look very upset as we say goodbye.

"Oh, Mario," says my uncle, turning the key in the ignition and putting the car into gear, "I feel I have just sent lambs to the slaughter. But what could I do? What else could I do?"

I'm sorry for the monks, but I'm not coming back. My uncle will return next week, but not me. I don't want to spend another three days hiding from the monster and I don't care what I have to do: I'll offer to do chores, help my aunt, I'll say I'm sick. If my uncle wants to come back and be eaten, he can, but I'm not coming back.

My uncle bends down and gives the monks a final wave, heaving a big sigh as he turns the steering wheel and rumbles the little car out of the piazza.

I'm back with the monks.

My aunt didn't believe I was sick this morning. She said I had eaten too well last night to be sickly, and that the only reason I might be feeling ill was because I had eaten *too* well. I suggested it might be an illness where you eat more like leprosy, but she insisted it didn't exist in Italy anymore. She pulled off my bedcover and forced me out to the kitchen.

Even Nonno's visit couldn't save me. I was told at the start of the week that my wonderful grandfather, Nonno Cesare, is coming to visit in the next few days, and may come up to the village to help us on the last day we are there. I asked if I could stay at home and wait for my *nonno*, but uncle said no, that he could not fix the church without my help.

Now I look with dread at the belltower as we drive up the last slope and come level with the village. Why couldn't I have thought of something else? There must be plenty of diseases that old monks shouldn't catch. I should have fought harder, cried in front of my uncle, refused to get into the car—but then there's my friends... After telling them the tale of the beast who ate people, and how afraid the monks were (but not me), my uncle interrupted—I didn't even know he was there listening!—to ask me whether I wanted to accompany him on the return trip. *So then I had to say yes!* My friends became excited and asked to be filled in on every gruesome detail when I got back—"*if* you come back," they added.

We pull up. There are people about in the piazza: two of the monks and an old woman who is chattering excitedly to Abate Marco, who waves hello. There are planks of timber, a wooden horse, hammers, bits of broken timber and sawdust, nails and a hand drill scattered on the ground in front of the church—and the front door is wide open. It looks dark and dusty inside. In the sawdust on the floor I can see footprints leading into the darkness of the old church. I wonder who is in there, and I shiver.

Fra Giuseppe runs over as soon as he sees us.

"Padre! Padre! So *good* to see you," he says, his belly wobbling as he runs. "Oh, it's been terrible, *terrible!* We can never find him, he won't work, he insults us... See, even now—" he turns and waves toward the tools on the ground—"he has disappeared and just left everything. No one has seen him for two days."

"And hello to you, Fra Giuseppe." My uncle puts his hand on the monk's shoulder. "Calm down, calm down. We will sort it all out."

As we get closer to the church, I hear what the old woman is saying and she sounds upset: "... but he's painting the Madonna *red!* And this week he told me he's going to put a hammer and sickle in the hands of our dear Moses!" She covers her mouth in distress and points to the mural above the church door.

"*Pace, pace,*" Abate Marco says soothingly, and then to my uncle: "Padre! Mario. Welcome back. We have had some excitement since you were last here." He signals toward the woman: "This is Signora Contini, the most devout member of our church. It seems our friend Dante has been having some fun upsetting Signora with his suggested changes to the church—"

"*But he did it!*" the woman cries, looking at my uncle. "He's painted the Madonna red."

"It was only *one* brushstroke, Signora, and he assures me it was an accident. It will be righted," says the *abate*.

"To think this beast has been invited into the house of our Holy Mother. *Him*—a sacrilegious red shirt. *Sciocchezze!*" She crosses herself. "Thank heavens you are back, Padre. Perhaps you can stop this madness!" She dashes off across the piazza.

"He never works, Padre—" Fra Giuseppe again—"we paid him for this week but he's never here. We cannot find him—he's not at his house. We have tried to do some work ourselves, but it is dangerous. I am too heavy for the ladder, Fra Giovanni too bent, and Fra Luigi . . . well, he cannot see the nails. As for Abate Marco, he is too busy with angry merchants and screaming women to lend a hand."

I almost laugh. I am terrified of this Dante, but *something* about him makes me want to laugh. He seems to make everyone around him jump through hoops while he drinks and smokes his cigars. I start to imagine the fat monk up the ladder with the rungs bowing and creaking, the bent monk trying to reach up with a nail, and the blind monk—the *blind* monk—hammering, perhaps with Fra Luca humming in the background . . .

I give a snort, and my uncle darts a look in my direction before addressing the *abate*: "Angry merchants?"

Abate Marco continues the story: "We gave Dante a small amount of money to purchase a hand drill and plaster down in the main town. He came back three days later with the drill, no plaster, and two flagons of wine."

"Well, at least he accomplished half the task," quips my uncle.

"Ah, not so, Padre," Abate Marco says. "It seems he swapped the drill for the wine and then took the drill anyway, saying he'd been cheated with vinegar instead of *vino*. And he didn't purchase the drill with the money we gave him. He 'bought' the drill with several boxes of Cuban cigars that turned out to be stale and made in Napoli. I have had both the produce merchant *and* the wine merchant up here wanting their money."

"And where is he? Nowhere to be seen!" laments Fra Giuseppe.

"Come on, Mario," says my uncle, "we have work to do."

I turn my head to breathe in the scent of cool earth; several blades of grass flicker up my nose, tickling and stinging at the same time. I spread my fingers wide and brush my hands back and forth across the damp greenness to absorb the moisture, and I get that same tickling-stinging sensation as the blades spike the soft flesh between my fingers. It feels good. I open my eyes again and look up at the sky.

I am lying on the grassy slope at the side of the monastery with my feet pointing up toward the mountain peaks. The back wall and belltower are just to the right of me, and a gnarled old apple tree stands to my left. I look at the blue Abruzzo sky through the tree's twisted arms, and then notice there are apples, tiny green apples, hiding in it. Are they bitter or sweet, I wonder? No, even the *thought* of climbing is too much effort...My eyes drift lazily across to *il campanile*. It is as if the belltower and the apple tree are two guards protecting me on each side. I imagine that I'm a soldier, back from some great battle, resting here under the tree with my armor next to me...Oh! I have one of those metal helmets with the brightly colored cock feather that flows down to my shoulders, and my beautiful white horse is resting—no! It was shot in battle, falling from under me—

Ouch! I rub my left eye, which is tingling and burning. The day has been long and busy, and I am very tired from helping my uncle and the monks to repair the church. I've had to follow them around with nails and pieces of timber, run out and get the tools, hold on to timber as they saw, mix the plaster, run up and down ladders, hold the paint can for my uncle, help lay down and fold up canvas sheets, clean the brushes and, finally, sweep the fine sawdust from the church floor at the end of the day. *I am worn out!* And it is only three p.m.

My body is sticky and dusty and hot; the sawdust is itching my eyes and every other part of my body. I just had to get out into the fresh air, the grass, the mountainside. I rushed outside as soon as my uncle said I could go. I didn't want to wait while they talked of repairs and slowly packed up—I just had to get *outside*. It is the first time I have been out of the monastery alone since I came to the village; even the priest-eater couldn't keep me inside a moment longer.

Mangiapreti. I wonder where he is? I figure I am safe to go outside, as long as I stay close to the monastery, for he is in hiding from my uncle. Wherever my uncle is, Mangiapreti will not be. I hope. I wonder if he stole that wine? And the drill! He must be bad—stealing is a mortal sin! (But, then, what of my cherries? And my uncle's broad beans?) And the "red shirt": what did that woman mean? And where did he get the cigars? I'm sure they said Cuba: I know it's a country a long way away—maybe he came from there? I think it's in South America. Oh! *Isn't that where they have cannibals?* Oh no, that's Africa—

Smoke! I quickly prop myself up on my elbows. Smoke is coming from the tower just above me, drifting softly, gently against the sky.

A tiny wisp . . . there it is again! A small puff of smoke from the top of the belltower. No one can go up there because the old stairs have collapsed. A *fire!* My uncle told me there had been a big fire here a long time ago and most of the monastery had burned down. Perhaps it's happening again! I have to tell someone . . . my uncle! No, it will take too long to get him; the fire could have reached the main part of the monastery by the time we get back. Right now it's probably a small fire, and if it's at the base I can put it out—and putting out a fire would make me a *hero* . . . I leap up and race toward the small door at the base of the belltower.

It's cool and dark inside the old stone tower. I am hit by the pungent smell of urine and straw from animals that have been kept here. Several pigeons fly off from a timber beam way above me: I see them head upward, to the very tip of the tower and freedom. I think I hear a noise, and then there's nothing. There is no smoke; I can't see or hear anything like a fire. There is no crackling, no smell. Perhaps it's right at the top.

A narrow window at the base of the tower lets in just enough light to enable me to take in my surroundings. There is a broken timber floor some sixteen feet above me, so broken that I can see up above it, but there are no stairs from the ground to this first level. The charred remains of one side of a staircase frame, leading from the ground to the first floor, rises black and decaying with none of its steps in place. It must have been that fire! From the first floor the stairs are intact, spiraling to the very top. I cannot see the bell because the top is obscured by another timber floor—perhaps the base of the lookout. The narrow stairs hug the wall, slipping through this top floor via a narrow gap, the gap the pigeons disappeared into.

Another doorway stands opposite the one where I came in, leading into the monastery; it must have been the one the monks used, long ago, when they had to ring the bell. I try to open it but it is locked, and I can see the lock and hinges have discolored, stiffened; intricate spider webs mass over the upper corners of the door—no one comes through here.

I look up to the top again: no smell of smoke, no sound of crackling, no noise apart from the coo-coo of a pigeon. I look at the charred stair frame—no steps! *Mannaggia!* There's nothing to climb, no way of getting to that first floor and the steps beyond—steps that wind their way right to the top. I want to go up and explore! And the smoke? Perhaps it was mist, or a small cloud drifting... *Phew!* This place stinks! Of straw, and damp, and animal dung. I head toward the door—

"What do you want?"

I stop. I'm sure I heard a voice, but I was moving—was it the crackle of my clothes, the sound of my footsteps? I hold my breath, tense, listening. Nothing. I go to move again—

"Well? *What do you want?*"

This time unmistakable—that voice. Mangiapreti: the priest-eater!

Suddenly there is a clatter above me as the fearsome beast slams open a manhole that allows him to exit from the very top floor. In those frozen seconds, I notice that he strides down the winding steps with great speed—toward me. But how does he get down *here!*

On the broken timber floor immediately above me, he drags out a long, makeshift ladder from a hidden spot and slips it down to the floor; it crashes and rattles as it strikes the earth, the bottom rung landing right at my feet. I look up. He is silhouetted against the light from above, a tall figure, waiting, demanding. I get the feeling he is not coming down. And he has in his hand a cigar. The smoke.

Panic. I have to run. But if I run without speaking I'll look like a coward; he told me he didn't like cowards. So I should say *something*. Then I can run.

"My uncle is looking for you," I say, in a shaky half-whisper.

"I don't care about him—let him call a monk! Get on!" he says, signaling for me to step on the ladder.

Get on? He wants me to go up...? No one would know he was up here—no one would know *I* was up here—oh Madonna! *Is this where he—?*

The slam of his heavy boot on the ladder brings me back to the present. "Get on!" he yells. "Stop hiding behind your uncle's robes!"

Oh, he's calling me a *bambino*! I'm *not*, and I'll show him...but I don't want to be eaten...and I don't want to be called a baby... I don't think he'd eat me *here*, in the monastery...

I take my first step forward. The ladder rattles loudly. I think it's me: my arms are shaking so much that the top of the ladder is clattering against the timber beam. It's a long, *long* way up, and at the halfway point, with the floor so distant, I flatten out, clinging and sliding the rest of the way. With mixed feelings of fear and relief, I finally reach the top rung of the ladder and slump down onto the smelly, mud-stained boot of Mangiapreti. He had been holding the ladder with his foot—one foot! *I could have fallen!*

As I stand, I see that he is very, very tall: at full height I only reach the middle buttons of his...*red shirt*. He doesn't look at me, just hauls the ladder up and begins climbing the stone steps to the top. I look down at the floor below—my only escape gone. My mind is racing. The ladder would be too heavy for me to lift, and it would take some time to drag it out and across the floor—enough time for someone to leap down the stairs and reach me...I look upward with dread. What else can I do but follow? I trudge behind him, finally sliding through the manhole and up and out—

172

Oh, the view! I gasp as we exit to the belfry. The wind grabs my hair, buffets my body against the wall, flickers and pulls at my clothing. There are large arched openings on each of the four sides of the tower, framing views that extend far into the distance in every direction: it is *beautiful!* An unexpected gust pushes me and I fall against the bell, which makes a dull *gong!* Dante grabs me and stands me up, holding his finger to his lips in a gesture of silence. He signals for me to look down and there, far below in the piazza, are my uncle and Fra Giuseppe, just closing the church door. We are so close to them and yet so very, very far! It is funny that no one down there realizes who—Dante's strong hand jerks me back.

"Sit," he says.

I slide down the wall into a sitting position, my knees clamped close. I am tense: what does he want from me? I watch as he too lowers himself; he half sits, half lies against the wall. I feel better now that he is not standing above me and I am just out of his reach. The bell is in the center, and if he tries to grab me I can run away from him, round and round the bell—but for how long? Strangely, I feel less afraid now that he is in front of me and not only in my imagination.

I study him carefully. A shaft of late afternoon sunlight strikes him, tinging him with gold. He seems kind of young for an old person, but he has lots of gray hair, so that proves he is old. Not as old as the monks, but maybe as old as Nonno Cesare. He looks sort of handsome, except for the wrinkles, and I am surprised that he is clean: his clothes are clean, his teeth are worn and crooked but clean (I notice this when he bites the end off a new cigar) and he doesn't have prickly hair all over his face like some of the old men do; his face is smooth except for a pointy beard on his chin. I notice there is a can next to him, for ashing the cigar, and a small wooden box with more cigars, and matches. The cigars are cut in half. The end of a loaf of *pane* peeks out from a cloth bag lying on the ground and I smell something else, a strong cheese. A book has been tossed to one side, some of its pages dog-eared. I look up to see him watching me. Without taking his eyes from me, he unwraps a piece of damp cloth that sits in the shade; in it is the cheese. He breaks off a piece and hands it to me. As I try to chew, he sits there smoking and watching...

"So what's your name?" he asks finally.

"Mario." At least this time my voice didn't shake.

"So, Mario, how far have the papists got with brainwashing your young mind? They training you to beg too?" He spits out a piece of tobacco. "Or perhaps they're grooming you for the top job in Rome." He gives a half-laugh.

Papists? "What are they?" I ask him.

This time he guffaws. "What are *papists?* Have a look around you, boy! Your uncle, the damn monks, all those behind that cursed crucifix down there—" he waves to the cross on the church below— "and your sweet-faced Madonna. Any supporter of your Holy Catholic Church is a papist and a *persecutor of the people!*"

I don't know what to say. I've never heard talk like this before. I know that persecution is something bad...is he saying the church is *bad?*

"Your uncle doesn't seem too bad, though—*for a priest*," he says, ashing his cigar. "Better than those spineless monks who've never done a day's work in their life and who think they can take food from the common man."

"They say you stole the wine," I blurt out. I don't know why I said it. I think I want the monks to be wrong, but I shouldn't have said it. What if he gets angry when I am here with him... *alone?*

174

"Oh, they said that, did they?" He seems to look at me differently. "And what else did they say?"

"They say you stole the drill, that you blaspheme, that you are a heretic, and something else called a com... com... that bad thing. They say you come from Cuba, that you wear red shirts, that you tried to paint the Madonna red, and that you eat..."

"Priests?" Dante proffers.

I nod.

"Well that last bit is true."

My eyes widen.

"Figuratively," he adds. "Do you know what figuratively means, *ragazzo?*"

I shake my head.

"Do you know what a 'red shirt' is?"

I hesitate and then shake my head.

"I can see I need to give you a countereducation, a bit like a counterrevolution—do you know what a revolution is?" he asks.

I shake my head.

"Ah, I can see we need to start right at—"

"Is it when they fight a war?" I blurt out, starting to feel stupid. "I know it's something to do with soldiers."

"It's more to do with the people. The battle of the people—the great mass of the people—against tyranny," says Dante.

I've never heard of Tyranny, but he must be a famous warrior like Genghis Khan for so many people to be fighting him.

"Can you tell me about the battle? Were many people killed? I like history, it's my favorite thing at school," I say.

He ignores me, looking at the mountains as he draws on his cigar. I feel less frightened, and straighten my cramped legs out in front of me.

"And why do they call you Il Garibaldino?" I ask. "I heard one of the monks call you Dante Il Garibaldino. Is that your name? Garibaldi is *famous*!" I say, delighted to be on a topic I know about.

"Ah! Garibaldi is famous, you say, *and so he is*! And do you know what he is famous for?"

He spits tobacco from his tongue and stubs the crusted black end of his cigar into the can.

Everybody knows this! "He is the father of Italy! We learned about him at school. He was very brave and fought the Austrian and French soldiers who were taking our country from us," I say with excitement.

Dante is now pulling chunks off the bread. "Go on," he says, handing me a piece.

"He went to South America and learned to fight in the bushes like a guerrilla—"

A sharp snort from Dante.

"—and that was why he could beat the other armies when he came back to Italy, because he was not only brave, he was also clever and sneaky. And because of him we have a united Italy. He rode up from the bottom of Italy with all his soldiers and met the king— who was coming from the north—halfway, and said to him: 'I give you Italy.' I always remember that: he did it all himself—*he gave the king Italy*!"

Dante is really smiling now: I think he is surprised at what I know.

"Well, let's just say he gave the *people* Italy," he says, "and not get too carried away with the king part. He gave Italy back to the Italian people, Mario—what greater deed than that?!"

We both stare out at the vista for a moment, not speaking.

"The great 'Red Shirts!'" says Dante finally.

I look at him, questioning.

"Garibaldi's army," he explains.

Ah, *now* I remember!

"And incredible as it may seem," says Dante, "that is why they call me Il Garibaldino. I fought with Garibaldi, young Mario: I was one of the famous 'one thousand.'"

I sit up. "One of the *thousand*! Truly? One of Garibaldi's thousand men who fought and won the battle against twenty thousand soldiers in Sicily?"

He nods.

"That battle is *famous*. Our teacher said it was what made the Italian people believe they could win back their country. She said that battle was the start of the victory!"

"Quite so! It was tough on the beaches. A bloody and brutal battle with not many of us returning . . . ," continues Dante.

Something isn't right.

"But wait," I say, "that battle was in 1860. You can't . . ."

Dante looks at me. He starts to say something and then stops. After a moment: "Well, it was my father who fought," he says gruffly.

I am still doing the math. "But that would make him *at least* a hundred and twenty. He must have been old when you were—"

"All right! It was my grandfather, all right? Damn school teaches you too much!" He looks across to the mountain peaks, and then up at the sky. "It was my *grandfather* who was one of the famous 'one thousand' and fought beside the greatest man who ever lived—*Giuseppe Garibaldi!*"

He looks back at me. "You still don't believe me?" he asks. "Just because I got a bit creative about *which* family member fought, you don't believe that any of it is true?"

I try to speak but nothing comes out.

"Come to my house tomorrow—the house everyone avoids." He smiles to himself. "Come visit tomorrow, and I'll prove it's true. I'll show you things you've never seen before and you'll never see again— armor and weapons from the most important battle ever fought in this country."

Oh, I want to see this!

"Come at noon. Tell your uncle I'll work tomorrow, but don't tell him *where* you saw me. No, come to think of it, don't tell him anything. But I'll see you there. And you'll need to bathe those sawdust eyes."

My eyes must still be red.

"And about the wine and drill: don't believe all you are told. Those merchants come up here regularly with stories to get money from the monks. Why? Because the monks are gullible and because the money they spend is not theirs—*it's ours*. You'd better go," he says.

As I stand, I hear my uncle calling. Dante puts his finger to his lips again and signals the exit to the stairs. He follows me down. As he drops the ladder, he says: "Tell me, Mario, does your uncle teach you things, like history?"

"Yes, all the time. He gives me his books," I say.

"Did he ever talk to you about Garibaldi?" says Dante.

I think. "No," I say, "I learned about him at school."

"Ask your uncle why he has not taught you about this most famous of men. Ask him *why* Garibaldi was fighting, *who* he was fighting against, and *who it was* that committed that most despicable of acts: using the French and Austrian armies *against his own people*. Ask him that. And then read more of those books—including the ones *not* in your uncle's study."

I nod and descend the ladder. This time I notice that Dante holds it firmly with both his hands.

Garibaldi was fighting the pope!

I can't believe it. My greatest of heroes was fighting against the church—this holy Catholic Church I have been brought up to believe in! I am even to go to the seminary because my family wants me to become a priest. But Garibaldi said the church was cruel, that it had taken the people's land, that the pope was killing people— cutting off their heads at the guillotine—just because they wanted their land back. Could this be true? It can't be true! But then how could a great man like Garibaldi be wrong? I'm confused.

And I can't ask another question of my uncle. He's not in a good mood. He wanted to know where I had got all these ideas from and why I wanted to know. Before I could answer, he asked me where I had seen Dante. I didn't want to reveal his hiding place, so I told Uncle I'd learned it all from a book—which was half true. I had gone straight to the monks' library and into a yellowing encyclopedia there: there was only a bit on Garibaldi, but it said enough. It said that the "papists" (Dante was right about that word) held a lot of the land in the center of Italy and were against giving it to the people so that Italy could all be one, that the pope had killed people and that he had used the French and Austrian armies to fight the Italian people just like Dante said. So the church *is* bad! Does this mean my uncle, too, is bad? It got me to thinking about him picking those broad beans . . . But then I love him! Nothing makes any sense.

I am keen to ask Dante more. I will tomorrow. But I have to keep the visit secret, as my uncle told me not to talk to him. I can't wait . . .

I drift off to sleep seeing my uncle's annoyed face; Dante's smiling one; heads rolling off guillotines outside the Vatican; and Garibaldi, riding high on his great horse, with a thousand "Red Shirts" behind him . . .

THUMP!

A great wheel of cheese is slammed on the table in front of me. I'm getting sick of cheese. We're in the kitchen of Dante's house, and he's invited me to eat.

"*Stop looking in there!* We eat first and then I show you."

I try to tell him I've already eaten, but he doesn't listen. He tells me that men don't show good will to each other if they don't eat together. I think that means I have to eat. But I've only just had lunch with my uncle and the monks and it was bread—with cheese! In fact, it was *exactly* the same cheese as the one in front of me now, with that same stamp on the rind. Fra Giuseppe said that Mangiapreti stole cheese from their *cantina*, but then, Dante would say that *they* stole the people's land, so now he and the church are even.

I had to sneak around the back of the village to get to Dante's house: crossing the piazza would have meant too many eyes following me. It was easy getting away from my uncle today. He is in a good mood because Dante turned up for work. I watched Dante fix the roof and plaster a section of the wall. He is fast and skillful, and got more work done in those few hours than the monks had done in a week. My uncle was *very* happy. Even the monks seemed less afraid, although I noticed they still didn't go near him: every instruction to Dante went through my uncle or me.

Dante's little kitchen is neat. There is a clean checked tablecloth beneath my arms, fruit in a bowl on the sideboard, and I notice the plates and cutlery are old but shiny and clean. And there are even cushions on the two chairs.

"Do you have a mother, Dante?" I ask. "Or—"

He laughs. "No, there is no Signora Garibaldino!"

He raises his arm as if holding a sword in triumph; he had told me the amazing story of Anita, Garibaldi's brave wife, who fought and died in battle.

"There are no women here, Mario, haven't been for a long time. There's no one left." His shoulders drop as he sighs. "This was a busy village twenty years ago: I should have taken a wife then. Every day that piazza was full of carts, horses and many, many people. You wouldn't believe it now, eh? All the *carbonari* and their families have gone, along with the fires on the hillsides from their coal-making stacks: the industry died with gas and oil, and everyone moved away. Except for *them*." He jabs his finger in the direction of the monastery.

"But I've got a girlfriend—*don't look so surprised!* She lives down in the town. Why do you think it took me three days to buy the drill?" He winks at me. "But she won't come here because I don't have a donkey, and she doesn't want to walk. Shows it can't be true love, eh?"

Walk up here from the town? It takes several hours in the car. Walking would take a whole day!

"Come!" says Dante.

He has finished his cheese, and gulps down what is left of a large glass of red wine. He doesn't seem to care that I haven't touched my cheese; I think he just wanted me to sit with him. I am his first visitor in years, he said. When I knocked on his door, he told me that entry here was a sacred thing, that I was coming into an area "free from the dominion of the church." Did that mean it wasn't a papal state, I asked him (I wanted to show that I remembered). Yes, he said. I felt proud; I think I was starting to understand.

Dante leads me to his bedroom of treasures; I could see part of this room from the kitchen. On the wall is a sword...oh, what a sword! It is large with a slight curve to its blade, and sits protected in a golden sheath. Below it is a dented trumpet. Above the sword is a faded cloth banner that reads: *He who dies for his country has lived long enough.*

"This is the sword and bugle of my grandfather, who fought in the *Risorgimento*—in Garibaldi's army." He leans against the bed and sighs, staring at the wall. "Not many men can say they have a Garibaldino in the family."

His voice is different: high-pitched and soft. I know to be respectful in this little bedroom. It is very quiet in here, as if it's sealed from the outside world; the only noise is the ticking of the small clock near the window. The room is crowded with a black iron bed, a sideboard and a large set of drawers; old photos sit atop dusty lace covers with pretty stitching. I wonder if his mother put them there a long time ago.

I turn back to the precious battle items. They are positioned on the wall at the end of the bed so that they can be seen when he awakes. Just think: the sword and bugle were in *that* battle . . . *could Garibaldi himself have touched them?* Dante sees me looking; he takes down the sword, gently, and pulls it from its sheath. He lets me touch it, hold it. I take it in, absorbing it, imagining the battle. After a while I notice there is a picture of Garibaldi on the wall, and next to it pictures of two other men.

"Did they fight in the 'one thousand' too, Dante?" I ask.

"Marx and Lenin were also great men, Mario. You could say that the movement Garibaldi started led the way for others to make great changes that would help the people—the common people. These three men fought for the right of *all* people to be free and happy, to eat well, and to be treated with the same dignity and respect as every damn aristocrat and pope."

He walks over and taps the picture of Garibaldi and smiles: "But, to me, this man was the greatest—the others even copied his damn beautiful red shirt!"

Nonno Cesare arrived in the village on the third day. He came just after lunch, getting a lift up in the timber merchant's truck. He wanted to see the church because it is our last afternoon here for a month, and Nonno's only opportunity before he goes back to Collemare. I *love* him being here. In contrast to the dress of the monks and his son, Nonno has on a bright green shirt, colorful braces and a smart white straw boater. He lights up the piazza with his loud talk, gesturing arms and laughter. I have been waiting and waiting... I *so* want to introduce Nonno to my friend. But I'm not supposed to be talking to Dante, though my uncle is very pleased with him: he has been working "like a mule," my uncle said.

Dante went back to work that first afternoon (after our secret lunch!) and worked late into the night. Yesterday he plastered two complete walls, and this morning he finished the altar, painted the small end wall, and repaired several pews. My uncle says if he keeps this up the work will be finished in a third of the time estimated. Uncle promised Dante a year's worth of cheese and apple liqueur as a bonus, on top of his wine and wages, if this is achieved. Dante didn't say much in reply, but I knew he was happy as he slipped off to have his after-lunch smoke.

That was two hours ago.

One of the monks says loudly that he is "up to his old tricks," and I quickly say: "He'll be back—he wants to work now."

My grandfather, who is nearby, looks at me for a few moments and then pulls me aside. "So where's your friend Dante, Mario?" he asks.

Oh no! I can't lie to my grandfather: "I don't think he's very far," I say, truthfully.

Not very far! He is in the belltower right above us, where he always goes to smoke, but I can't tell—

"Let's have a break," says Nonno, signaling for me to come outside with him. He lights up a cigar. "My one delicious vice..."

For the first time I really look at the cigar. Something about it is familiar...

"That's just like—" I stop mid-sentence.

"Just like *what*, Mario?"

CHEWING GUM IN HOLY WATER

"Dante smokes them," I say.

"Ah, this Dante who terrorizes all the—"

"He doesn't!" I say quickly.

Nonno looks surprised. "You know, I'd like to meet this Dante. He sounds quite a character." I look away as my grandfather continues: "I hope I don't have to go all the way back home without meeting him. Do you know where he is?"

I dart a quick look at the belltower. Oops, *shouldn't have done that*, I think Nonno saw.

"That's a beautiful view of the valley on the other side, Mario." Uncle and I had taken him around behind the monastery earlier. Nonno *loves* the mountains. "That view would be *magnificent* from just a little higher."

He runs his eyes slowly up the full length of the belltower, halting at the very top. "You're right, Mario. You shouldn't judge a man by what others say. You have to find out for yourself." He blows out a great waft of cigar smoke.

Dante let my *nonno* up.

I told him I had checked that Nonno wasn't a papist, but Dante said it was the cigars that mattered. He told Nonno he was welcome because he was my grandfather and doubly welcome because he also smoked *toscani*—the cigars of the proletariat.

I was surprised at how fit my *nonno* is: he scaled the ladder faster than me. When Nonno asked about the burned-out stairs, Dante quickly said they were too hard to fix. As we got to the first floor, my grandfather commented: "I see the stairs on the upper levels are better repaired—easier to fix, eh?"

Dante took in the smirk on Nonno's face. "I work better at higher altitudes," he said, slapping my grandfather's back. The two men smiled at each other and Dante signaled for us to follow him up the stairs.

For two hours I have been sitting in a blissful haze of sunshine and cigar smoke at the top of the belltower, listening to their talk. Just the three of us, up here in our special place—where no one can find us: *il campanile*. I feel grown up as we talk of tyranny, and Garibaldi, and "politics." Dante tried to explain that politics are the ways you think about life: he said Nonno's are "in the middle," in between him—he's a communist (and they *don't* eat babies!)—and my "papist" uncle. But I'm not to call Uncle that to his face.

Nonno and Dante didn't agree on a lot of things, and at first I thought they might fight. But they explained it was a *discussion*, and that people can have very different ideas and still be friends; it doesn't make one person bad or one good—it just makes them *different*. But how could a communist like a papist who had chopped off his head? And how could a papist be friends with someone who swore and threw potatoes? But then Nonno *and* Uncle had made friends with Dante! That means they know about people being different, but the monks don't seem to. Was this why they *still* ran away, thinking Dante would eat them? I asked my grandfather.

"Ignorance, Mario," said my *nonno*. "Ignorance is a terrible thing. It's when you close off your mind and refuse to learn more about something. You will find the more you learn about a thing the less you are frightened of it."

Nonno is now enjoying a short black *toscano* from Dante's box. Dante says he cuts them in half so he can "enjoy more cigars."

"The church still has a lot to answer for," says Dante, continuing their former conversation. "How many of our people had to emigrate overseas because the church would not give them back their land? Certainly they took the church states from the pope *pretending* to sell them to the people, but they kept the prices so high that in the end the land went to the *borghesia*. The common man could not obtain it—land that was likely his in the first place! The church was very much in bed with the rich *pescecani*..."

The church in bed with *sharks*!

"But then, history always has its dominant few who run the show and take from others—," says my *nonno*.

"And *needs* the fighting few to curtail them and bring things back to the middle," cuts in Dante.

"Quite so," says my *nonno*, "but in the end we all still have to work, in the end we all still have to eat, in the end the farmer still has to till the soil, ready for another year. Mostly we have to 'live and let live.'"

"*And keep watching the bastards!*" says Dante proudly, smiling at my *nonno* and me and stubbing out his cigar.

It's three months since we returned from the village of *il campanile* and my aunt and uncle are acting... *different*. It began when I told my aunt she was doing tyranny to the cat. She stopped talking, stared, and then sent me inside.

My aunt had thrown a wooden spoon at Rusciu and chased him outside, booting him down three steps, just because he brought in a rat. I told her he brings dead rats inside because he's a hunter, and that we should leave the rat on the kitchen floor for a while so Rusciu knows we're proud. Aunt said *she* wasn't proud and for me to get the rat out, *velocemente*! But I had read it in a book, I protested. Aunt said she didn't care for books and didn't care to know about cats. I told her that not wanting to know would make her... *ignorant*.

I was in my room for a week.

And then my uncle: when he tore off another of those posters from the church door that make him *almost* swear, I said that I knew the face on it. It was a man called Marx! My uncle paused for a moment, and then went on ripping. Later, I heard him tell someone he was going to advise the congregation not to frequent the village bar where the communists met, and I asked him why. He said I wouldn't understand. I asked him whether this was like that bigotry thing my aunty was good at. He said it *wasn't* bigotry, it was that communists were a bad influence, and he tried to explain to me they weren't *Christian*—I didn't tell him I already knew. So I asked whether that meant they didn't have a soul, because my friend Dante seemed to have one, and did he remember telling the monks that *all* people do—or is it only papists? My uncle went very red, slammed the church door open and gave me the worst of the *chierichetto* duties. I waited and waited, but he didn't mention the communist bar in his sermon.

I pull the covers up to warm my icy cheeks. It seems like a long time ago that I sat in *il campanile* in the sunshine with Dante and my *nonno*. I look across at my special shelf—there sit the two small wooden Madonnas that the monks gave me as a parting gift and, behind them, half hidden, is a small picture of Garibaldi that I tore from a magazine and stuck on my wall. It's on the wall at the end of my bed so that I see it when I wake up.

The little Madonnas sit there guarding Garibaldi, or maybe he's guarding them. The wooden figures were grimy and discolored when I got them, and I had to do a bit of work. I look at the shiny Madonna on the left: I cleaned it carefully and rubbed it with oil, so now you can see the grain of the beech in the lovely curves of the figure.

I look at the other Madonna. I painted that one red.

Something worse than Lucifer. That was what my uncle just said.

We all stop what we're doing. There's no movement in the room at all, no tapping pen or ruler, no rustle of legs—Libero has even stopped picking at his nose. We're at *catechismo*, the class that prepares us for *cresima*—holy communion—and there are eight of us, all forced to give up our Saturday afternoons to study church teachings under the watchful eye of my uncle or a nun. At least it's not as bad as school because we're allowed to talk a bit, and the *best* part of *catechismo* is discussing what we will do in the two hours of free time between class and dinner.

"Next week I will tell you about something *worse*—something more dangerous and more powerful—than *Lucifero*," my uncle repeats.

He *did* say it. I look around. I've never heard such a long silence. Even during prayers there's always a cough, a shifting foot . . .

My uncle looks into each of our faces. We all look back, intently.

"Yes," says my uncle, holding our gazes, "something more subtle, more sneaky, and therefore much more dangerous than Lucifer."

Something worse than the devil? How could it be? What he has said throws into confusion everything we've been taught. What could be worse than the worst of all the demons? What could be more dangerous, more evil than *Satan*? My mouth is wide open. I close it and try to push aside the monsters already crawling around in my mind.

A boy shoots his hand up eagerly.

"Next week," my uncle says.

"But what could be *worse* than—?" I start.

"*Next week*," he repeats, smiling.

There is excited chatter and whispering in the room. A few of the boys are looking at me. *Me?* They must think I already know, because I'm the priest's nephew. But my uncle has never even *hinted* to me before that there could be something worse than Lucifer.

My uncle's still smiling because he's got our attention. And he knows that not one of us will miss *catechismo* next week.

"What is it, Mario? What's worse than Lucifer?" asks Giovanni.

A crowd of boys has gathered around me outside our *catechismo* class.

"I don't know, *honest*," I say.

"It's an atheist—atheists eat babies!" cries one boy.

"*Communists* eat babies, not atheists!" says Giovanni.

"No, they don't!" I exclaim, thinking of my friend Dante. But then I've only met *one* communist...

"It's not a *person*," says another boy with a shiver. "If it's more powerful than Satan, then it's not a person."

We disperse, my friends all seem deep in thought—I'm eager to follow my uncle.

Marcello thinks it has two heads. I think three: one head for ripping things apart (screaming people), another for continually sucking up their blood, and another head for keeping watch on all the things that are "more good" than it is—which is *everything*—so that it can kill them.

Giovanni says that *his* monster-worse-than-Satan is invisible (so that even God and Satan can't find it). It rips up and eats *whole countries*, not just people—that's why they tell you some islands sink and have to keep changing borders on maps. It peels off your skin and eats you slowly from the inside out so you see it chewing all your guts before you die, and it lives outside the known universe. We didn't believe the bit about the universe. How could it live outside the universe if the universe is *everything*? Giovanni repeated, the *known* universe; he said we don't know yet if something is outside of it. We then agreed his monster was the most believable.

Worse than Lucifer.

I tried to get it out of my uncle at home, pleading with him, but he wouldn't tell. I even took down the picture of Garibaldi—just for now—and showed him, pointing out that it *could* be damaging my Christian thoughts. I thought this would please him so much he would tell me what I wanted to know, but he just said, "It's up to you," and walked off!

And I've had nightmares all week. Nightmares of monsters and demons, things crawling all over me, eating my guts, dipping me in boiling oil, demons with wicked, yellow eyes, sharp teeth and long tails hovering across burning flames. One is a black demon that keeps pulling me over to it with a signal from its claw. Its horrible face is partly covered and I can't stop it pulling me and pulling me until I am on the edge of the flaming hole and I can hear my friends screaming in the fire below, with holes right through them where their guts used to be—*Aargh!* Have to stop thinking about it ... I'm worn out.

Today is the day.

In the *catechismo* class a few of us are yawning and bleary-eyed, but everyone is keenly sitting up, waiting. I notice there are fourteen of us this week: six boys we haven't seen for a while have decided to attend. I hear the clock outside strike the hour. It will be another fifteen minutes before the lesson begins and most of us have already been here for a while. There was some fighting over seats near the front, and I'm sure some were hoping to get to my uncle before class: he is always early.

But not today: he's not here. The start time comes and passes. My uncle is late. Strange. None of us talk very much.

Suddenly my uncle sweeps in. All eyes are on him. He smiles at us, taps his wrist to indicate that we are very prompt today, and begins unstrapping his books. He takes his time: a long time. He sets his books, papers and pens out neatly, brushes a mark or two from his robe and then turns to us, leaning against the table.

"Welcome, boys, *come stai?*" he asks brightly.

There are a few tired mutterings of: "*Bene.*"

We go through the usual prayers—they seem to be taking *so long*—and then my uncle brings up church topics: boring things like church festivals, coming *catechismo* subjects, and homework for next week.

Finally: "So, did you boys have a good think about that powerful thing I mentioned last week? It seems some of you are keen to know." He glances around at us.

There are a few reluctant nods.

"Did you all consider carefully what could be *worse than Lucifero?*"

Silence.

"Does anyone *know?*"

More silence.

My uncle pauses. He reminds me of the wolves my *nonno* told me about, the wolves that prowl around you, watching, waiting, silent, getting ready to pounce. He must know our minds are churning—*why doesn't he say something?*

"I'll tell you what is worse than Lucifer," he finally says. It is so quiet that I can hear the soft ticking of the clock on my uncle's table.

"*La carne,*" he says.

Tick, tick, tick goes the clock.

"*La carne,*" he says again and looks into each of our faces.

My mind is scrambling. *La carne? Meat?*

"*La carne?*" cries one of the older boys, disappointed.

My uncle slowly nods, watching us.

What does he mean? Which sort of meat? Lamb, beef...oh, now I remember that some religious people don't eat pork! Maybe that's what it is: when you're taking communion you can no longer eat pork...

"*La carne!*" repeats my uncle, who suddenly seems awkward. "*The flesh!*" he emphasizes, eyeing us intently.

We look at each other, shrugging our shoulders, all of us feeling disappointed—and *confused.*

My uncle gives an exasperated sigh: he seems tense. "*The flesh!*" he yells.

I hear one of the older boys say, "*Oh,*" in an embarrassed kind of way just as my uncle says: "The temptation of the flesh!" He sees a few blank faces still, and adds: "The temptation of women!"

A shocked silence.

"For you boys what is more dangerous, more powerful, than Satan is the temptation that is coming, the temptation of girls. *La lussuria—lust!* The most subtle of the seven deadly sins, and therefore the most dangerous."

I can't believe what my uncle is saying. Is he saying that those lovely things we look at in magazines: the legs, the tight dresses that show bosoms and curves, all the things that make us go red, laugh, feel excited and that we enjoy more than anything else, these things are *worse than Lucifer?*

I look at my uncle. He is still talking but I don't hear him. For the first time he doesn't look so important, so clever, so scary, so *right.* This time he's *not* right, and I know it inside. *I won't believe it.*

Around the room I see a few disbelieving faces like my own, but others are listening to my uncle and looking worried as they hang on his every word. I thought this thing-worse-than-Lucifer must have been a monster, the most horrifying, evil monster of all time, and now my uncle is saying that it is the soft curves we look at in the women's magazines at the *edicola*, or the sweet nakedness in the magazines under Giovanni's father's bed. He seems to be saying that even our *dreams* are evil: the ones we have about the girls we like at school.

For the first time I want to yell out, "*No!*" to my uncle. "*No, no, NO! I don't believe you!*" Everything inside me is screaming out against his words, and I won't believe them, *ever!*

I look at my uncle. He's still talking.

Soon I am to go to live at the seminary where they will train me to become a priest. I am supposed to stay there for the rest of my school years and beyond. I don't want to go, but my uncle and my mother want it. My aunt wants it too—she says I'll make the worst priest ever, but she can't wait to get me out of the house. I think again about my uncle's words: about this thing-worse-than-Satan. How can I be a priest if I enjoy the *worst* mortal sin? I will just have to go to the seminary and keep it a secret that I'm not really going to be a priest.

But then what should I be? If I don't become a priest, like my family has decided, then I'll have to be something else! I think about the painter and his book with the best bosoms of all. I could be a painter... or a farmer like my papa and Nonno. And then there's Dante. Maybe I could be a communist like him, but I'm not sure if that's a job—

"Padre! *Padre!*" young Emilio calls out from the back of the room. The frightened tone in his voice gets our attention. His bottom lip is quivering.

"Yes?" asks my uncle.

"Padre, how will we know when the *lust* thing is there? If we can be friends with girls, then how will we know when they are doing this bad thing?"

193

There's a snort from the back and a few of us glance around, heads down to hide smirks. Slowly, we all look at my uncle, waiting for the answer.

He looks up as if searching for the answer on the ceiling. Maybe he's asking God...

"*That*," he says after a long pause, "is such a powerful and dangerous thing that we can't speak about it here..."

I'm going straight home to put Garibaldi back on the wall.

Il Monsignore e il Fiume
THE MONSEIGNEUR AND THE RIVER

C runch! Crunch! THWACK!

    "Oh, *mannaggia*! Tie it again!" someone whispers.

"Not too tight. Don't squash it—*don't squash it!*"

"Kick it and see . . . Oh!"

Paper flies into the air: lots of it. The tightly scrunched bits return to the floor quickly, drifting and flickering along the ancient tiles of the long corridor; the softer pieces dance for a while in the dusty light that streams in from the far window and then waft softly to our feet.

Our paper soccer ball has disintegrated. All that remains in the center of the hallway is a lonely, looping piece of string.

We are in the seminary. I'm living *in* the seminary, and I'm supposed to be here now forever and ever . . . I hate it. The only good parts are my new friends, and—soccer. The long upstairs hallway we're now in is our one place of brief freedom in between awful classes full of praying, scolding and Latin. We snatch a few precious minutes at the end of lessons to play our paper soccer: boys scrambling and kicking alongside hallowed walls heavy with crucifixes, Madonnas and old paintings. Hoping always that the ball only ricochets into *empty* rooms off the hallway—may the Madonna help us if it flies into one where there's a class! No one ever gets a goal—the hall is too long and the goalposts too far away—but we have such fun! We have to talk in loud whispers so as not to attract the attention of the priests or novices in the classrooms, and it's hard to snort and guffaw quietly but we have to, because there is to be no laughter in the seminary. *No* laughter.

Right now six of us are desperately, and *very* quietly, scrambling after paper. One bit floats up the wall again as I rush to it, sitting itself happily on the corner of a heavy gold frame that surrounds the portrait of some old, stern and very ugly bishop. I don't want to look at him, not close up. Why are these pictures all so grim and *dark*? And if they're men of God, why do they all look so *unhappy*?

"Quick, *quick*! The bell is about to go!" yells a boy.

The bell. I soon discovered that life in the seminary is run by bells. Every moment of the day is timed and has its bell: a bell rung by the novice who struts and yells his way through the *dormitorio* to wake us in the early morning, a bell for attendance at prayers, a bell for breakfast in the *refectorio*, a bell for first classes, a bell for every class ending and beginning throughout the day, a bell for lunch, a bell for day's end, a bell for evening prayers, a bell for the evening meal, a bell for evening study, a bell for lights out ... *aargh!!!* We love and hate the bells, depending on which end of our small freedoms and pleasures they sit.

Several months in the seminary and I've almost forgotten what freedom is. I wish I was back with my uncle: even my *aunt*. As well as giving me religious instruction, my uncle gave me room to run outside and explore, to question everything, to *think*: here at the seminary they don't. After two canings, I stopped asking the questions no one else asked in class: how come Jesus didn't wear a crucifix around his neck like we have to? Why do we covet the robes of a priest when we're not supposed to covet? And how come we have to have our hair so short when Jesus and his disciples had long hair? One of the younger teachers started answering my questions, hesitated, started again, and then stopped. By next lesson he ignored my hand: he had been told to stop encouraging me. The strictest teacher caned me, twice. The teachers must have talked together, because soon they all simply said, "*Valentini!*" and nodded toward the cane whenever my hand went up. So I stopped asking. It was difficult when I wanted to go to the toilet.

And then there's the "creeping *Monsignore*." We fear him more than anyone. He is the head of the whole seminary and is like God to us. I think he's a bishop or something. No one but the very top priests speak to him without being spoken to first, he never talks to us boys, and he walks around during the day, up and down the hallways with his *messale*, always reading his *messale*. He has his head down reading his book, but you can hear his footsteps and woe betide you if you are not paying attention in class when he walks past, for he is able to see without looking up. Anything out of the ordinary comes to the attention of the teacher if the *Monsignore* has walked past the classroom at that moment. If we want to talk or pass a note, we have to watch for the teacher *and* listen for the footsteps.

And it isn't just in the classroom that we have no freedom: *outside* class they're also strict. Worse than my aunt! We have to make our beds, bathe, fold our clothes, clean our teeth, nails and shoes, and sweep around our beds, all before leaving the *dormitorio* at six a.m.! Meals are taken in different sittings within the great *refectorio*, underneath the entrance hall of the seminary, with its dark, wood-paneled walls. About forty of us are seated on benches at several great tables, with two elegantly set tables at the end of the room for the priests. *Orzo*—which I no longer like!—is ladled out from great copper pots at breakfast, and you can have seconds. I don't want seconds. I don't even want *firsts*. The things I want more of are the sweet, crunchy cookies made by the nuns from the convent, but you can't have seconds of them. And even here, eating, we are watched every minute, and if we get into trouble we are forced to go without breakfast and lunch, and have to do extra chores like cleaning the kitchen. At the seminary we have to eat a certain way, walk a certain way, dress a certain way, *talk* a certain way—we even have to walk in a neat line when we leave class! We can't *do* anything—and we can't *go* anywhere.

That's the worst of it. Not going anywhere. There's no chance for adventures or exploration, no chance for anything that isn't supervised by some priest or novice priest. And the novices are the worst. The big important priests we never see except at ceremonies or from a distance down a hallway, and the normal priests are strict but not mean, but the trainees... They are not yet twenty and they're recognizable because even though they wear the robes (the ones we covet), they don't yet have a tonsure—the *chierica*—and they are the bossiest and meanest to us. They make us do their chores and get things for them as though we're servants.

I complain to my friends that we're in prison. We're *told* that it's a seminary but our families really sent us here for punishment: to a prison full of Greek and Latin. Yes, we've all been bad and they've locked us up here, and that means we have to break out now and then. One boy said I was talking rubbish, because he was always well behaved at home. I asked him how many times he'd been to confession. He said lots, so I said: "If you've had *lots* of confessions, you've done *lots* of bad things and that's why you're here in prison."

We tried out several plans of escape in order to get out for an hour's rock climbing or down to the village shops, but none of them worked. Mostly we just couldn't get out: once I managed it and got spotted outside the walls and ended up with the cane—again. The novices watch us too closely, especially after hours, and especially me. So we are stuck with doing the rounds of the garden—the seminary is in a wing of an old castle, so the gardens are large with clipped hedges and fountains, but there are also *hundreds* of windows looking down on them.

Once a week we are taken on a walk to the village—it is our "outing," our *passeggiata*. The good things about it are getting comics and seeing people who aren't priests; the rest of it is awful. We have to line up in double lines inside the seminary and then one of the head novices leads us out the gate and down to the village: *at all times* we have to stay in our line and not move out of it; to do so means a caning.

We aren't to talk to people on the way, apart from nodding our respects to any elder who says, "*Ciao!*" or "*Buongiorno!*" and we can't go *anywhere* ourselves, not even to the *edicola* to buy our comics! We have to wait patiently in line until the novice reaches us and takes our money and then he goes and makes our purchases. We can't even look at what is on the stand! Once I pulled the line over to the stand, forcing those around me to move and turning the straight lines into a big bendy snake. The novice yelled when he noticed a few of us, still in line yet right beside him, turning the pages of comics on the stand. I was banned from the outing for the next two weeks.

"Quick, Mario!" yells the Venezuelan.

I reach up to retrieve the bit of soccer-ball paper from where it has come to rest on the bishop's frame, but I can't quite get it. The painting rocks dangerously after I knock it when I leap up. The Venezuelan quickly steadies the painting and snatches down the paper. At twelve, he is the eldest of our group by only a few months, yet already looks a man: he is tall and solidly built. He's also very strong, and good in a fight, and he can bend his finger back so far that *it touches the back of his hand*! Yuck! It horrifies and fascinates us, so we ask him to do it again and again. He's one of my best friends here, and I discovered that he has a funny accent because he's from Venezuela, in South America. Because he's the only one here from Venezuela, we nicknamed him that. I told him Garibaldi lived in South America too, so he's going to ask his *nonno* if he knew him.

I've tried not to make too many friends here at the seminary, though. If it's hard to leave people after *two years* in a village, imagine how hard it would be to leave after only a few months! Because I think I will convince my uncle any day now to let me out of here— and I just don't want my friends to be upset, and to miss me—and maybe even cry about it at night ...

"*It's had it!*" says the boy scrambling to tie up our soccer ball.

"Leave it! The bell's about to go," says another. "I'm getting a drink."

"Me too," says the boy with the ball.

The nuns have jugs of water and biscotti for us in the *refectorio*, which is where we're supposed to be right now. The others head off, leaving only the Venezuelan and me in the hallway.

"Coming?" he asks.

I hesitate, glancing at the great window at the end of the long, long corridor. The window that lets in the soft golden light that seeps toward us, trying to warm the ancient hallway, the somber walls, and the dark faces displayed on them. The seminary is in a

200

wing of a great ducal castle that was built in 879. It sits high on an outcrop, overlooking the village on one side and the great valley on the other at a place called Trivento, which means "three winds." The window at the end of the hallway looks out toward the valley where two rivers join, facing directly into the fierce "three winds" that fly up the gullies and gorges cut by the waters. It looks down and out to the mountains, the valleys, the trees, the rivers. It looks down and out to *freedom*.

"I might just—" I begin.

"You and your window!" laughs the Venezuelan as he follows the other boys down to the *refectorio*.

I rush toward the window, stopping to walk slowly past the two full classrooms farther down the hall, and then rush again, sliding the last several feet along the smooth tiles until I grip the edge of the window frame.

Well, it's more a *wall* than a window frame. The castle walls are ten feet thick: this means you can't see out the window fully from the hallway. I climb up into the window cavity and slide myself along until I reach the glass. I stretch out inside the great stone cavity, with still more than a yard between my feet and the inside wall behind me, and from here I can look down and out. *Oh, what a view!*

The mountains, the villages, the valleys and hills of the Molise! I like to look out here because the village that I can just make out on a distant peak on the other side of the valley is in the Abruzzo— my home!

But it's what's *in* the valley that I really like: the great glistening, rippling, dancing river. The Trigno. It calls to me, inviting me to come down and splash and play and jump about in it. It invites me because it's not deep—living in the mountains, I don't know how to swim—and it seems the most wondrous place, for I love both water *and* rocks! The river ripples and tosses itself about in a narrow, shallow stream with several feet of white shiny pebbles on either side of it. The white is broken up by the soft feathery green trees that dance around in the breeze up on the higher banks and among the pebbles. There are boulders to jump off, pools and swirls of water, small ripples and large, deeper surges, and little rapids where the shallow water bounces and froths itself over the rocks...Oh, I *so* want to go down there. It looks like *heaven*!

Footsteps.

I just heard footsteps. Soft shuffling footsteps...

It can't be. The bell hasn't rung! Or *has* it? Maybe I've been here longer than I...but surely my friends would have called me. Unless *they* were running late...I'm too scared to look around. My body is clenched tight, listening.

More footsteps.

I turn my head ever so slowly and strain my eyes back down the long corridor.

It's him. The Monsignore! Halfway along the corridor and heading this way. The bell *must* have rung, and the others are in class and the Monsignore is now doing his rounds...

I flatten and squash my full body length in against one corner of the cavity, hoping I will not be spotted. Trouble is, the window sits in direct alignment with the corridor, and in a dead end, leaving me in full view. Still, he might *not* look up. He usually turns back several yards before the window so maybe he won't look up because he knows there's no classroom this far down, and no boys to catch out...I flatten myself even further against the wall, wishing there was a hole, an opening, somewhere to hide in this stone!

The footsteps are very near. They stop. Maybe he's turning? Yes, he's turning to go back. Oh, *wonderful*!

The footsteps stop again. There's a pounding in my ears, and the distant rumble of a teacher's voice in one of the classrooms. Otherwise there is only silence. Maybe he's gone—

"Mario," says a deep voice very close to me.

I jump and then freeze. He's here! And he used *my name*! I didn't know he even *knew* my name...

"What are you doing?" asks the voice.

I slowly turn and try to sit up. What should I do? Bow? Stand? Not look at him? I don't know how you are supposed to address a *monsignore*.

But he's not looking at me! The *Monsignore* stands quietly with his eyes still on his *messale* as he speaks: "Well?"

"I...um... I was looking at the river," I blurt out. It was the first thing that came to me. Oh no, I should have said I was looking up at *heaven*—

"Shouldn't you be somewhere else?" he asks. I notice his voice is not angry.

"Yes, but I was looking at the river. I've never been there—I'd like to go there!" I blurt again.

"You really dream of the river?" he asks, still without looking up.

I can't believe he's not scolding me, he's not threatening punishment for being out of class—he's just talking to me about the river.

"I'd like to go there," I repeat, "and collect rocks from the water and...fossils and shells and gold."

"Please go to your class now," the *Monsignore* says firmly, turning on his heels and beginning his gentle pacing up the hallway again. He didn't once look at me.

I scramble off the window ledge and head for my classroom, relieved that I just escaped a close call, but also aware there will be some punishment to follow.

But first, a more pressing problem: late to class. The toilet. I'll say I went to the toilet. They'll understand; I never go during class.

Passeggiata, stupid *passeggiata* in two lines, like puppets, down to the village ... still, it's better than being inside the seminary.

We're all lined up in rows out in the garden, ready to go, and the novices are hovering, giving us the eye or a nudge if we move a fraction out of line. Still, I'm happy. Each day that I don't get called somewhere by one of the priests I'm happy: it's now *three days* since the incident at the window and I haven't had any punishment. It *should* have happened by now, so hopefully the *Monsignore* forgot or got kind or something, though I'm still a bit worried.

There is a sudden ripple of excitement through the lines: the boys in the front rows quieten. All eyes go to the front. Someone important is coming: I can tell by the way some of the most annoying novices stand up really straight and start acting nice to us.

I hear the word "*Monsignore*" whispered. I look through the heads in front of me. It's him! The *Monsignore*! What's he doing here? He *never* comes outside for simple things like our outings. It seems strange to see him in his elaborate robes standing in the garden, in full sunlight, with us. Oh no! It dawns on me that he is going to announce my punishment out here in front of everyone ...

"*Dio sia lodato*—God be praised," says the *Monsignore*, greeting us.

We all reply: "*Dio sia lodato*," and wait, keen-eared, for what is coming.

"There's been a request about outings," he says. A murmur through the lines: the *Monsignore* pauses until he regains everyone's attention. "So today you will be going to the river."

I'm stunned. I can't believe the words I just heard. We are going to *the river*? The *Monsignore* listened to my request and we are going to the river? The other boys jump around me with excitement, but I stand still, waiting for it to sink in.

"Isn't it great?" yells a boy next to me.

Yes, it's *great*, but did he . . . was it . . . ? The *Monsignore* meets my eyes briefly before turning to leave. *It was!* It was because of me that he did it!

Oh, I'm so happy! Not just no punishment . . . but *the river*! I look at the other boys. They don't know that I did it, except maybe for the Venezuelan . . . yes, he looks across at me and smiles. I told him about the *Monsignore* at the window and he knows I did it. The other boys don't, and I suddenly decide that I'm going to keep it a secret, just between me and my good friend the *Monsignore*!

The trip down into the valley is quick: all I can see in my mind is the glistening water. The two novices have great trouble controlling all of us as we slide and scramble and laugh our way down the trail to the river. This is *my* special trip because *I* got it, and I am going to enjoy every moment of it and do what I want. Watch out if any of the novices are mean to me today because I *could* report them to my friend the *Monsignore*.

I'm in! Shoes off, pants rolled up to my knees and I'm first in! (I had to be—it is *my* outing!) Ah! It's cold, colder than I thought it would be, but I don't care!

The boys are screaming and yelling and pushing each other behind me. There are whoops and squeals of delight. One boy falls over on the rocks as someone pushes him just as he is balancing on one leg, trying to roll up his pants. Another thumps someone in the back as he enters the water and he *almost* falls in face first.

"*Behave!*" yells a novice, but no one takes any notice.

Anyway, I don't care what they're doing, the novices *or* the boys. I'm in *and I'm in heaven!* The water swirls around my legs as I slip about over smooth pebbles. There's a gushing, gurgling pool just to the left of me, and a bit farther on is a large branch stretched out over the water. I wade to it and try to climb it, but it's slippery with moss and I can't get a foothold. I finally scramble up, the seat of my pants already wet. I look at the other boys—some are too scared to go in past their ankles, and no one is in as far as me!

Rocks. I love to collect rocks and pebbles and shells, and here they are everywhere, all around me! I slide off the branch and back into the water, heading for the bank on the other side. There are millions of glistening, smooth white pebbles and rocks of every shape in among the trees and shrubs. Maybe I can find a fossil—or even some gold! I've read that people find gold in rivers.

"Not too far!" yells a novice, I think at me. I don't even turn to look. I clamber around, filling my pockets with pebbles, rocks, a small glass bottle, a piece of patterned crockery that I found wedged in a branch. There are stringy bits of bark and grass halfway up some of the trees, which means the river must rise this high sometimes. Imagine how deep it would be! *That* thought is scary . . . The breeze chills my cheeks as I scramble and play and yell, and my pants become more and more soaked, but who cares? *We're at the river!*

Both of my pants pockets bulge out sideways, filled with rocks and the rest of my weighty collection. In fact, my pants have become *so* heavy that I have to keep yanking them up because my backside is beginning to show. I decide to dump my rocks on the bank near my jacket, and then return to the water. I have to go slowly and carefully as I no longer seem to have my balance. Halfway across, I get stuck. There's a sharp piece of rock and I can't use my hands to lean down because they're busy keeping my pants up. I try, but my pants half slip off, along with my undies, and I almost fall sideways.

"Look at Valentini losing his pants!" yells a boy.

A couple of others laugh.

"I'm in farther than you!" I yell back.

I slip again and go over on my side. The boys watching roar with laughter. I'm angry. They're making fun of me when they don't know that this is *my* river and I got them the outing! I have to do something to show them that I know what I'm doing—and quickly.

"I can jump off that rock!" I yell, pointing to a boulder about seven feet high sitting in the middle of the river just to the right of me.

"Yeah, yeah," one calls back derisively.

I use all my strength to stand up and pull myself across to the boulder. The water is a little deeper just in front of it, so I skirt around the side and manage to clamber up to the top, pulling one leg after the other by gripping my weighty pockets.

"Go on!" yells a boy.

I jump.

Water swirls around me, clouding my eyes, and there's a dull roaring sound...can't find my way up...can't get...*it's over my head!* It can't be... I've just slipped sideways...the river is shallow! I try to come up again. *I'm up!* There's the sky! But I'm going under again! The water is deep...deeper than me! All I can see is greenish gray water, and I'm choking...*drowning!* There's a swirling, rushing noise in my ears, and I'm too heavy to get up. Can't float, the weight in my pockets is pulling me down... I can hear the muted sound of people yelling somewhere, but there's only a rushing noise close to me. The panicked feeling is turning into a dizzy, quiet feeling...can't breathe, my nose, mouth and throat are burning, full of water...can't breathe... I relax into the soft swirling sound of the river...

"*Shake him!*" someone yells.

I'm being rolled and shaken, and I realize I'm on the riverbank. Someone is slapping my face—hard. My chest feels tight, like I'm about to burst, and I want to vomit. I try to get my breath...sucking, sucking in: I can't breathe...*the air is not going in.* I heave and desperately try to suck in another breath: I lurch up and vomit out water, sending several boys near me running. I sit there, gasping.

"He's all right!" yells one of the novices, relieved.

Peering through swollen eyes, I see everyone gathered around me. Someone tries to shake me again, but I push him away. I'm cold and begin to shiver uncontrollably. All down my side I can feel a burning where I must have been scraped across the rocks. I feel dizzy and faint, and very, very ill.

"Get him to the infirmary!" yells the senior novice.

I hear scrambling around me and feel myself being lifted.

The infirmary is nice. All quiet and white. The sheets are white and crisp, and they're folded down neatly. Very neatly. I keep looking at the edges, which are exactly the same width right across the bed, like someone measured them with a ruler.

And the nuns are nice. I've had every drink I've wanted, not just water like we usually get, but *lemonade,* and I've had a lovely piece of cake. I vomited it up soon after, but at least I got to *taste* it.

When I tried to impress on the nuns that I *could* still die and should therefore have more cake, they refused. They said my tummy was in shock and couldn't hold food yet, but that it would be all right by tomorrow, and that from the point I started breathing down on the riverbank, I wasn't going to die. One nun said the person who probably should have been in the hospital bed beside me was the novice whose back I almost broke as he tried to lift me from the water: they had stripped me of my pants when they discovered the incredible weight was coming from my pockets. The nun then leaned over and gently took the thermometer from under my arm. No, no fever. And, *no,* still no cake.

It's nice here, nice and quiet. And the best thing? No classes for two days. All my friends are in class right now, and I am here with lemonade, cake (when I can get it) and a book. And not a church book either: they let me have one of my own books. The Venezuelan came to visit and brought me one of my Conrad books about sailing on the high seas. He said all the boys think I'm a hero and that it was *still* the best outing ever, even if it was cut a bit short. I look at the glass of lemonade on my little table, the smooth, white stone that the Venezuelan collected at the river and has now given to me, and back at the ship on the cover of my book—yes, it's *very* nice here. Think I'll just doze off back to sleep...

Footsteps. Coming down the hall outside. I know those footsteps: soft, rhythmic...It couldn't be...could it?

I look up and see the *Monsignore*. He has just entered the main doorway of the infirmary and is heading toward me past the rows of empty beds. As usual, his head is down reading his *messale*. He stops at my bed. Silence.

The *Monsignore* stands there for a full minute beside my bed, silent. Should I say something? What? No, wait for him to speak—*never* speak first! I try to smile, but it turns into a grimace. No matter, he's not looking at me anyway.

"So, Mario," he finally says in his deep, gentle voice. "Did you find what you were looking for?"

What does he mean? I ended up with *one* rock, but I don't think he—

"It seems you wanted the river so much you almost gave your life for it," he says quietly.

The *Monsignore* walks from the infirmary, his eyes never leaving the *messale*. His words ring in my ears. Looking down, I realize I am rubbing the smooth river stone, tucked under the fold of my sheet, in time with his fading, rhythmic steps.

I swing my wooden sword around my head as I stand on the stone battlement and whoop a loud call down the valley to the coming invaders. *Hannibal!* Today it's the army of Hannibal. I can see the great elephants lumbering up the valley with the thousands and thousands of soldiers all around them! I call to my friends that they are coming!

It's summer, I'm at Castropignano—the new town we have moved to—and I'm happy—very, *very* happy. I'm not a *seminarista* anymore. After more than a year in the seminary, *I am free!* I could not believe my uncle agreed when, in the middle of my second year, I asked to leave. I wish I'd asked earlier—like on the second day! But my uncle said he would not have let me go earlier: he always had in mind, he said, to give me eighteen months there and then to see.

My aunt isn't happy. She remarked that putting the priest's robes on me was like dressing a wolf in fleece and telling him to go tend a flock of sheep, but quickly added that I needed strong discipline to *learn* to be good, and the best place for that was in the seminary. But it was too late. My uncle had already said I could come home!

One of the best things is not having to wear the dorky clothes anymore. As a *seminarista*, a boy training for the priest's life, I had to wear my seminary uniform all the time, every single day of the year. I had to wear it when I was at home with my uncle and aunt, playing with my friends, and even when I went back to my home village of Collemare! It was just like a prison uniform. All the kids— all the girls, *everyone*—knew that I was a *seminarista* and I got a lot of teasing. In front of several other kids, one boy in our new town said that I must have forgotten about girls and now only knew how to kiss boys; he said it just once. I pushed him so hard he fell back off the low wall he was sitting on and I jumped on him. He yelled that priests weren't supposed to fight: I told him we were allowed to defend our faith just like the crusaders as long as it was done with loving intent. I said this as I rubbed dung into his face. No one in Castropignano picked on me again.

My home village of Collemare was harder. Not because they teased me, but because they looked on me as a sort of hero there, someone who came back to tell them of wild adventures and far-off places. They had seen me as brave and fearless and *free*—and to have to go back there in the shackles of a seminary uniform ... but I fixed that. I told them I was in the seminary because of my wildness, that it was a sort of prison, and that soon I would escape ... *And I have!*

On my first trip home to Collemare after I left the seminary Claudio looked startled when he saw me, and he pointed at my clothes. "I'm not a *seminarista* anymore—*I escaped!*" I yelled loudly, holding my arms out. Then I realized that my uncle, in full priest's robes, was glaring at me and that others in the small crowd around our house—neighbors, my grandparents, other villagers—were all looking too. I turned toward our house to meet the equally scowling gaze of my mother—she hugged me but her attitude was a little cool. My mother *wanted* me to be a priest, and this was the first time I had seen her since that all ended. My father doesn't care. In fact, I heard he was *happy* I had left the seminary, which made me begin to think, now that I know more things and can remember my father always talking about "the people working together," that perhaps this wonderful papa I hardly see is a little bit like Dante ...

"So how did you *escape* from the *seminario?*" Claudio asked me that day.

"It was difficult," I began, and then, seeing the eager, honest face of my friend: "Well, I didn't really escape, Uncle let me leave. The seminary was happy, because they said *I* was difficult. Anyway, how could I be a priest if I like bad magazines, and ... and *Tarzan?*" My friend agreed.

So now I'm getting used to being back home with my uncle and aunt in our new town of Castropignano. They moved while I was in the seminary. It felt strange to come back and find everything in another place, all my things moved and in another bedroom—a *strange* bedroom. Aunt made a joke of it, saying that they *tried* to get away while I wasn't around...

This place is bigger than where we've lived before. It's a large town with several *piazze* and beautiful old buildings. It's still high in the mountains, and *this* time I didn't have to ask where it was, or whether it was in Italy: I looked it up myself on a map. And on the edge of town there's a Norman castle! That's where we are now.

"Hannibal's coming!" I yell. "Quick—to your battle stations!" I call to my friends as I leap up to the next wall.

"Wait, I have to have a piss," says Adamo, who is scrambling down to a walled corner below us.

"You can't take a piss when Hannibal's coming!" yells Lorenzo.

"Yes, I can—I have to," yells back an indignant Adamo.

"You can't do it there, that's the kitchen!" yells Cecio. "*Ugh!*" he says in disgust as Adamo's pungent stream strikes the wall, pools at its base and then snakes along the ancient drain that would have taken the runoff from the preparation of meals long past. Meals prepared for princes, knights—maybe even crusaders!

The great ruin of the castle sits on a crag just outside Castropignano. The castle is at the very end of this outcrop with a drop on three sides down to the Biferno valley, its entrance facing down to the town. The outcrop is high and its sides steep, with no chance to build there, leaving the village with only one way to grow and that was down and away from the castle, so that the very oldest buildings sit close and the newest buildings farthest away. The newer part of town is the most lively, leaving many of the older buildings close to the great structure deserted, which means we are almost always alone when we become knights at *our* castle.

It is a massive place. Time may have toppled the upper levels, but the castle is still enormous. Many of its rectangular windows and great arched doorways are still in place, several floors remain intact, and its jagged gray walls rise high into the sky. We ride in on our steeds under the great arched double entrance that still stands fully intact, past walls twenty feet thick, coming out into an open-air arena—what we imagine would have been the great hall and meeting rooms. We've spent excited hours trying to work out what each of the *three hundred and sixty-five* rooms were used for.

Cecio, who is mad about the castle and loves it more than any of us, told us its history: it was built by the Normans, with one room for every day of the year. Before the Normans, there was a Roman fort on this site that was later built over by some people called the Lombards, and then came the medieval lords and knights who built the great structure that looms above us now. The fact that it's half ruined makes it fascinating, because there is enough of a castle to *truly* be a knight in, but it is also a mystery, a giant maze of low walls, ruined steps and drains, wells, and half-buried sections.

When we're not playing Lancelot or Ivanhoe or trying to work out what room we're standing in (Lorenzo insists that the small room in the corner tower would have been the beautiful princess's bedroom, and Adamo keeps spoiling it by telling him that towers usually held mangy prisoners, people with leprosy, and witches), we're looking for *treasure*. Not just gold but any treasure, for we figure if rich people lived here for hundreds of years, and half of the castle has toppled with the great stones still sitting beside their walls or in wells and holes, *and no one has yet looked under them*, then there *has* to be fantastic treasure waiting to be found.

My *nonno* said people would have looked. They would have looked under the stones that sat on top of the ground and were easy to get to, he said. I told Nonno about my castle when I went back home to Collemare—I told him because Collemare was a little village that had no castle, no church, no big or really old or famous building, and I knew my grandfather had lived all his life in this little village and had not traveled very far, so I thought he would want to know about all the things I saw. But he *had* seen a castle or two, he told me, and he *had* traveled to several of the castles not far from Collemare *and* the Roman towns, and he *had* been to many great churches with his son, the priest, but he still wanted me to tell him about everything I saw.

My *nonno* told me that if I wanted to find undiscovered treasure at the castle, I had to use *strategy*. I remember Dante using that word when he spoke of Garibaldi: he said Garibaldi won because of *strategy*, so it must be a weapon. I asked Nonno where I could get some strategy and how to use it to find treasure. He tapped his head. "It's all in here," he said. "Strategy is a careful plan you make in your mind to go in, under and around things: to go beyond the thinking of other people in order to achieve things—to get what you want." (*Get what I want?* I remember the *Monsignore* and his warning...)

"Think about your *nonna's* skirts," he said next. He reminded me of the game my *nonna* regularly played with me—not Nonna Custodia, who is his wife, but my other *nonna*, my mother's mother: Nonna Anna. She lives just across the valley from Collemare, in San Martino, the little village where my mother was born. There is a joke in our family that our father didn't go too far to get a wife: if you run down to the back end of San Martino and call out loudly enough across the valley, you can talk to people in Collemare. On my visits back home, Nonna Anna would rush down and call across to me as I was always outside, and our backyard faced the gorge. "*Mario! Mario!* I have something for you!" she would yell out in her laughing, cheeky way. Nonna Anna was completely different from papa's mother, the stern and critical Nonna Custodia. Nonna Anna would lovingly tease me, spoil me and play lots of games.

Her favorite was the "money in the skirt" game. After hearing her call out across the valley, I would rush over, half walking, half running the half mile or more around the ridge, knowing I would be rewarded. She would be standing outside her house dressed, as always, in her traditional Abruzzo costume with her tight, colorful bodice, sometimes her cap, and her six or seven layers of thick, swirling skirts. No one ever knew what shape she really was from the waist down: you could never see, not even a *hint* of it, because her thick skirts billowed out like a bell all around her, dropping to her ankles. She was very proud of her Abruzzo heritage, and my mother said she could never be persuaded to wear modern clothes. And Nonna Anna wore her tradition with a smile—the biggest, cheekiest smile you could ever imagine.

"What do you have for me?" I would call out, breathless, as I reached her door.

"Oh, I've got nothing for you," she would tease, and then walk away, jingling the coins in her skirt pocket loudly as she did so.

"What have you got?" I would yell, laughing and grabbing at her pocket.

"Oh, leave me alone!" she would shriek in mock horror. "Don't steal my money—oh, *he's stealing my money!*"

What followed were ten minutes of laughter, frustration and squeals of delight, with me tickling my *nonna* and her wriggling and squirming away as I tried to get through the layers of her skirts. It wasn't easy. The money was in the pocket of the *bottom* skirt—the seventh layer: the top six skirts had slits at the side so that you could reach through to this pocket, but the problem was *lining them*

CHEWING GUM IN HOLY WATER

up. With my *nonna* squealing, squirming, laughing and running away from me, it meant I had to be persistent. If I got the money, she would yell, "Rascal!" with a laugh, but sometimes I had to give up and wait for her to dig out the money herself and hand it to me. That was, until I finally worked out a way to do it quickly: I would stay beside my *nonna* as she ran, and keep scooping my hand back and forth, back and forth inside her skirts—a bit like a wave—and I found if I did this I could reach the bottom pocket quickly!

"You see," said Nonno Cesare, "*that* was your strategy, and when you worked out this strategy and kept to it, you quickly had success each time. So, if you want to find your castle treasure, use strategy: plan, use a system, look in ways and places that others aren't looking, and you are likely to find your treasure—just as you found treasure in your *nonna's* pocket."

"We should look in the well," I say, peering down into the round opening as I stand high on the castle battlement. "That would be a good hiding place for treasure. It isn't easy to get into a well and no one would have moved *those* rocks." I clamber down from the wall with my broom-handle sword. No point in fighting Hannibal's army now—I've lost interest since listening to Cecio and Adamo argue over whether he's just peed in the kitchen.

"Do you mean the well at the back of the castle, the small well in the northern corner, or the main well?" asks Cecio from the kitchen. I keep forgetting it's *Cecio's* castle.

"*That* well," I say, pointing down.

"But there's no—" begins Cecio.

"We could go down on the rope and stack the rocks to the side as we move them," I say. I won't tell my friends this is a *strategy*—they wouldn't understand.

"Hang on!" yells Cecio excitedly. "That wasn't there before! That well—*it wasn't there!*"

"The earthquake," says Lorenzo.

There was a tremor recently. They happen now and again, and it's exciting because always, *always*, they move something in the ruins: forcing something down, shifting large boulders, opening up hollows that might just contain surprises!

"There was a floor there before, see . . . it's fallen away," says Cecio, pointing. "The well was under it—*wow!*" He jumps down to get to the well before the rest of us. *Nothing* excites us more than the possibility of being the first to see something old that the earth has exposed.

Lorenzo beats us all to the well. "Something's slipped down here, the wall and the floor . . . this part's new," he says, pointing.

We all look.

He's right. Parts of a room have crumbled and fallen into a small ravine, exposing the earth underneath the room, and a large well. The ancient hole no longer contains water, having long since filled with rocks: but they're not the same color as the stones of the castle around us. Perhaps the well is even *older* than the Norman castle! I shiver: it's exciting *and* scary.

We all peer in over the edge.

"Still going in?" asks Lorenzo.

There is a frightening thirty or more feet from ground level to the top of the rocks in the well. The rocks I want to search under for treasure. The well didn't look so deep from up on the battlement.

"Sure, this is where there'll be treasure!" I say, my voice not sounding as certain as my words.

"Get the rope," says Lorenzo to Adamo, who runs up to our hiding place: the hollow under a large rock at the back of the castle where we store our wooden swords, our knights' cloaks and our rope. We intended using the rope to climb up to a tower window that we couldn't reach from the inside because the steps had given way. We were convinced something exciting was in that high room . . . maybe a dead body! Then Adamo said he wasn't touching any body because it was probably someone with leprosy—we reminded him the person would have been dead for seven hundred years, and we were sure you couldn't catch leprosy from a skeleton. Anyway, we never went up: the window was too high and no one was game.

"Who's in?" I ask as I knot the rope around a large boulder close to the well.

"Not me," says Cecio, looking nervously down the hole.

Lorenzo looks away, not wanting to admit he's afraid of heights. Adamo pipes up: "I will. I'll come down."

Adamo is loyal, but I was hoping for someone stronger. I don't know how he'll go lifting rocks. Neglected by parents who spend all day drinking at the bar, Adamo is the smallest and thinnest of us, with matted hair, dirty nails, and always the same grimy jacket on which he wipes his streaming nose. I'm happy I can feed him. He comes to school without lunch, and he's always hungry: I don't think he gets fed some nights. Most of the people in town are not very well off—my aunt says because of the war—but in our house there's always plenty of food, good food, because my uncle is paid well as a priest and because he gets regular gifts of food from his parishioners. My aunt tries to keep it, but my uncle gives most of it away to those in need. So I copy my uncle: when my aunt isn't looking I snatch away morsels—my friends and I filling up on cheese, *pancetta*, fruit and bread—and I make sure Adamo gets the most.

"Good," I say to Adamo. "Come on!"

"That's where they chucked the bodies," says Lorenzo. "The ones with leprosy—"

"*Did not!*" I cut him off, watching horror creep over Adamo's face. I don't want to lose him—I need *someone* to come down the well with me! "Why don't *you* come down with us, Lorenzo?" I say, knowing this will end his talk. "Cecio can watch the rope up top."

Lorenzo snatches up the rope, quickly making himself above-ground rope handler by tossing the loose end toward the well and then leaning against the anchoring boulder with the base of the rope gripped firmly between his hands: he won't look at me. Lorenzo can be a bit of a bully, but he makes up for this by being very loyal to us—his gang—and a great fighter...you don't want to get him angry, as one of our rival gangs discovered when *two* of them went home with a bleeding nose. Lorenzo didn't get into trouble: his father is something to do with the legal system and Aunt says he "knows the right people." And most of the time I can stop his bullying: I've worked out where he is *not* so tough.

"I'll keep lookout on the edge," says Cecio, realizing he's just lost his safe job above ground. "You know, I'm not sure that we *really should*..." His voice trails off. None of us is listening.

I tug at the rope for assurance it will hold, and then, with my heart racing and not daring to look down again, I tightly grip the grimy, fraying rope and lower myself into the well. It smells damp and old: very, *very* old. At least the sides are uneven, with plenty of places to wedge in my feet: still, it's scary. Scary because I'm worried that something else might fall in—just as all the rocks below me have done—on top of me or, worse still, that there may be something very creepy down here. Something strange that has only recently been exposed to the light of day after hundreds of years! I put my feet against the wall to halt my climb and shiver: I'll pee myself if I don't stop thinking scary thoughts. Have to think happy thoughts, about finding treasure, and keep climbing down...and not think about some withered old hand reaching up from among the stones and pulling me in...

As I leap out from the wall again, my feet touch something solid. Shocked, I quickly realize that I'm already down on the rocks at the base of the well. I gingerly let my full weight rest on the rocks, keeping a tight hold on the rope just in case. Nothing moves.

"I'm here," I call up, hearing my voice echo off the walls.

"Is it safe?" asks Adamo.

I look up at my eager friends, their three heads silhouetted against the bright sunshine. I look down again—can't see a thing, it's so *dark*! For a few seconds I panic, forgetting that my eyes have to adjust . . . As I stare into the blackness, things slowly become visible around me: loose rocks and broken walls. I can hear the sound of water trickling, and all around and through me is the smell of damp, damp earth: there may be treasure here, but it's *not* a place I want to be in alone.

"It's great," I lie, my voice shaky. "Come down *now*," I tell Adamo.

Adamo, being light in build, descends very quickly and lands next to me with a thud.

"We need a candle," I say.

"*We need a candle!*" Adamo screams up to the others.

"Well, I haven't got one—and *I'm* not going back home," Lorenzo calls down.

"Me neither," says Cecio.

"Great help they are!" I mutter to Adamo.

Adamo faces upward: "*Great help you*—" he begins screaming.

"*Don't!*" I say, grabbing his arm. "You don't have to repeat everything!"

"Where's the treasure?" asks Adamo.

"Over there in that old chest," I say, grabbing him back as he goes to find it. "Don't be stupid. You know I haven't even *looked*. Why don't you start digging over there and I'll start here?"

After pulling up rocks for several minutes I realize we're not getting very far. Besides, Adamo is putting his rocks over near where I'm looking, and I'm starting to dump my rocks closer and closer to him, filling in the parts that he has exposed. I suddenly remember Nonno's words.

"We need a *system*," I say.

"Huh?" says Adamo.

"A plan. We need a plan, so that we can dig deeper and not muck up each other's work. How about we both dig here, stacking the rocks up the wall to one side so that we can dig deeper and know that at least we've done this half right?"

Adamo thinks. "What about the other half?" he asks finally. "What if the treasure is in the *other* half, and we do this, and then there's a *million more* rocks on top of it?"

"Well, *I don't know!*" I say. "I don't know whether the treasure's in the other half. And what else are we going to do? We can't lift the rocks out!"

"Okay," says Adamo as he bends and begins lifting stones, stacking them against the wall as I suggested.

We're down almost three layers of heavy rocks, my hands are grazed and burning, my shoulders and back are *aching*—I'm hot, sweaty and itchy, and all we've found is some broken pottery. Things aren't going well. Worse still is the worry of having to keep a check on the tall, tottery pile of rocks beside us. I keep telling Adamo to stack them farther back, *not* right next to us or they're going to fall! Added to this is Lorenzo's annoying voice: if he asks *once more* whether we've found the treasure yet, I will go back up and—

"Wood," mutters Adamo. "Flat wood . . . it's heavy." He tosses the item aside. Adamo mutters every time he picks something up.

CHEWING GUM IN HOLY WATER

I keep lifting rocks, but his words float through my mind. "Flat wood" and "heavy." It doesn't sound right. A small piece of wood isn't usually flat *and* heavy, unless—

"Give me a look!" I say suddenly. Adamo looks startled and then scrapes around for his find. "If it's flat and heavy, it's metal," I say. "Could be part of a treasure chest!"

I grab the object from him. It's darkish brown and lumpy from the clay stuck to it but too heavy to be wood, and it's long, about a yard long, and thin, with one end flat and square and the other end more rounded in my hand with a good . . . a good—*grip*. I quickly hold it up to the light at the opening so I can make out its silhouette.

"It's a *sword!*" I gasp.

"But it's . . ." begins Adamo.

"Its tip is broken, but it's a *sword!*" I say in awe.

There've been fights over who should keep it.

Along with the sword we found a metal hook and two large pieces of broken pottery, so at first it was decided that we should take turns keeping one of the objects at home—one week the sword, the next week the hook, and the next week a piece of pottery— but it didn't work. No one wanted to give the sword back. And then it *disappeared.*

Adamo accused Lorenzo, Lorenzo accused Cecio, Cecio kept out of it, and I accused Lorenzo. Well, he *was* the last one to have had it.

"I didn't, I swear . . . I had it in my room and I didn't take it *anywhere,*" Lorenzo kept saying.

"Maybe the ghost of the long-dead knight came and took it back," said Cecio in a low voice. I saw Lorenzo shiver, and realized then that he really *didn't* know where it was.

"It's got to be at the castle," I said. One of the keeping rules was that whoever had the sword *always* had to bring it with them when we were knights at the castle. Obviously we had been playing at the castle and the sword had been left there, no one remembering to bring it home. But when we looked around the castle—up on the highest battlements, down among the rocks and plants on the slopes below the ramparts, every single place in the castle where we played—there was no sword.

"There's one place we *haven't* looked," said Lorenzo, his eyes wide.

We knew what he was going to say. "Oh, that's *too* creepy," I responded with a shiver.

"But why would it be back—*oh!*" said Cecio. "You *can't* think . . . but there's no such thing as . . ." He couldn't finish the sentence.

It took almost an hour for us to work up the courage to go near the well. Lorenzo had run home and come back with four small, fat candles, but these were not much help because we couldn't lower them down and all they did was blind us if we held them out or, in the case of Adamo, singe all the front of his hair.

"Throw them down," someone suggested, "that way we can get a quick glimpse inside." The first one spluttered out halfway, but the next one made it to the bottom.

"There it is!" said Lorenzo, reeling back in horror. "The sword!"

And there it was. The flickering light of the candle danced around in the well, but we could see clearly enough that there was a sword with a broken tip jutting up on an angle from the rocks—*our* sword.

"But what's holding it?" I cried in horror. "There are bones near it, there's a—"

The candle went out. We quickly lit another one and threw it down.

"There is!" screamed Adamo. "There's a skeleton holding the sword!"

He was right. There were bones near the sword, a shattered skeleton. Perhaps that was its arm near the sword, trying to stretch out and reach it. We all jumped back from the well with horror: wide-eyed and staring at each other.

Cecio was the first to dare to look again. Blackness. The candle was out. There was one candle left. We threw it in. It sputtered for a few seconds, revealing the odd-shaped skeleton resting near the sword.

"Might be an animal," I said nervously. "I'm sure it's too small for a—"

"*It's a small knight!*" Adamo screamed just as the candle sputtered out.

We all looked at each other and ran, none of us stopping until we were well into town. We didn't go near the castle for *months*.

Nonno said it was probably a goat or sheep skeleton in the well, but I hadn't told him about the sword—that was our sworn secret— so there was still no explanation for how it got back in the well. And anyway, why would a goat be minding a sword? I think Adamo was right: something strange had happened. I remember my uncle telling me that people hundreds of years ago were smaller, so I think the spirit of a very small knight came back to get his sword. When we eventually found the courage to go back to the castle, no one went *near* the well, and no one did any more serious digging. We figured it was better to leave things where they were.

We soon began being knights again, and our wars and battles resumed at the great castle. One day when I was whooping and yelling from a lower battlement—so glad to be free, so free that I no longer even *thought* about the seminary—I looked up and saw Cecio on the wall above me. He was silhouetted against the fading afternoon sky, and he really did look like a knight as he stared across the valley with his cloak flapping in the wind behind him. The thought flashed through my mind that he was the happiest of all of us that the digging had stopped around *his* castle . . . and I realized that what he looked like was the proud *ghost* of a knight who had, gallantly and secretly, taken steps to protect his castle, a knight who was a farmer's son and who regularly had to bury sheep, a knight who made sure things that belonged to his castle were kept sacred and in their rightful place . . .

La Ragazza con il Coltello
THE GIRL WITH THE KNIFE

"**S**pill it and I'll thump you around the ears!" yells my aunt in reply to my question.

I just asked whether she thought there might be hidden treasure in the *palazzo*. The one we're living in. I've given up on the castle. And this is the most *amazing* part of being in our new town: where we *live*. My uncle is always offered large, comfortable houses—he being the respected priest—but this time, with no house available in town that was grand enough and empty at the right time, we were moved into the large, baroque edifice at the top of the hill— the palace! We are living in a *palazzo*! So now I have *imaginings*... about who lived here, how grand they were, and whether there is any hidden—

"The only gold you're to worry about is that liqueur, *so keep pouring*!" screeches my aunt. "I've told you this was no more than an aristocrat's country house, and now a run-down one at that. There were no princes here."

"A *conte?*" I ask.

No reply.

We are making *nocino*, a liqueur created from fermented walnuts. I have watched my aunt halve hundreds of soft green walnuts with a wooden knife—metal knives oxidize the tender, developing centers—and place them in the *damigiane*: the large, glass wide-shouldered bottles that hold fifty liters. I hope the nuts were picked from the right side of the tree: my *nonno* told me that walnuts for *nocino* are to be picked only from the side of the tree facing the sun, because on the other side they're not developed enough—and he said *always* thirteen walnuts to a liter of wine. My aunt just put in *fifteen*. I won't say anything: she'll only get mad.

I pour the red wine in over the soft nuts—the bottles will be sealed with gauze, and then set in the sun for forty days. Each year I help my aunt carry the bottles out. They sit in wickerwork cradles with handles and a loop at the neck to assist with lifting their great weight. They're wide at the top and narrow at the base so that most of the fruit sits up high and less sediment collects at the bottom. After their bask in the sun, the bottles are taken inside where the fruity pulp is strained through linen and pure alcohol added to the syrup; the *damigiane* then remain inside for several more weeks. The result is a delicious, brownish gold liqueur that burns like spice and tastes like nutty honey. Unbeknownst to my aunt, my friends and I *love* it.

My aunt thumps me on the shoulder: I was thinking about treasure again and had stopped pouring.

"Watch what you're doing!"

"A baron? Maybe it was a baron?"

"Keep pouring, Mario!"

My aunt doesn't know—and doesn't *care* to know—who lived here or what happened. How could you live in a *palazzo* and not want to know these things? My aunt only seems to care about us being better than others, baking the best *pane casareccio* in the street, competing with the neighbors over liqueurs—and gossip. I'll ask my uncle. He knows lots of things and seems to *want* to know things. He said it's because he listens and *reads*, and so I copy him. I discovered very early that reading transports you to another place, a place full of knights, magicians, lords and sea battles, wild beasts, Roman soldiers . . . and now, when I read, I keep my uncle's atlas next to me to see where these fantastic people and places are. Some of the books I pull off my uncle's shelves are very old and the writers must be dead . . . which makes me think of the Jesuit: *words fly away and the writing stays.*

I sneak into my uncle's library when I have to do homework or religious study. I drop the *interesting* book inside my schoolbook, so it looks like I'm reading that, though it doesn't work when the adventure books are big. My uncle pretends he doesn't see, but my aunt yells when she catches me, saying such books will make my imagination "fervid"—which I think is a sickness—and forcing me back to my religious studies. I don't care. I don't care if I catch this fervid thing. I have fantastic stories in my head, stories my aunt will *never* know, and now, *right now*, it's like we are living *in* a fantastic story because we're surrounded by walls embedded with three centuries of loves, secret plots, battles, maybe even murders. *We are living in a palace . . .*

"It was built three hundred years ago," I say, "so it must have been a rich nobleman because most people were poor then." Bet my aunt didn't know *that*.

It must have belonged to someone important, because the place is so *big*. Two stories high and in the shape of a U, it has wings, and even outbuildings. The oldest part of the palace—the bottom of the U—sits atop the hill and faces down toward the center of the village. I watch for my friends from a window here: you can see all the way down to the bar where the men play pool, and just across the road is a low stone wall surrounding an *orto* full of low, clinging zucchini plants and tall corn. If I stretch my neck, I can just see the great white rock protruding from among the houses in the center of town. The *palazzo* is solid, but so old the stonework is crumbling in the beautiful patterned surrounds of the windows on the first floor, and I've even found a stone crest engraved with Latin words that are so worn I can't read them.

And there's the amazing courtyard, covered in white, sun-bleached flagstones with a thousand dips and grooves, worn—*just think!*—from hundreds of years of footsteps, hooves and carriage wheels! On either side of the courtyard are the east and west wings where no one lives, and at the very end of the east wing is an arched carriageway that both joins the house to and divides it from the stables and workshops. Behind these outbuildings is a stone wall that signals the end of the estate; beyond it is a sheer drop to the valley below. My friends and I figure it is a good place to throw someone off, and we plan to go to the valley floor one day to dig up the bones and jewels of the rivals and unwanted guests we're sure met an ugly death there.

But everyone talks about the doors. My uncle says the *palazzo* is famous for the magnificent carved timber entranceways at the front and back of the building. I love the door at the front: it stands at the center of the oldest part of the *palazzo*, and when it was built carriages actually *entered* the house, so the giant arch rises to about twenty-five feet at its peak. The door has *five* parts that can be opened separately: the two main leaves open as far as the beginning of the curve of the arch; two smaller leaves open in the arch itself (only for the tallest of coaches); and a smaller "daily use" door is cut into the right of the two main doors. This door was made for people to enter, but they must have been *tiny* because even I have to duck to get through. Once opened, the doors lead into a great, covered atrium that my uncle says was built to allow several carriages to stand as the gentry alighted under cover . . . and safely away from the street.

I never see much of the atrium, because I always run through it. The great doors close off the daylight from the outside and the only illumination comes from a small window near the roof high above. This creates a ghostly half-light, and it's easy to imagine faces at the deserted kitchen windows as I pass: long-dead cooks and scullery maids still tending to their chores—kneading, gutting, scrubbing—awaiting the return of their master and wondering at me, this strange intruder. I race through and up the stairs to the safety of our brighter living quarters on the top floor. But in no way is the atrium the scariest place in the *palazzo*. *Nothing* puts a shiver up my spine like the abandoned wings on either side of the courtyard.

I can't look in the direction of these wings once it's dark: no one has lived in them for years, yet I fear something *does*—a ghostly, awful something. I can get into the east wing, and I'm not afraid to enter during the *day*, but I have to be careful. Long abandoned, this wing has rotting floors and crumbling walls: my foot has gone through the floor twice, and I've now learned to walk along the nail lines. The place fascinates me, and I can't resist going there—to explore and *imagine*.

The west wing is different: it is locked up, and no trespassing is allowed. Uncle said the owner of the *palazzo* (perhaps the *conte?*), who lives abroad, shut off this section years ago. The doors are bolted, the windows screened. Occasionally I've scaled pipes and sills to peek in, but could only catch glimpses of dust-covered furniture and old things. This is the only part of the *palazzo* I can't explore, and I *so* want to. I imagine that this wing holds all the secrets, and maybe *the treasure*...

"Give me that bottle!" says my aunt, snatching it from me.

Some wine slops down the side of the *damigiana*, adding to a large pool of red already on the table.

"You now have more wine *out* of the bottle than in it! I don't know what gets into your head. Go and see if your uncle needs you," she says, shoving me aside with her hip.

Good, I can go! And my uncle's not back yet. That means I have time...

The musty smell hits my nostrils as I push open the door. It is mysterious, musk-scented, dusty, old: I'm sure it could tell a thousand stories. Some plaster cracks from above the door and lightly sprinkles my face. Soft, powdery, it caresses and tickles as it falls from eyebrow, to eyelash, to cheek. I breathe in the stale, enclosed air and close the door behind me. This is the east wing: my secret place.

Silence. It's so *quiet* here...

The corridor in front of me has several great windows—their casements faded and cracked—overlooking the courtyard. A million specks of fine dust play in the muted light slanting in from outside. There's only one window that can be forced open, and I have to do it carefully, to avoid its loud screeching. My uncle says it would be more than a century since servants cleaned them and thrust them open to let in the summer air. Now they stand like silent sentinels, facing the outside world: the chipped stonework on their exterior the only hint of the collapse and decay within.

And this place is all the more wonderful because I'm not supposed to be here. No one can find me: no one else even knows how to get in. It took me some time, but eventually I worked out how to shift the door—ever so slowly, so that the planks on the other side don't jam against it—forcing it open just wide enough to slide through.

And I'm safe...I think. In the daytime, the sunlight makes everything sinister fade and melt away. At night it's different. This abandoned wing joins our living quarters *right next to my bedroom*: my aunt and uncle are farther away, where it is safer. I am the first port of call for *anything* that comes from here. At night I imagine the east-wing ghosts dissolving under the door and entering my bedroom to tell me about their murder...And then...they think I'm a descendant of their killer and decide to get *me*...*aargh!* I tried to swap bedrooms with my aunt, but she wouldn't do it.

In the daytime the abandoned east wing doesn't frighten me at all, and I wonder how I could possibly be scared at night. My secret place becomes peaceful, quiet—and here my aunt can't find me for chores. I can enjoy my banana (all the tastier because I'm not supposed to have it: I took it when Aunt wasn't looking) and stare out the window, down to the courtyard and across to the west wing, and imagine... *imagine*...what it was like here with princes, and great coaches, and...

Wait! Something just caught my eye. A light, flashing onto one of the windows across from me in the deserted west wing. I peer through the murky glass. There is movement, a sharp light reflecting off something shiny: perhaps a mirror. Of course! It must be the small penknife in my hand catching the sun, but...there's no sun on me here. I glance across at the window hoping the flickering has stopped: no! It's still there. Something—or *someone*—is in that room. But how can it be? It is locked up, forbidden: no one is allowed there.

I suddenly feel cold, *icy* cold, and the pasty, sweet banana in my mouth turns to mud. Who, or *what*, is at the window in the western wing? I don't want to look, but something makes me. I don't want to look, but I am frozen, staring.

And then I see her.

The light flashes and jumps away as the window is pushed out, and I see her. She looks about my age, with long fair hair pulled back at the temples and falling freely down past her shoulders. She leans forward to grasp one of the windows and lock it into place. I get a glimpse of slender arms and billowing sleeves, a tight white blouse and a high collar that has something sparkling pinned to it. It must be a clasp or brooch—perhaps *diamonds!*—and *this* is what reflects the light.

She is *beautiful.* I have never seen a girl with such fair hair—it is almost white—nor one dressed like this; she's from another world. And framed in the window of the *palazzo,* it can only mean one thing. *She is a princess.* I stare for several seconds until she turns, as if someone has called her, shuts the casement, and is gone.

I shake myself. Could it have been? After all my imaginings, was it some vision? A dream? I look again at the somber west wing: shuttered, worn, enclosed, resolute. Nothing has moved, nothing has changed; all is as it has been for the long months I have stared across there.

But no! There is another movement at that window: a curtain being shifted, ever so slightly. I peer intently. *Yes!* A hand and the curtain pulled at an angle and—I suddenly realize I am being watched. *Oh!* What must I look like, leaning out over the windowsill, ogling, my open mouth stuffed with banana? I feel myself redden. I turn as if someone is in the room behind me, and quickly jump back out of view.

Racing to the next window, I peer through: here I am protected from outside eyes by the grimy glass, and I can just make out her window. But she is gone. I wait anxiously, tensely, for several minutes, but there is no further movement. She is gone.

Who is she? What's she doing here? *Did* I imagine her? I slump back against the wall, my pulse racing, wondering: the house suddenly alive.

"Don Fernici and his daughter Letizia, *Mario!*" says my aunt.

The emphasis on my name means that I have to give more than the usual respect to those I am being introduced to. This time I don't mind. It's *her*: my princess.

Her father is tall and well dressed—my aunt said because he's rich and *from the city*. I study him. His jacket and trousers are new and tight-fitting, not like the loose clothes I see on the people around me. His buttons look like gold coins, and he has on *cufflinks*. And even though it's Saturday, he is wearing a *cravat*. But it's the hat and cane he's carrying that *really* make him look rich. And it's not just the clothes: his skin is pale and smooth, his nails pink and clear; not a hair is out of place on his scalp, and his mustache is thin and *curled*, something I have never seen. And he speaks differently—very properly, the way my aunt likes—not dragging out his words. He stops talking to my aunt and offers me his hand to shake: I take it, feeling clumsy.

Don Fernici is the owner of the *palazzo* (I'm too scared to ask if he's a *conte*). We are in the atrium, my aunt and I on our way out to the shops, having just bumped into them as they returned from an excursion. They arrived only yesterday, and my aunt was in a fluster because she had been given no warning. ("Well, it is *their* house," my uncle said, "and I'm sure they can come and go as they please without having to consult us—their *guests*.") I feel awkward in front of them in my old clothes, but Don Fernici's expression relaxes me. He has a warm smile, though I don't catch the end of it—for my eyes are on his daughter.

Che bella! Pale-skinned and slender like her father, she has silvery hair that is now braided along her temples and tied at the back with a blue satin ribbon and yellow flowers. Wisps of soft hair drop around her neck. She is tall, but her face seems young—surely she is no more than eleven? Twelve? The girl spins and turns as she holds her father's hand, as if bored with this meeting. My eager nostrils take in the delicate floral scent—the scent of *her*—that gusts to me with her every move.

I can't take my eyes off her. I've never seen a girl like this. I had no idea people like her existed, except in storybooks. *So this is what a princess looks like.* I take in her flowing, pale blue dress, pulled into little patterns of stitching across her chest and inlaid with what look like tiny pearls—her perfectly formed lips, clear blue eyes and smooth, unmarked skin; her graceful movements. Our eyes meet fleetingly, and I realize that I've been staring: I look away, embarrassed.

Then she speaks: "Papa, may I stay? Nonna will be here." Her voice is quiet and dutiful.

Her father turns to her; he has been telling my aunt about a visit to one of his country properties planned for the following Saturday.

"Letizia, I would like you to come," Don Fernici says. And after a pleading look from his daughter: "Well, if you do stay, then music practice, please, and no going into the courtyard sun." He casts a fleeting glance at me.

Me! As if I would encourage her outside, as if I would lead his daughter—this delicate princess—astray. I wonder what time he is leaving?

"No, Papa, thank you, Papa."

With that, she is gone—into the bowels of the west wing. Not a look, nor a backward glance. Only her scent lingers.

* * *

My friends are sitting in the gutter. I'm standing. I don't want to be caught out sitting down just in case...

My friends don't believe me: they think I made it all up. They think I made *her* up. So they're all here *again*—Adamo, Lorenzo and Cecio—waiting to catch a glimpse. We're outside the main doors of the *palazzo*, waiting, waiting, and my friends are getting agitated. I *need* them to see her before...well, in case she disappears again.

It's three days since our meeting in the atrium, and I haven't seen her at all. My princess. I have heard her voice, but by the time I rush to a window or outside she is gone. They go out a lot, my aunt says, to their estates. So now I've been trying hard to bump into her, especially when my friends are around, and I have to do this *outside*. To begin with, my aunt won't let my friends into the *palazzo* at all—not with the owner home—and besides, I can't reach my princess once she's inside: the west wing was always forbidden territory, and it is even more so now. We're all here, outside the *palazzo* doors, because I know she went out today and my friends and I are hoping to catch a glimpse of her when she returns.

"Put it *away*, Lorenzo—do you want to get me *killed?*" I whisper fiercely, looking up to see if my aunt is at any of the windows.

Lorenzo has pulled a wrinkled cigarette out of his top pocket and is tapping the black ash off its tip, as if getting ready to light up. This is why I don't usually invite them anywhere near my home. My aunt has eyes like a hawk: one wrong move out here and I'm in big trouble. Anyway, Lorenzo's only doing it to annoy me, breaking one of our important rules. Cigarettes are expensive—we can only afford to buy one or two at a time—so we stub out and reuse them, and they are *only* to be smoked when looking cool is essential: when rival gangs are around, or to impress girls...*particularly* to impress girls.

"Any more bananas, Mario?" he asks, irritated. "Oh, Adamo, *shut your mouth!*" he says as he repockets the cigarette.

While the rest of us talk, Adamo eats: he is devouring some cheese I gave him. His teeth are a bit green, and I try not to look. We all try not to look. As usual, he does his regular sniff and then wipes his nose on his sleeve. I tell him he needs to learn to smoke or he will never get a girl.

"I don't want one," he says between mouthfuls.

"Well, practice just in case," I say.

"Mario—the *bananas?*" repeats Lorenzo.

"I'm not going back inside," I say, not wanting to sneak past my aunt one more time.

"Well, I don't think there *is* a princess," he continues with a sneer.

Cecio darts a look at me: he doesn't like fights. Although tall and quite solid, Cecio is like the rest of his farming family: gentle-natured—sometimes *too* gentle, with Lorenzo bossing him at every turn. Lorenzo always acts cool and takes no nonsense from anyone. Cecio *tries* to look cool but can never quite hold the cigarette right, or anything else for that matter. And as for Adamo—

"Go home if you want. *I'm* waiting for the princess," says Adamo, his teeth stuck with cheese.

"More likely the ugly stepsister! No one has *white* hair," says Lorenzo.

"If Mario says it's true, it's true," says Cecio.

Adamo must have breathed in some of the gritty Parmesan, because he coughs explosively in the direction of Lorenzo, spraying him with cheese and saliva.

"*Porca miseria!*" yells Lorenzo, leaping backward. "You're *disgusting!*" A horrified Lorenzo looks down at his shirt.

I glance up at our windows.

Cecio starts laughing and then begins a fit of coughing, holding his crotch in between convulsions.

"Let's go," I say, knowing that my aunt will be out any moment.

"You've pissed yourself," says Lorenzo to Cecio.

"No, I haven't—"

"Mario!" whispers Adamo fiercely, pointing behind me.

A large black car purrs noiselessly to the doorway beside us, its engine so quiet none of us heard its approach up the hill. Don Fernici's car. Oh *no*.

I glance at my friends: Lorenzo has cheese stuck to his chin, Cecio is holding his hands in front of a wet patch on his pants, and Adamo is still sitting in the gutter, his wide open mouth displaying chewed food. *Oh Madonna!*

Don Fernici alights from the driver's seat to open the great door. "Ciao, Mario!" he says brightly as he opens the latch.

I nod mutely, glancing back at the car. I can't see through its dark, tinted windows and I pray that this time he is alone.

The back window of the car rolls down. Letizia. Her fair hair and white clothes contrast with the black paintwork as she leans out. She seems even more beautiful. I hear Lorenzo gasp.

"Ciao, Mario!" she says, smiling. "Are these your friends?"

I feel myself redden. "You've been out?" I ask, not wanting to answer her question.

"Up to our land, mushroom hunting," she says.

There's an awkward pause. What should I say next? Can't think . . . oh, I *wish* her father would hurry up with the door.

She continues: "I love *porcini*, they're my favorite, but we didn't find any." She looks around at my friends again: "Is this where you all hang out?"

"No," I say.

Perhaps I could actually *pretend* they're not my friends. They haven't said anything yet, although I think Adamo is about to: he seems agitated and keeps looking from the girl to me.

"Mario," he finally says.

From the corner of my eye, I can see he is offering me something.

"What?" I ask curtly.

"Your cigarette," he says proudly, looking at Letizia to be sure she heard.

He holds up the crumpled white fag that Lorenzo has passed him: I see Lorenzo snickering. I snatch it from Adamo and put it behind my back just as Don Fernici steps in front of me.

"Help me with this door, will you, Mario?" he asks.

Quickly shoving the cigarette into my back pocket, I help push the great door open. Letizia alights from the car—I thought he was going to drive through, so why did he open the big—? Oh, his daughter doesn't step through *small* doors. The girl sweeps graciously past me: I give a last mortified wave as she disappears into the *palazzo* and I close the doors behind her and her father.

Lorenzo is speechless and just stares at me. It's all *his* fault. If he hadn't carried on like an idiot Cecio wouldn't have laughed and then pissed himself and . . . and I'm going to kill him if that cigarette is ruined. I pull it out: it's bent, but smokeable.

"She's *beautiful*," says Cecio, who is still holding his hands over the front of his pants.

I suddenly have an idea. "What did she say she liked—*porcini* or *prugnoli*?" I ask.

No reply.

"Which mushrooms did she say—*which*?" I ask, panicky.

"*Porcini*," says Cecio.

"I'll go tomorrow. There's a patch near Rossini's."

The others stare at me.

"But that's an *hour's* walk," says Lorenzo.

"I'll go tomorrow," I say.

Adamo hasn't said anything at all. He stares wistfully at the black car and then in the direction Letizia has gone. Finally: "Mario, can I have your cigarette?" he says. "I've decided I want to practice."

Whump! I thump the ball hard against the coachhouse doors.

I look up at the windows: no movement. I thump the ball again: still no movement. I drop the *zizzola* bat onto the courtyard flagstones, its clatter reverberating off the three walls that surround me. I look up at the windows of the west wing again. Nothing.

It's Saturday. The Saturday Don Fernici has gone away.

I pick up the bat and am about to thump the ball hard against the doors again when I hear: "You can stop it. I'll come down."

My princess! Roused from her flute practice, for I have been listening to the notes floating down from above.

I shrug. "If you want."

If I want! Of course I want! But what did she mean, *you can stop it?* Surely she didn't think—!

I watch her close the casement and disappear inside the building, and I realize that my stomach is all aflutter. I have to stay cool; this is our first meeting alone, and with her father away and my aunt and uncle out, perhaps my *only* chance to impress her.

The carved doors directly in front of me blast open and there stands my princess. Behind her is an old woman—must be her *nonna*—rapidly scolding in some dialect I can't understand, though I make out the words "lessons" and "sun."

The girl turns to the old woman behind her: "Nonna, I will not stay outside. We will play in the rooms here, I promise," she says.

She turns to me: "Stupid old ... *vecchia caffettiera.*"

Old coffeepot? I'm shocked at her rudeness, especially because it is in full hearing of her *nonna*. I look anxiously at the old woman and then back to Letizia.

"Don't worry, she's deaf," says my princess. "She can only lip-read—watch."

She turns to the old woman: "Nonna, I love you dearly and you know I would never disobey you, Papa, or my darling mama."

The old woman smiles and visibly relaxes. The girl turns back to me. "But in truth, Nonna, your breath smells like dung, and I shall do what I like."

Her *nonna* remains smiling behind her and then, with a wave of her hands, walks off muttering: "*Bene, bene . . . bene ragazza . . .*"

Letizia turns to me with a captivating smile: "You into knives?" She looks away before I can answer, and then says: "Oh, and thank you for the mushrooms."

I realize my mouth is still open. I close it.

"I've heard of boyfriends giving girls chocolates and flowers, but *never* a bunch of mushrooms!" she laughs.

I feel my cheeks burning red.

"No, it's sweet of you. But when did you go there—in the *night?* I hope you didn't go to any bother."

I quickly shake my head.

A pause.

"So, are you?" she asks.

"Am I what?" I say.

"My boyfriend? *No!* Only teasing! Are you into knives, I mean?"

What sort of knives is she talking about? The carving knives on her *nonna's* table? I'm beginning to think not . . .

I study her in the full sunlight. She looks angelic in her yellow dress, her braided hair descending into soft curls on her neck. Close up, I see that her eyes are a piercing blue, and she has long brown lashes. She catches me staring, and I glance down. Even her shoes are soft! They look like slippers, made of shiny fabric with lots of little beads. They seem to have no heel and don't look like they should be out on the rough flagstones.

"So, are you?" she asks again.

Think of something clever, *quick . . .*

"So, do you?" I ask.

"Do I what?"

"Have a boyfriend?"

She is caught for a second, and then smiles. "Not one that brings me mushrooms."

Very clever. She hasn't given *anything* away with that answer. *Oh Madonna!* How do I impress a girl like this?

She looks at me for a moment, waiting, then says: "Aren't you going to ask me where I'm from?"

"No," I say. I already know, having quizzed my aunt for an hour.

She looks startled at this unexpected reply, but gathers herself quickly: "So, *do* you want to play knives?" she asks haughtily.

I'm catching on. "I presume by *knives*, you don't mean those on the dinner table. If you mean switchblades, then yes I can play. I'm quite good. Knives are my hobby: I have several."

"Like *this?*"

She pulls an object from the sash at her waist, quickly thrusting it at me and flicking the blade open so close to my nose that I feel the breeze of its movement.

I gasp. *What a knife!* Twice the size of any knife I've ever handled, and beautifully crafted from ebony and stainless steel. I have only seen such monsters in magazines. I can't believe she pulled it from that pretty, satin-draped waist. How did she manage to hide it there?

The blade is so close that my eyes cross trying to focus on its silver tip, and I step back. What a beauty! But what would a girl . . . ?

I look again at her lovely face, at the large knife, and then at the slender arm holding it...

"Automatic—look." She pushes the blade in and then flicks it out.

An automatic switchblade! *No way!* This is new, and a city thing—no one I know has such a knife. Besides, I can't imagine the cost of such a treasure; a knife like this would be well beyond the pocket money of anyone I know. *What I would give to own it!* Even just for a day! As we say in our gang, "I would lick the whole street to have it." If that knife was mine I'd feel like a king!

"But before we start..."

Oh no! She's rummaging in that sash again.

"Have you got a light?"

She shoves the knife at me to hold, and returns to fumbling in the soft folds of her waistband. A silver cigar case appears. It must have been cold against her soft skin. She snaps the case open. My delicate princess is now standing with cigar in hand: not the thick, coarse ones enjoyed by the men in the village but a smooth, slender *sigaretto.*

"Papa doesn't count them. Want one?" she asks. She tosses me a cigar. "Better than a crumpled cigarette," she says.

Oh! She's having a dig at the cigarette Adamo threw me; there's still time to say they're *not* my friends... I study her and try to reconcile this girl with the one I watched take leave of her father an hour ago, standing beside the shining black car, kissing her father on each cheek, and then waving politely as the car swept away, the dutiful daughter with her *nonna* by her side...

She clicks the cigar case shut. A window above us rattles open. Like a shot she moves under the doorway so she can't be seen, and I am left out in the open with the cigar *and* the knife. Nonna smiles and waves to me as she shakes a rug from the window.

"Did she leave the window open?" my princess inquires eagerly.
I look up.

"Did she?"

I nod.

"*Cavolo!* She may be deaf but she can smell smoke at a thousand paces—comes from being a cook."

"Cook?"

"Oh, *porco diavolo*! She's not our real *nonna*, I just call her that. She's been with us since I was born. You'll have to say they're yours."

"What?"

"The cigars. If she smells them and comes out, which she will, say they're yours."

I'm not *that* stupid. "*No way!* I'll get—I don't have a light," I say.

"*You*—don't have a lighter? Come on!" she says.

"My Zippo's being repaired," I lie. "Get some matches from your kitchen."

The bluff works. She looks at me defiantly for a moment and then stuffs the cigars back in their case, and the case back into that magic place against her skin. I am thinking about that magic place when she suddenly snatches the knife from my hand and takes several steps backward, her eyes locked on mine all the while.

"Let's have a competition," she says.

Before I can respond—*thwack!* The great knife shears past my nose and lodges in the carved doors to my left.

Adrenaline pumps through my system as I look at the door. Oh my God—the *door*! My first instinct is to run. This is one of the two great doors of the *palazzo*, prized for its beautiful carving. I watch as the wood slowly splits, the protruding knife handle still reverberating from the impact. I feel shock, shame and *fear*.

"Your turn." She gestures flippantly toward the door.

I don't move. She looks from me to the door and back again, as though directing me with her eyes.

I shake my head as the words come, slowly: "No way, no frigging way; we'll be killed for this!"

"By whom?" That voice again. Clear, precise. "It's my house," she finishes.

She yanks the knife from the wood and throws it again; it strikes the door an inch and a half from her first hit. She's good.

"*Blast!* I usually get a bull's-eye on the second throw," she says, as if to herself.

I know it's a lie, but I can't help responding. "You'd do better if you lined your body up before you threw," I say.

"Show me," she says.

Oh no, *what was I thinking?* We can't do this! I look around to see if anyone is watching, witnessing this awful thing. "No," I say.

She goes to throw again, her stance all wrong. Is it my imagination or was her posture better the first time?

"No, not like that!" I yell. I move into position, posing as if about to throw an imaginary knife. In a flash she has the knife in my hand.

"Show me," she says. I can smell her perfume.

The knife comes alive in my hand. Perfectly weighted and contoured, it is beautiful to grip—it demands action. I grip, stand and throw. The knife lands directly between the first two gashes. My pulse is racing.

"Your turn," I say with urgency, handing her the implement.

She throws, and it lands to the right. I throw and bring it back to the center.

"We need a target—carve a target," she says.

I begin carving a square into one of the panels; she grabs the knife from me.

"It needs to be round," she says.

She carves a large circle outside my square, then an inner ring, and finally a bull's-eye.

I snatch the knife from her and throw. *Three-quarters of an inch from a bull's-eye!* She throws: the knife wedges a fraction closer to the center. I throw again, landing inside her mark—I am ahead... *just!* She throws—oh no, she almost hit the center! I snatch the knife again and stand to throw—

Thump! A hand lands heavily on my shoulder—so heavily that my legs buckle from under me. The hand then grips—*tightly*. I look up into the face of my uncle.

With a rush I remember where I am, what I'm doing and—*the door*. Great gashes, crooked and deep, mar it. Our target—an ill-carved canker—is highly visible as it sits in the very center. I wince at the deep gashes in the elegant door that was probably carved by some great craftsman in the 1600s... perhaps my uncle won't notice?

Ever so carefully, *slowly*, I look up at my uncle again. He's staring grimly at the door, shaking his head. My stomach churns for the second time that day.

"These are three-hundred-year-old doors," he says, still shaking his head.

Then silence. I can hear a dog barking somewhere, and a distant bell in the village. I am aware that Letizia is somewhere to the right of me, out of sight. My uncle continues to grip my shoulder. I wish he'd say something.

He does: *"Who did this?"*

"He did!" says a girlish voice.

As if coming to life, my princess springs in front of us. She is wearing the same expression she wears for her father—coy, shy, innocent. *I don't believe it.*

"And whose knife?" asks my uncle, taking it from my hand.

"*His*," she says. "It's Mario's—" pointing directly at me—"I told him not to."

My uncle looks at me. Why don't I say something? Why don't I tell him that it's *her*: her knife, she started it, carved the bull's-eye—*her*. Why don't I protest? Is it honor? No. Is it because, as the owner's daughter, she will win, be believed, and have last say, regardless? Maybe. Or is it something else? Is it that I want to leave this beautiful thing—my princess—unspoiled? All I know is that things will get uglier, messier, if I start to deny her words, so I stand silent.

"Come with me," says my uncle.

I flash a last look at Letizia, who stares at me steadfastly. No meekness, no regrets, just a straight look, as if this is the way things are. She is still, silent, in her beautiful yellow dress, the breeze flickering at her softly braided, silver hair...

I give a half-wave goodbye and turn to follow my uncle.

The room is cool and a little musty. I blink, trying to adjust my eyes to the darkness after the bright sunshine outside. We are in my uncle's study. He begins rubbing his spectacles.

"Anything to say, Mario ... *anything?*" he asks, and before I can answer: "*This* is the way you say thank you, is it, to Don Fernici, who has allowed us to be guests in his beautiful *casa?*"

Palazzo, I think to myself.

My uncle picks up the knife and turns it over in his hands. "So ... you can proudly remember this as the day you assisted in the destruction of some irreplaceable history..."

"I'm ... I'm sorry—"

"*Sorry* is hardly going to repair that door!" he says angrily. "And what will you tell Don Fernici, for you shall deal with him—"

"Oh no, *please*! I'll do whatever you want, but please don't make me see her father, *please?*"

I have grabbed my uncle's sleeve. He looks surprised, and is silent for a moment.

"Then it's a full week of *pane* and *acqua*. You eat in your room, stay in your room, and no soccer—understand?"

I nod. This is harsh, but better than humiliation in front of my princess and her family. Besides, I have had several weeks of *pane* and *acqua* before, and by the third day my aunt starts sneaking me in meat with the bread. It's one of the rare times my aunt is nice to me.

My uncle turns to the large oak bureau behind him and opens a drawer. He has the knife in his hand. "Who does this belong to, Mario?" he asks, with his back to me.

Relieved, I blurt out: "Well, it's *not*—" I don't finish the sentence.

My uncle pauses for a moment, and then places the knife inside the drawer and locks it. He purposefully removes the key and slides it into the pocket of his robe.

"To your room," he says solemnly. And as I reach the door: "Mario, I'm being kinder than befits this great transgression because I feel that this time your devil may have come in sweet disguise. Think about that in your room . . . but I'm sure you will." I catch a chuckle as he turns away.

Sometimes I don't understand my uncle.

Out in the hallway I catch sight of my aunt with Letizia's *"nonna"* at the top of the stairs. My aunt has her hands to her face, moaning. They spot me: I know better than to stay around, so I bolt for my room.

My aunt screams after me, *"Ragazzo, ragazzo, scostumato, oh Madonna, Madonna . . ."*

I shut the door against her railing, relieved to be locked in. I feel the weight of my uncle's punishment, but nothing cuts like my aunt's words.

* * *

Three months have passed since my misdemeanor. The bottles of *nocino* that sat for so long in the courtyard sun have finished their fermenting and are inside, waiting to be savored. My friends and I will test them. Lorenzo now believes me when I tell him things, Cecio no longer smokes, and Adamo smokes *more*—he says he wants to marry a girl with white hair. The Fernici family have long since packed up and gone, back to the city. The west wing stands silent once more. I have watched the bureau drawer all this time, passing through my uncle's study to my room rather than taking the shorter route down the hall. Increasingly, I had noticed that the key to the drawer was being left out on top of the cabinet, or left resting in its lock.

As I stand in the courtyard and look up at the west wing, I think of my princess and her window—for it is hers now, and I will know it as no other. My princess in yellow with the long silver hair... my beauty. I never saw her after the day with the knife, as she only stayed for a week and I was locked in my room. But I could hear her, the notes from her flute, her musical voice in the courtyard, and outside in the street. I wondered what could have been if I had not been my uncle's prisoner...

I jump as I notice a flicker of brightness—a spike of light on the pane of her window above. Movement? No. This time it *is* the reflection off my knife, my silver blade; it dances and plays on the windows around me. What were her words to my uncle? *It's Mario's.* I turn the beautiful ebony and silver knife over in my hand: it's been four weeks and my uncle has not questioned its whereabouts. It is mine.

I look around me. No one is here. The marks are still there on the great door, a reminder of our tryst. Would one more gash be noticed? I have been practicing elsewhere, and it would be good to know... I throw the knife and it slams into the wood just to the right of her last hit—and closer to the center. I look around me, and then proudly pull out the knife; I imagine her face at the window, smiling.

"*Che ragazza...che cattivella*," I say gently, tenderly, and blow a kiss to the window.

I did find treasure in the *palazzo*. My princess. In storybooks they leave behind handkerchiefs, glass slippers...Mine left a knife.

"I don't want the bit on the end, it's smaller," says Adamo.

"I will get it...yust...yust wait...," I slur, trying to pick gum off my back tooth.

I throw him the packet.

"What should we do?" asks Lorenzo.

We're sitting on the front step of his house. His mother must have scrubbed the step not long ago because I can feel the damp seeping into my pants from the stone. We were going to play knights at the castle, but Cecio has just been called home for farm duties and now we're not sure what to do. It's one of those dull, overcast days that makes you feel tired, and no one is keen to move. Still, we have to do *something*.

"What about the rock?" says Adamo. "What about climbing the rock?"

Yes!

We jump up without another word and head up toward the rock: a large, white mass protruding upward, right in the center of the town. It's steep and as high as a three-story house with clumps of grass and shrubs growing along its craggy sides and on top. Red-roofed houses huddle around it, and lean in against it, as if pretending it's one of them. It's fun scrambling up the great rock, grabbing on to roots, twisting our feet daringly into narrow cracks and indents and lifting our bodies upward, our fingers mostly trusting a grasp at smooth rock. We race to see who can get there first.

From the top we can view the world. Our world. In front and to the sides we look down on the town. I can see our house, and over to the left is Adamo's. We watch the people come and go, the carts, the donkeys, the activity near the shops. It is like we are in charge of the world. Up behind us some houses sit along the slope leading to the mountains. Many have fields behind them with their *orto* full of vegetables—I can see the rows of wooden braces that support the beans—and fruit trees beside grassless patches that hold a few chickens, a scraggly goat or two, maybe a pig. Most of the *cantine*—the cool storage areas under, or next to, the houses—have long chains of garlic and onions hanging from horizontal poles protruding from around their doorways. I always like the way the women thread them, knotting the bulbs together in a great, long necklace so they can dry.

Reaching the top of the rock, the wind whips at us: it always surprises me how there can be no wind down on the ground, and yet so much up here on top of the *roccia*, just a few feet higher. It feels fresh and exciting, if a bit cold.

I look down.

The building directly below us has been built in against the base of the rock. It looks abandoned. There is a house farther along, also built against rock, and we have seen people come and go there, but they don't seem connected with the building directly below us. A lot of people build their houses hard up against the *roccia*, with the bare rock face exposed inside. I used to think it was to hold their house up, or so they didn't have to build another wall, until Nonno explained that the rock keeps the air around it cool and therefore makes it a good place to store food. This area of a house, the *cantina*, is stacked with barrels of wine, wheels of cheese and oil-sealed jars of vegetables, tomatoes and other fruit; sacks filled with potatoes, *ceci*, or apples; sometimes bottles of homemade liqueur; and dangling prosciutto, salami, sausages and pale yellow, glossy bulbs of mozzarella. The chill air keeps the food preserved throughout the warm summer months.

There doesn't appear to be anyone in the building below. And I've always wondered what was inside—it *looks* like a *cantina*. With no house attached, perhaps it is used as a communal *cantina*, given its good position against the rock. But the terracotta tiles on its roof are faded and chipped, and several are missing altogether, so the rain must get in.

None of the holes in the roof are big enough to slide through. Perhaps the doors into the building aren't locked? There's one this side. It's out of view of the house next door and if we're quick, no one would see us from the street. Besides, it's starting to spit rain and become very cold up here on the rock, and my aunt would *hate* me to be getting wet and cold...

"Let's go down," I say, pointing.

"Where?" asks Adamo, hugging his thin jacket against his body.

"To the *cantina*."

"Someone might be there," says Lorenzo.

"We can peek through the roof," I say, indicating a hole.

"You first!" he replies.

I begin sliding down the rock, signaling for the others to go slowly so that we land lightly on the roof. There's a loud cracking noise as a loose tile flips up when I step on its edge. We all tense up and look at each other, but there is no sound from inside the building. We continue down on our hands and knees as beside and above us there are numerous *casas* from which eager eyes might be watching. I crawl toward the nearest hole in the roof.

Dim. Can't see. It takes a full minute, with one cheek squashed hard against a cold tile and my nose protruding inward, before I can make out anything inside. Wood. It smells of old wood and dust and damp earth. *Ouch!* I graze my cheek on a nail protruding on the beam beside me as I shift, trying to get a better view. A table. No chairs, just a table. And something on it . . . can't quite see. There's a rake or broom leaning against it—I can see a handle— and what looks like wood and junk in a corner. Oh, no wonder I can't see! *Shutters!* The window has its shutters closed, allowing only dim strips of light to enter, and it doesn't help that the day is overcast. No one seems to be there. I can only see part of the room, but there is no noise, no movement, and no one would be inside with the doors and shutters closed.

"Come on!" I say, clambering less carefully along the tiles.

We help each other as we do the last, biggest drop, from the roof to the ground: Adamo goes too far to one side and almost ends up in the barrel of rainwater by the door. Realizing his mistake mid-jump, he grabs at the pipe that drains from the roof to the barrel and snaps it in half.

"Great," says Lorenzo, "now they'll know we were here!"

We tilt the iron latch and push at the graying, cracked wooden door. It's locked. We push again. Something moved! We push harder, and suddenly all fall in against it, Lorenzo landing on the earth floor inside. The bottom edge of the door is jammed hard against the ground and, lifting together, we manage to force it open further, letting in more light.

Barrels! Lots of barrels and things for making wine: wooden buckets, copper ladles, large pots hanging on the wall and, below them, a three-legged stand for heating them over a fire. Jugs and bowls sit on sagging shelves along one wall; we crash into a row of *damigiane* by the door, and slats of wood and metal rings for barrel making are stacked in a corner. I can just make out what appear to be large wooden cupboards at the far end, the darkest part of the room.

"Candles!" I say, finally making out what it was I had seen on the table.

I pull out my matches—always handy for our cigarettes—and light the two candles. Rough and yellow in color, their drip-riddled shapes are half burned down and stuck to the table from being rammed into a pool of their own wax. There are hard drips and blobs of wax all over the table.

Now that we have light, I signal for the others to help push the door closed again. We shove, groan and lift until it is shut.

"We could read comics!" says Adamo as the candlelight brightens. I give him my cast-off comics to take home, but he only wants to read when we're all together because he likes to swap me for my *very latest* comic: this means I end up reading old stuff whenever we're together and then have to fight to get the new one back. But I let him because Adamo's family never buy him comics—they never buy him *anything*—and it's worth it to see his face.

"Look over here," says Lorenzo, who is near the *damigiane*. "I think there's some liqueur!"

"*You* can drink it," says Adamo, heading toward him. "It's probably poison!"

"Look over *here!*" I cry.

I am facing in the opposite direction from my friends, looking at what I'd thought were large wooden cupboards. They are not cupboards. They are barrels: huge, *huge* barrels. Two are the size of my uncle's car, but the *third* one . . .

"*Wow!*" yells Adamo.

"*Porco diavolo!*" cries Lorenzo, who drops the *damigiana* he was inspecting. "It's as big as a house!"

254

The three of us stand in front of the barrel. It *looks* like the usual wine barrel, sitting on its base with bowed sides and metal rings holding the slats in place, but that's where the similarity ends. We look up: the top of the barrel is only a hand's width from the ceiling, and the *cantina* roof is high, and the sides...

"I bet you could live in there," says Lorenzo. "I bet a whole family could live in there."

"It's open," says Adamo, looking at me.

A thick wooden door that must belong to the hatch sits propped up beside the barrel. The opening itself, cut into the lower half of the barrel, is big enough for us to get through if we squat and crawl. Looking in, it smells funny, and it's very dark inside.

"We need a... *the candle!*" I say.

I snap one off from its waxy base and take it to the barrel. Kneeling on the floor, we jostle until all our heads fit in through the opening: I hold the candle up high.

"Wow!" says Adamo, then: "Uh-uh-uh-oh," he sings in a high-pitched voice, trying to catch the echo that bounces back dully from the heavy wood.

"Smells yuck!" says Lorenzo.

"Must be the wine," I say.

The smell is strong: very strong. A sickly smell that has that whiff of my aunt's liqueurs: a smell that burns your nose a little, and catches at the back of your throat. I know it's the smell of wine, because my *nonno* has allowed me sips of his, but here the smell is *much* stronger.

"Must be in the wood," says Lorenzo, who leans in further and flattens his nose against the timber, taking a deep sniff. He reels back: "*Ugh*... I'm going to be sick!" He pulls his head out from the barrel and staggers backward, sucking in fresh air.

"I'm not going in," says Adamo, quickly pulling his head out. "I don't want to be sick."

"Well, I'm going in," I say. "It's a great cubbyhole—it's cozy, and a good hiding place. I'm going in to read my comic."

I step inside with my candle, reeling from the smell for a few seconds, but soon I don't notice it. Pulling the comic from my back pocket, I sit, placing the candle in front of me. Adamo is watching from outside.

"Do you feel sick?" he asks.

I shake my head and begin reading. Lorenzo is coughing somewhere in the room, Adamo is still watching me. I hold the comic up higher so that he can see the cover.

"Is that Tex?" he asks.

I nod.

"The latest one?" he asks.

I nod again.

"Well, if you're not feeling sick, I think I'll come in," he says, clambering across the wooden beam.

Lorenzo yells, "Wait!" and follows Adamo in: he has his hand covering his nose and mouth and is looking fearfully around at the walls.

"It's all right," says Adamo, and Lorenzo slowly lowers his hand.

We sit there for a few moments, looking around. Lorenzo makes a *who-o-o-o-o* ghost noise and then suddenly leans over to blow the candle out. I snatch it away just in time.

"Get out!" I say, not wanting to sit in the barrel in the dark. I keep the candle to the side of me, well away from him.

The others pull out their comics. I try to read mine, but begin feeling strange . . . Lorenzo snatches the comic from me, giggling.

"Hey!" I say, but I don't fight to get it back: I wasn't reading it anyway. The pictures seemed to blur and move. Must be the candlelight.

Lorenzo opens my comic. He is swaying a little and falls over on one elbow. He pulls away as Adamo snatches for it, and then slowly gets up again, trying to hold the comic straight. "It's crooked," he says.

We all start giggling.

"What do you mean it's crooked? It's crooked because you're holding it crooked," says Adamo, laughing.

"No I'm not, the page is crooked!" says Lorenzo.

We all begin to laugh and laugh and laugh. We're rolling over, snorting, guffawing. Adamo falls on his back and tries to get up, but he can't.

"I'm a—" He snorts with laughter. "I'm a cock—I'm a cockroach—and I can't get up!"

We all roar with laughter again.

"I feel weird...silly," says Lorenzo, who is trying, unsuccessfully, to stand up.

"You *look* silly!" says Adamo, who's still on his back, and we all laugh again.

"Watch out, watch out!" I say as Lorenzo knocks the candle over. It splutters and almost goes out as I grab it. I pour more wax on the barrel to try to anchor the candle, but it keeps moving... *the barrel keeps moving...*

I just manage to put the candle upright before my eyes close. I'm swaying as I sit...

"I'm tired," says Adamo.

Opening my eyes slowly, I see that he is going to sleep on the floor of the barrel.

"Me too!" says Lorenzo. He gives up trying to stand and slumps back down, spreading out flat on his back.

"Now *I'm* a cockroach," he giggles to himself.

The candle has gone out. It's pitch black: only a small patch of light creeps dimly into the barrel from the candle in the room outside. I can't see my friends, and I'm too tired to light the candle again ... too tired ... Not a sound from Adamo and Lorenzo: they must be asleep. I roll over on my side and curl up, closing my eyes against the darkness. I feel dizzy, and so, *so* tired ...

I'm in a dream. I think it's a dream. I'm walking up a mountain with my *nonno*, the flowers are out everywhere ... but they smell funny: they have this awful, sour smell, like old wine. I drift in and out of being with my *nonno*, and every now and then I realize I am in the barrel. Something tells me to get up, that it's *important* to get up, but nothing works. I can't move my arms or legs, can't move *anything*—I give up, and close my eyes again ...

"Get up! *Get up!*"

I hear a faint voice calling from far, far away. It must be Lorenzo ... no, it's a man's voice ... but it can't be ... funny how Lorenzo's voice sounds so *old*.

Something's moving ... *I'm* moving. No, the barrel must be moving. And my arm—it *hurts* ...

Kersplash!

"*Aah!*" I cry, opening my eyes. I've just had water thrown on me! I'm soaking wet, and there's sunlight, dull sunlight: it's bright, even through my squinting eyes, and I feel sick ... so dizzy and sick! I close my eyes again ...

"Get up! Get up, you boys!" yells a man's voice.

We're outside the *cantina*, and there's a man ... But how did we get ...? The man has gone to the rainwater barrel with one of the wooden buckets and is now coming back toward me.

"No, no!" I say, getting up on one elbow and putting my hand out to stop him. Oh! I feel *so sick*, I drop down onto my back again.

Kersplash!

The water hits me directly in the face. *It's so cold!* But it wakes me up a bit more. I can now hear Lorenzo and Adamo moaning. They're near me on the ground, rolling around. They're wet too—I can see mud all over the back of Lorenzo's shirt.

"Fools!" says the old man above me. "If I hadn't come back when I did...!"

I'm shading my eyes trying to look up at him...the light is so *bright*. I go to say something, but my tongue won't work.

"You were breathing pure alcohol in there, that barrel wood is saturated with wine," says the man. "You'd all collapsed from alcohol poisoning. And if I hadn't got to you when I did..." He grabs my arm and yanks me to a standing position. "Wait until your parents find out!" he yells.

I'm swaying on my feet, trying to make sense of things. If my uncle discovers *this* ... he *still* hasn't got over the knife throwing...

"*Scusi*," I manage to say.

"*Scusi!*" mimics the man, angrily.

He drags me to the water barrel and grabs the back of my head. "Here—baptize yourself!"

He pushes me headfirst into the water and holds me down. I force my way back up, gulping for air, trying to catch my breath. He grabs my head and is about to push it down again but stops.

"Wait," he says. "There's a way to make up for this. You three boys can do a week of boiling and lifting for me." He looks intently at each one of us: "*Si?*"

We all nod eagerly, knowing this help is in exchange for his silence—*none* of us wants our family to find out.

"I'll see you all here after lunch on Saturday," he says, tossing the bucket back hard against the barrel.

My friends are now standing, wobbling and squinting in the light: I'm bent over, still sucking in air. We're all muddy, disheveled and dripping.

"Besides, you've had enough humiliation for a first drinking session," the man continues, looking behind me.

What does he mean? I turn to see several people gathered in the street: neighbors who've come out with all the noise and shouting. Oh no, I recognize a boy from school. They're all laughing.

"So, we'll see you Saturday then, boys?" asks the old man, smiling. "And if you do a *really* good job, I'll make sure you get to enjoy a large glass of my best red wine before you go home!"

Lorenzo grabs his mouth and runs for the drain.

Il Tocco **THE TOUCH**

O ne cheek icy; I turn up my collar. I can smell the mountains, their coldness: the snow, the drifting chill.

But today there's something different. Waves of gentle warmth waft in and out of the cool—the bite of spring drifting toward the mellowness of summer. For it is *Mese Mariano*: the Month of Maria, and I now watch for the shepherds and their flocks moving along the ancient grassy roadway through the mountains.

Plop! It takes several seconds before I hear the pebble strike the water. My legs are swinging, and the cold iron grating is now starting to chill through my shorts to my buttocks: more rusty marks to explain to my aunt.

"The moon's coming—*the moon's coming!*" says Lorenzo.

We all look down, except for Cecio. "Stare at the moon in the water and you'll go mad, *I'm telling you!*" he says, keeping his chin in the air.

"*Will not!*" says Adamo, looking down into the water and then up to the dulling, late afternoon sky. "Is it true it's made of cheese?"

We are sitting on the great well above the town. It is several yards wide with an iron grid on top to protect people from a drop of more than sixty feet. We sit daringly in its center and dangle our legs through the gaps, looking down, down to the water—always searching for the moon or the sun.

Even though we are within the boundaries of the town, this well does not belong to Castropignano, nor does the land it sits on. For this land is part of the mystical *tratturo*: a pathway of green that winds through the mountains, traveling along the spine of the Apennines from Abruzzo in the north to the plains of Puglia in the south. The *tratturo* is sacred land that has been used for thousands of years by shepherds and their flocks to journey south to the warm tablelands where there is feed for their animals: no *erba fresca*— fresh grass—remains in the mountains during the freezing winter. This journey, called the *transumanza*, still happens, with the flocks traveling south at the start of autumn and returning northward in the spring. The grassy pathway they follow is both a route and a feeding ground for the animals, and the shepherds have to arrange their journeys to make sure the grass has grown back before the next flock passes.

Farming the *tratturo*, or using it without permission, is against the law, but at least now you don't get killed for it. The medieval kings made a law that the *tratturo* had to be kept at 111 meters wide—I always remember the three *ones*—although there are very few places in the mountains where flat land is that wide. This law was made to stop people from stealing land from the pathway where it *was* flat, so that the *tratturo* could remain open. I thought they were being kind to the shepherds until I learned these kings owned the lands at Puglia and made lots of money out of the flocks grazing there each year.

My *nonno* told me that a great writer from the Abruzzo, Gabriele D'Annunzio, called this pathway *erbal fiume silente*—silent river of grass. I imagined a rippling green river of grass, and big ships—hoisted with the Roman eagle—flowing through the mountains, for Roman soldiers and crusaders did journey along the *tratturo*. And sometimes, when I lean against a rock here, I pretend I'm a Roman legionnaire dropping my great helmet by my side and resting, away from the clattering of my halted legion...

My friends and I would often get stuck behind a flock during the *transumanza* and have to wait at the well for up to an hour, watching the passing of the shepherds with their staffs, their food packs and tools for making pecorino—the creamy sheep's milk cheese—that they would sell along the way, and the thousands of smelly, bleating animals that would push and fidget and dart around them. The only time *we* darted out of the way was when we got too close to a *maremmano*—or they to us. *Maremmani* are the huge white mountain sheepdogs of the Abruzzo that are so tall they come up almost to our chins: they can rip the throat out of a wolf and they wear sharp, spiked collars—with spikes as long as our fingers—so that the wolf can't return the favor. They're fiercely protective of their sheep and brave: when there's a serious attack from wolves, the oldest dog will stay behind to sacrifice himself while the other dogs get the sheep away. This means that we certainly don't frighten them, but they do us, and they know it, quickly sending a low rumbling growl in our direction if we even *look* at their flock for too long.

Being white and long-haired, these dogs blend in well with the sheep and surprise any wolves that dare to close in on the flock—but this means they also surprise us. One time Adamo and I were laughing at the rams with their *parnanza*—the little aprons tied around their lower backs that flap down under their tummies. (I asked my uncle what the aprons were for and he said it was to stop them being too friendly with the ewes; when I asked him for further details, he changed his story and said they wore them there to keep their private parts warm. While my friends and I giggled, Adamo asked my uncle why the ewes didn't have aprons too.) On this particular day we were laughing so much—at a ram that had its *parnanza* caught up under its bottom—we didn't notice that one of the white creatures moving in close to us was *not* a sheep. Before the *maremmano* had finished growling against my leg, I had leaped over four sheep in a single sideways move, and Adamo was nowhere to be seen. I found him at home later—he'd run all the way.

After that we made sure we watched the sheep from a distance, or from the well, because even if the dogs *could* jump it, they couldn't walk across the grating. We figured if we perched in the middle of the grid we'd be safe; then Adamo suggested we wear spiked collars too, just in case.

I shift my leg as the metal digs in and look up and across the *aia*—our village common ground—for the well sits close to its edge, just where the land rises again to join the Apennine peaks. A wonderful pine smell wafts from the tall cypresses that surround the *aia*—the cypresses that supply us with the large, hard seeds for throwing at one another—and if I lean to one side I can just see one wall of our Norman castle. Our village *aia* is actually situated on a section of the precious *tratturo*, the town having to officially request use of this land. It was only granted because the *aia* is very important to a community, being used for markets, festivals, harvest collection and *trebbia*, the threshing of wheat. But shepherds still hold right of way here, and everyone has to leave the village common ground when a flock approaches. And after the *maremmano* incident, my friends and I always move quickly.

264

"It's coming, no, no—*yes*—oh it's not," says Adamo.

We peer down into the well.

"But you have to get them *together*," I say. "I was told you find gold when the moon and the sun are in the water *together*."

"That's impossible," says Lorenzo, "isn't it?"

"Why would they say it, if it's impossible?" asks Adamo.

Lorenzo slowly nods in agreement, and we all keep looking.

"You won't find out now: the sun's almost behind the mountain," says Cecio, clambering off the grating. "*I'm* not watching—"

"Wait . . . wait! It's coming—*make a wish!*" says Lorenzo.

The three of us stare down at the gleaming orb as it dances in the well water. The pale globe pulses, throbs and flickers in gentle liquid movement as we watch, mesmerized. We have never seen it in the well before.

"You're all going to go *ma*—" yells Cecio.

"*We are not!*" I cut him off. "Seeing the moon in the well means anything you wish comes true."

Lorenzo looks at me. "If *any* wish comes true with the moon, why do you need the moon *and the sun* to find gold?" he asks.

I look at him, thinking . . .

"*Quick*, you're missing it!" yells Adamo.

Lorenzo squeezes his eyes shut and Adamo mutters. I quickly make my wish. I don't have to think what I want, *even for a second*.

Amelia. Dark hair, dark eyes, exciting glances over schoolbooks, the thrill of her touch (even if it was accidental), thick braids that swing when she turns and give me a sudden sweet gust of her scent. *Ah, Amelia!*

It happened not long after my princess left. I was broken-hearted for almost *two weeks* when I noticed that stirring again, that same thrill and sense of wonder, but this time it was at school. Two desks ahead of me sat a tall, dark girl who laughed a lot and who had a smile . . . a smile that made me turn to jelly. Every day she just looked *more and more beautiful*, until I realized that I didn't like fair hair but jet black locks, that I didn't like fair skin and fancy words but dark skin and warm, warm laughter . . . I was in love.

"Bet I know what you wished for," says Adamo, who has finished wishing and is now watching me.

"Bet you don't!" I say quickly.

"Amelia, Amelia, *Amelia* . . ." Lorenzo mocks, making a kissing movement with his lips.

"*Shut up!*" I say.

Cecio giggles from a distance.

"Mario's going red—that means he's in love," says Adamo. "I bet there isn't *anything* you would do for her, would you?"

"Huh?" says Lorenzo, pulling a face. "That doesn't even make sense."

I'm sick of Lorenzo embarrassing us, and the way he makes fun of Adamo: it's time he was taught a lesson. I turn and pound my clenched fist on my chest as I face him: the Roman swearing of an oath. We rarely use this oath because it means a promise sworn with truth and valor, a promise you can't go back on. But right now Lorenzo needs it.

"You're right, I'd do *anything* for Amelia," I say.

The others stare at me, Lorenzo looking the most surprised. It's the first time I've talked seriously about liking a girl. We all knew the princess was a dream, but this—*this* is a local girl. It's the first time *any of us* has talked seriously about a girl we all know. Anyway, last birthday I turned *thirteen* and my friends are all still twelve— so perhaps it's time to show them the way . . .

Proud at having finally declared my love, I hold my fist against my chest and imagine what I *would* do for Amelia: save her from a pack of wolves with my sword, scale the Majella to reach her as she lies trapped on a narrow ledge, swim out to sea to rescue her in a mighty storm—

"Anything?" asks Cecio, who, in the excitement, has rejoined us.

"Anything," I reply emphatically.

"*Anything . . . ?*" begins Lorenzo.

There is a moment of stillness. Lorenzo has a strange look on his face, and I sense that I have gone too far into something. My clenched fist starts to slip, and I'm feeling strangely nervous. Suddenly, I realize what he is about to say—

"*Touch the bull?*" he asks.

I swallow hard. The bull. *No one* has touched the bull, and lived. We're not sure if anyone has *died*, but we know that no one has touched the bull and *lived*.

The bull is a massive gray beast that lives in a walled paddock two hills up. A one-ton mass of heaving, snorting rage with high sharp horns—one alone is the length of my arm! He grazes in a bare paddock surrounded by a six-foot-high stone wall: a paddock containing no buildings or trees, except for one tree in its very center that *il toro* always stands under, which means there is no protection once you are in: nothing to climb or hide behind. In this dare you are supposed to cross to the center, touch the bull, and then race the beast back the forty or more yards to the wall—race a two-thousand-pound, massively horned beast that is fired up, ferocious and *fast*. And *then* climb the wall. This is the dare we threaten each other with, the dare you don't really *do*.

I seriously try to imagine meeting this monster in the middle of his paddock and touching him—alone, unaided, without a tree, ladder or anything to climb: it's something we all *dream* about doing but in reality we'd rather leave it to someone else—someone daring, courageous and *fast*. I try to feel brave at the thought of it, but the only image that comes to mind is me skewered to a wall by an enormous bull's horn.

What am I to do? My hand is on my chest, and our code is that if you say yes to a dare—if you take on a dare under oath, as I have—you *have* to do it. If you don't, you lose the respect of your friends, your peers, everyone—and you can never be leader of any gang ever, *ever* again.

"Only joking!" says Lorenzo, seeing my expression.

I breathe out. Adamo's sigh is even louder. My fear turns to embarrassment, then annoyance. "Good, because I wouldn't have done it for you. For Amelia I would have, but not for you," I lie.

The wind buffets us as the sun finally disappears over the peaks, and I suddenly realize how dark it has become. The excitement over, Cecio has begun trudging down the slope, his jacket pulled tightly around him.

"*Andiamo*...I'm hungry!" I say, leaping off the well and trying to be cheerful, although I can still feel my heart pounding. I remember there is something I have to do. As I bend, I hear Adamo chatting happily.

"What did *you* wish for, Lorenzo?" asks Adamo, as he slides off the grate after him. "I asked for a switchblade. What did you wish for?"

"Not a stupid girl, and you shouldn't *tell* what you wished for 'cause now it won't—" Lorenzo stops suddenly as he notices what I am doing.

I quickly squash the wild roses into my coat pocket. *Ouch!* Thorns. I had hoped to pull them up without anyone seeing, but Lorenzo never misses a thing. The tang of the snapped stalks mixes with the sweetness of the petals, the scent strong on my hand as I flick back my hair and stare into the faces of my two friends.

"What?" I ask.

No reply.

Adamo breaks into a smile. Lorenzo looks from my pocket to my face with disgust, turns, and starts thumping down the hill.

There's a thunderous flapping as the *piccioni* fly out from the tower and briefly darken the sky over the small square. The clanging bells have flushed them out from their nests under the ancient church roof. The clamor makes us look up: the sky is half blue and half gray, half stormy and half sweet, but I don't care, for it is Sunday and that means I get to see Amelia.

"You still playing?" yells Cecio.

I pretend to watch the birds a little longer, but my eyes are really on the church steps. My friends have gone back to the game. The birds above are common pigeons. Soon the graceful *rondoni*—swifts— will arrive: small, fast birds that never stop flying except for when they nest. They migrate back from Africa in the spring, sweeping and swirling together at such great speed that they make your head spin if you watch for too long. They will make their nests, as always, under the tiles of the church roof, with the lice-ridden pigeons as the downstairs residents inside the roof alcove.

People are *still* coming out, pouring down the steps that lead from the church into the ancient piazza. Mass has recently finished and my friends and I always get out of church early, quickly pulling off our white *chierichetto* smocks and shoving them into the drawer in the sacristy cupboard so that we can start our game—we only have an hour before we have to be home for Sunday lunch.

Right now my mind isn't on the game. I continue to stand with my back to my friends and my head tilted upward, pretending to look at the bird-filled sky. My eyes strain down toward the church portico. *She should be out by now . . .*

"Your turn!" calls Cecio, thumping me impatiently. He looks up. "What are you looking at?"

The sky is empty.

I turn and join in the game, crouching and flicking the coin in my hand against the wall. No idle flick, but an age-old technique, for we are playing *battimuro*. With my hand clutched downward and the coin balanced horizontally between my bent thumb and the inside tip of my forefinger, I sweep my arm forward and flick my thumb so that the coin ricochets off the wall and lands near or on top of the other players' coins on the ground. If you can reach between your coin and another player's coin with your *palmo*—your outstretched hand—and are able to touch both, the other coin is yours. That is how you win.

This time I miss. Completely. My coin spins and rolls, landing about three hands from the nearest.

Cecio leans forward, excited: his chances are now better. As he takes aim, I hear Adamo whining to my left. He is talking with Lorenzo, and I tune in.

"I'm *not* doing lookout again—*I'm not!*"

"Then who's going to do it?" says Lorenzo, not taking his eyes off the game. "We'll give you a turn down the back, I promise."

"Don't say I'll get a turn, because I *never* get a turn!" cries Adamo. "You know we're not allowed to change seats during the trip unless someone says they're sick and has to move up to the front, and you never say it! So I'm stuck up the front with all the nuns—and they make me sing with them!"

The trip he speaks of is a *pellegrinaggio*—a pilgrimage to one of the holy sites in the area that people do in May: the Month of Maria. My uncle organizes these pilgrimages, and we eagerly join in: not for the religious part—we put up with the hours of prayer and ritual—but for the fun of the bus trip, the great picnic afterward, and the freedom of an afternoon exploring the ruins and historic sites of the town we are visiting. And there's the excitement of getting up early in the dark, and arriving back home after dark! This time we are going to Casalbordino to visit the sanctuary of the Madonna dei Miracoli, the Madonna of Miracles, a church where Mary was seen. After mass, we will hunt around the hills to find a good spot for our picnic, and then we will head down to the coast and the beach. *The beach!*

And because there are adults on the bus, including the priest, it is one of the rare times we have the freedom to mix closely with the girls for *several hours*. I didn't like girls the last time I went on a *pellegrinaggio*, but this time there is Amelia...I have dreamed of this trip for weeks! And I will have to push even *harder* to get the right seat. The battle is always to get seats as far down the back as possible, away from the adults, and to save seats for those you want with you, so there is a lot of pushing and shoving when we line up to board. My friends and I have already packed the cards for playing *scopa* and other betting games down at the back of the bus, and now we just need to pick the person who'll be lookout halfway up the bus: the one who will whistle a warning should any of the adults decide to head down the back. It's always Adamo, and this is why he's complaining.

"You don't have to do it this time," I say to Adamo. "It's someone else's turn—*bags not me!*" I finish, crossing my fingers before someone can pick me.

Cecio jumps in: "*And not me!*" he yells, crossing his fingers.

Lorenzo, who has been flicking his coin, turns to us, scowling. "That's not fair! You can't vote until everyone is ready—I was *playing!*" he screams.

"You're it," I say. "You're lookout on the bus!"

"I'll do it *one* way, but I'm not doing it on the way back!" Lorenzo yells, slumping sulkily against the wall as Adamo grins.

"Oh *porco diavolo!*" cries Cecio, whose coin has just flicked over the wall and down to the street below. "Why do we have to play on such a low wall?"

We used to play our Sunday game against the side of a building in the next street, but I recently convinced my friends to change to this low wall in the square. It's the most stupid wall to play *battimuro* against: low enough to flick over, with a precipice on the other side that leads down to clay-tiled rooftops and a cobbled street full of drains and cracks where coins can easily disappear. But it has to be this wall, for one good reason: Amelia passes this way. Our low wall ends at the corner of the narrow street her house is in.

I look across the piazza to the great church that is still emptying; it dwarfs the other buildings in the square. I wonder if the Normans built it? They built the castle, and there are supposed to be older foundations beneath the church. It wouldn't be part of a Roman town—we're too high. I read that the Romans liked space and so built their towns and cities in the valleys where they had lots of room to spread, with great roads leading north, south, east and west. It was only later that the Normans and others built high up to protect themselves from invaders. And on the flat the Romans could attack and defend effectively, using their great army formations. This is why there are Roman roads, lookouts and an occasional fort up here in the mountains, but no Roman towns. The Romans felt safe in the valleys, and I felt proud when my uncle told me they feared no one.

"Ciao, Mario!" says a voice behind me. *Amelia!*

Instead of taking the direct route across the piazza, she has run up the side of the square, close to the buildings, and jumped out beside me. Does she think I was watching for her? *Oh!*

"Ciao, ciao!" she says again, panting.

"Ciao!" I reply, trying not to smile too much.

People jostle past and accidentally push her so that she bumps up against me. She's so close I can see a rivulet of sweat trailing down her smooth, olive-skinned cheek and I can smell her sweet scent—or is it the rose pinned to her dress...*oh!* One from the bunch I gave her? Her eyes are bright, luminous, from the excitement of the run. The people behind mutter, "*Scusi!*" and go on their way. I must be staring because she laughs at me, showing her white teeth and a dimple in one cheek. She is beautiful.

Say something! Say something clever, *ask* her something; it's only seconds before her mother or my friends join us!

"You going on the *pellegrinaggio?*" I ask. Stupidly, because she *always* goes on the *pellegrinaggi*.

"*Sì*, and you're going?"

I'm glad she asked a stupid question back. Oh, there's Amelia's mother! I can see her coming toward us across the square.

"We're going to the *curvone* this afternoon," I begin. The *curvone* is "the curve," the bend in the road just outside town where all the young people meet. It has a low wall that we sit on to talk, and laugh and smoke away from the prying eyes of adults. "Do you want to—"

Whack! Someone thumps me on the back, almost knocking the wind out of me, and then pushes in between Amelia and myself. Caterina. She leans on Amelia's shoulder, and eyes me as she pretends to tighten a shoe strap.

"Oh, it's Mario—*wonderful*," she says sarcastically.

No one likes Caterina: except Amelia.

Caterina can be counted on to tell on you, break promises, blurt out secrets and humiliate you at every opportunity, and she hates me especially because I like Amelia. She found out about the incident in the wine barrel and told *everyone*. She even lied to Amelia, saying that I had thrown up along with my friend. *I didn't!* Only Lorenzo was sick there; I managed to hold on until I got home. Caterina is *known* for her nastiness. So *why* is Amelia friends with her? My uncle said that sometimes opposites attract: this must be the reason because Amelia is sweet and *beautiful*, and her friend is a liar, a tattletale and—

"*Ugly!*" says Caterina. "Ugly's here." She jerks her head toward Cecio, who has come up behind me.

"I'm out, I've lost my coin," Cecio says, looking from me to Amelia.

Adamo runs up. "Ciao, Amelia," he says, smiling. "Ciao, Caterina. I'm not bus lookout this time."

"Well, don't think you're sitting close to me!" says Caterina, pretending to sniff an unpleasant odor.

"Are you going in the water at the beach?" Amelia asks me. "I'm still trying to convince my mother, but I think I'll be allowed to this trip."

Oh, Amelia and me with our shoes off *in the sea . . .*

"Amelia, come on now, please," says a voice. Her mother. She smiles and nods hello to us and continues on her way, signaling for her daughter to follow.

"Do you think . . . ," I begin, wishing Caterina would look away— or preferably *go away.* "Do you think we could, you know . . . sit together?"

No one speaks.

"On the bus?" I finish.

"I'll . . ." Amelia flashes a look at Caterina. "I'll see," she says quickly, her cheeks reddening. She looks down and then runs off to join her mother without meeting my eyes.

Caterina is glaring at me. She hasn't moved.

"*You,* sit next to Amelia? That's where I sit. What makes you think she'd want to sit with *you?*" she says with a sneer. "Anyway, she's got a boyfriend!"

She's making it up . . . but what *if* . . . Oh no, who could it be? I'm not going to ask—

"Who is it?" Adamo interjects, watching me anxiously.

"I'm not telling you!" she snaps back. "That's for Mario to find out!"

She does the two-fingered cuckold point at me as she steps backward, laughing. Adamo leaps after her, but I pull him back. "Don't!" I say to him.

"Anyway, Mario was going to touch the bull for her," Adamo yells across the square. "Mario is brave and can beat anyone!"

"*Shut up*, Adamo!" I say, hoping no one has heard.

Caterina turns. She was running away from us and didn't quite catch the words. "What did you say?" she asks.

I can see Amelia several feet away with her mother, who has stopped to talk to someone—Amelia is now looking back, watching us . . .

"And he even swore the Roman oath!" screams Adamo, holding his fist to his chest.

"But . . . what was the *dare?*" Caterina asks Adamo curiously as she moves closer.

I have Adamo's shirt pulled so tight behind his neck that he knows I will choke him if he says another word.

"Nothing!" yells someone behind Caterina. Oh! It's *Amelia!* She's come back. Did she hear? *Did she hear what Adamo said?*

"Come on, Caterina," says Amelia, pulling at her friend's sleeve.

"I'll find out," says Caterina, "and if you weren't so *putrid*," she says to Adamo, "I'd pummel you now until I got it out of you. But . . . I'll find out." She darts a last look at me.

As the two girls walk off, Amelia turns and flashes me a smile.

The smile thrills right through me but . . . *oh Madonna*. Did Amelia hear what Adamo said about my dare . . . my oath? *How embarrassing!* And how am I ever going to get her away from that monstrous

Caterina? It will be humiliating—*so* humiliating now that I've asked her in front of everyone—if she doesn't sit with me on the bus. I won't go. That's it—I'll say I'm sick and I won't go on the *pellegrinaggio*.

I look at my friends, who are watching me closely. If I don't go, they won't go, and we'll all miss out on the beach—Adamo's never been. As I look at him, something strikes me about the words he just yelled across the square.

It's only a week until the bus trip, and before then there's something I *must* do . . .

"Stop pushing! *Stop pushing!* I'll go over!"

"Can you see it? Oh! *That's it over there!*" yells Adamo, in awe.

The stones of the wall look whiter in the dusky, late afternoon light. I'm studying them up close because I have my head against my knees, too scared to look up. Lorenzo and Adamo are staring across the paddock but I don't want to look at what's there, moving and fidgeting underneath the tree.

"Look at those *horns!*" cries Lorenzo.

Sometimes I regret having friends.

"They don't look *that* sharp," he adds ruefully, seeing my face.

We are at the bull's paddock, and late afternoon is quickly turning to dusk. The three of us have just mounted the stone wall, which is high—half our height again—but not too hard to clamber up on the outside because there are footholds in the large chunks of jutting Abruzzo rock. The wall is smoother on the inside, which is just *one* of the things that worries me. We're all supposed to be in church at *rosario*. Lorenzo, Adamo and I got away, but Cecio could not get past his mother, who knows where he is in a room without turning her head. We *had* to get up here before dusk, because today is the last day I can do it. Tomorrow is the *pellegrinaggio*, so today is the day I must touch the bull.

It seemed like a good idea a week ago, when I decided on it in front of my friends, so that I could win Amelia over, sit with her on the bus...and become a hero. I promised my friends—and I told them I wasn't afraid. So I have to do it. Now.

I was going to do it every other day this week, but couldn't. I've had nightmares since I agreed to the dare. I even went to the paddock by myself to look, *twice*—which only made things worse, and now I'm *really* scared. But I have to do it, not just for Amelia but for *me*, and—I look at Lorenzo sitting on the wall expectantly, Adamo hunting for grass to appease the bull, and think of Cecio waiting eagerly after church for news of the victory—*my friends*.

I look up and over at the tree. Oh no. It's big. The bull seems much bigger than it was yesterday. I should have blessed it.

I had thought of getting holy water from my uncle's font and giving the bull a benediction—it's the only thing that could make an angry bull sweet, gentle, docile. I got the idea after I remembered the time we sprinkled holy water on our essay: a group essay that we had to do for class. With no idea how to do it properly, and running out of time, we figured a benediction could make all the difference. So I snuck the *aspersorio*—the ball-shaped sprinkler containing holy water for blessings—from my uncle's study. It was agony trying to get past my aunt while hiding it under my coat and holding it steady so it did not spill a *drop* (the water burns those who have sinned, and what greater sin could there be than stealing the holy water itself?). With great relief I got it to my room. In the end we didn't get a very good mark for our essay: I said it was because we *stole* the holy water; our teacher said it was because we didn't even answer the question.

I gave up on the idea of blessing the bull because it stands in the middle of the paddock, which means I can't reach it anyway;

besides, I'm sure I'd be even more damned if I stole holy water to bless a *dare*! But still. . .

"Should have blessed it," mutters Lorenzo.

"*I told you!*" says Adamo, who was pushing all week for the benediction idea once I had mentioned it. "Told you you should have done it. I would have done it for you!"

"You would have dropped it in a bull turd!" says Lorenzo, laughing at the idea, "and Mario would have had to take the precious *aspersorio* back to his uncle with little grassy bits sticking out of the sprinkler holes, and stinking of dung!" He guffaws until a low snort stops him.

All eyes go to the tree. We watch for movement, but the bull has his back to us and is still.

"I'm sure he's asleep—they sleep in the afternoon," says Adamo, whose cousin in Sicily owns a bull, making him the expert. We wait another tense, silent minute. "It's asleep, I tell you—they sleep standing up," says Adamo.

"If you're so sure, why don't you jump down and kiss it goodnight?" replies Lorenzo.

A louder *SNORT!* and we all pull up our legs together. There's a scraping sound, the stamp of a hoof, and the great left flank of *il toro* comes into view as he shifts around under the tree.

"Asleep, huh?" says Lorenzo.

THWACK! The tree bends slightly to the left, its tip silhouetted against the sky above the wall so that we can see the foliage rustling and rattling, and then flicks back. The bull is scratching himself, causing the tree to bend: the *whole* tree. Another snort sends me spinning around to drop my legs down the outside of the wall; Lorenzo has scrambled to his feet, ready to jump. The only one seated—with legs bent and ready—is Adamo.

"Wait, maybe the bull is *more* alert in the afternoon. Maybe I got it the wrong way around," he says.

"*Cretino . . . !*" says Lorenzo.

I'm focused on the tree. "How many paces to the tree, do you think?" I ask grimly. "Fifty?"

I know how many paces, I've counted them over and over each time I've been here, but I just want my friends to make me feel better. I want them to say it's *less*. My friends don't say anything.

After a moment's silence: "He hasn't turned around. Do you think he knows we're here?" whispers Adamo, with a shiver.

We all stare out across the paddock, no one speaking. The paddock seems *so* wide, the distance between the tree and the wall *so* far, and the wall itself *so* high—and smooth. It's impossible. I've seen this bull run, and there is no way anyone could make it safely from the tree to the wall once they'd prodded and annoyed him. How do you get away from a powerful, enraged beast that can scream across a field like a freight train?

"Got the pole?" I ask Lorenzo anxiously. I know he's got it—I just want to *see* it again.

He nods and holds up the long, gnarled branch resting on the wall beside him. We hunted high and low for this branch. It had to be thin enough to grab, yet solid enough to take and lift my weight. This stick will be what gets me up and over the wall, for it's too high and smooth to scale, and too far for my friends to reach downward. This stick could be the very thing that saves my . . . no, don't think about it.

"And I've got mine!" says Adamo proudly, holding up his shorter "tapping" stick. This stick is for distracting the bull. We decided that, should the bull come after me, Adamo will be situated at a point on the wall well away from Lorenzo—from where I'm headed—so that he can get the bull's attention by tapping the wall frantically with his stick.

"I'm off!" says Adamo as he slides down the wall and begins the run around to his position.

The sun finally dips behind the mountain; it is only minutes before dark. This is it. It's now or never. I can do it, I think...no I can't... I *can't*—Suddenly I hear Caterina's words in my head, the words she will say in front of my friends, Amelia, everybody: "You're a coward, Mario, *sei un pauroso!*"

I have to do it. My stomach churns, my heart is pounding. I look across at the bull. He has turned and is now looking at us. Irritated by the unexpected visitors, he stands and watches us closely. He is taller than me by two hands; he has a *very* large head, with great flared nostrils above a mouth that is moving sideways as he chews his cud. But I'm staring at what's *on* that head...have those horns got bigger since yesterday? Or do they just seem longer and sharper because I know they could come into contact with...

Aargh! Don't think about it or you'll never do it! Just jump in and *do* it! I slide forward to begin my drop into the paddock. Lorenzo grabs me.

"Wait. It would be better if you went straight across," he says.

"What?" I ask, panicked at this last-minute change.

"It would be faster if you touched the bull and kept running straight across the paddock to the other side, that way you won't waste time turning to come back."

He's right, it *would* be faster. Lorenzo is already making his way off the wall.

"I'll go over to the other side. Wait until I get there and give you the signal," he says.

"Quick, it's nearly dark!" I yell at him as he starts running around the outside of the wall.

Panicked by the lowering sun and the words in my head, I just want to get it over with. I'm nervous about the change, but it will be okay, I'm sure, and it *will* be quicker. The plan is that I wait until the bull has fully turned away, and then race up behind him. With a quick touch I am now to race directly across to the wall opposite, where Lorenzo will lean forward with the stick to pull me out.

"Okay," yells Lorenzo, waving his arms from the other side.

The bull has turned away.

I'm down and in the paddock. All night I said prayers and made my *mea culpa*. Maybe I should have left a note for my mother, and my uncle and all those who will miss me, even my...no, not my aunt. And then there are my friends. I look across to Adamo and then Lorenzo. They both give me the thumbs up.

I look back toward the bull, get my bearings, and run.

"Wait, *wait!*" I hear Lorenzo scream, but there's no time.

I tear across the paddock. I have the rear of the bull in focus, and I'm not taking my eyes off it. I make sure that I stay exactly in line with the back of him each time he moves slightly to the left or right. As I run I am aware of some noise ahead of me, but it is quickly drowned by the scream of the wind in my ears: there is no time to think or feel, only to watch. *Watch* that rear end and make sure it does not turn or shift before I get there: I don't want to see a flank or, worse still, a face, I just want the bull's rear end in front of me.

In the background Lorenzo is still screaming, something about a pole. I wish he'd wait until I get there!

I'm almost there. The bull's moving, turning—*No*, I'm all right, he still has his rear to me, hasn't seen me. I hope. I run up and prod his back end, which is softer than I expected...Oh, that was his tail! It seems like everything is happening in slow motion as I lean back in again and do the touch—*il tocco*—on the bull's tight, hard haunches. My hand slides off him, and the bull turns his head slowly...

There's a yell from the wall, and then loud screaming as I begin my run toward Lorenzo. He is waving his arms and I see that he... *he doesn't have the pole!* It suddenly dawns on me what it was that he was yelling. He has left the branch in our original position! Without a pole they can't get me out!

To the right of me I see Adamo racing along the wall toward Lorenzo with his short stick, trying to make it there in time...

I head toward Adamo, who is now not far from Lorenzo. *Oh Madonna!* I think I'm going to make it... Adamo is now kneeling on the wall and lowering the stick, Lorenzo reaches him—they are getting in position...

I glance away and then back to see Adamo disappearing over the other side of the wall. *Why?* I turn to Lorenzo: he too is standing on the wall, backing up with a look of horror on his face, about to jump down to the other side. Why would...?

Oh no! I just felt a rush of air against my legs, a snort... I scream along as fast as my legs will carry me. I'm sure I felt something, a movement of air near my legs—did I imagine it? *No!* There it is again! Oh Madonna!

Heart pounding and legs flying, I look at the wall: *no one's left on it!* Who's going to pull me out? How am I going to get out? I have a one-ton bull on my heels and no one is there to pull me... I'm dead; *I'm dead! Adamo!* Adamo is there, and Lorenzo! They've just reappeared on the wall and they're trying to get their footing to reach in and grab me.

I hit the wall, stretch upward with force and grab the first hand I can find, pulling on it and almost tipping its owner in as I stride up the six-foot-high wall in one quick movement.

But not quick enough. I feel a stabbing pain in my left calf as I go to pull my other leg up. For a split second I can't move, but I pull hard, *hard*, and my leg is released. There is *no way* it's going to get me and drag me back down now...

On the wall: *I'm on the wall!* Half laughing, half crying, I bend to get my breath as my friends joyously slap me. Adamo rubs his burning wrist and Lorenzo shows me how he pulled on Adamo's pants as he leaned outward from the wall, to stop us all from tumbling in.

But as we congratulate each other we are careful not to lose our balance, for there, right at our feet—heaving, snorting and glaring at me with blazing eyes—stands *il toro*.

The water tickles and laps at my feet and ankles. I squeeze the soft slithery sand between my curled-up toes, let it scrunch and then release it again. I'm not in a rush.

I look out across the Adriatic Sea. It's weird. I'm not used to having nothing but water in front of me for as far as my eyes can see. It takes your breath away and makes you feel like you can do anything. Today I feel like I can do anything.

I turn back: the others are almost at the bus; I am the last.

Bright yellow buds of flowering *ginestra* dot the slope from the beach to the road where the bus is parked, which means soon it will be summer, and it all looks so, so beautiful. It's spring, we're on the *pellegrinaggio*, the *transumanza* is about to begin, with the sheep and baby lambs heading back up into the mountains, and... Amelia is my girlfriend. I think.

Ouch! My leg jerks up from the sand. That pain again! Surely this time something has bitten me. I look at the back of my left calf. There is no mark—nothing—yet the pain jabs regularly. I get a rush through me and remember that I touched the bull—but that *he* had the last touch...

Amelia waves to me from the door of the bus. She *must* be my girlfriend, because what were her words as we paddled in the sea? *I have a seat next to me on the way back, Mario, Caterina has moved.*

All the boys laughed at me on the bus. No one believes that I touched the bull; and I had to stop a tearful Adamo from screaming in their faces that I had. In the end it doesn't matter: he and Lorenzo know I did it, *I* know I did it and...and Amelia is saving me a seat.

I like the back corner of the classroom; all the interesting stuff is on this wall.

The Latin professor has his singsong voice on again: "*Si parva licet . . .*"

Bombs. I look again at the bomb poster. Virgil and bombs: in our classroom.

"*Si parva licet . . .*" repeats our teacher. He's saying something about bees and the gods...that ugly one with the eye in his forehead: Cyclops.

I like the bomb on the left: it has a pointy nose and looks more frightening than the others. Wish I could find *that* one... No, I think I prefer the bomb at the top...it's not pointy but it looks *bigger*. The poster's old: yellowing and curling up at the corners. It sits beside me in the far back corner of our classroom, fourth in line from the world map, the mammals chart and the multiplication table for the younger kids, and just above the row of iron hooks that carry the weight of bags, hats and coats. The bomb posters were put up because of the war. At the top it says "*Attention!*" and tells us not to touch or play with any of the objects below if we find them; it tells us to call the *carabinieri* instead. Wish I could find just one bomb: I'd *look* at it, but I wouldn't touch it. We know that farmers are still blown up as they plow their fields, almost two decades after the war has ended...

"Mario? *Mario!*"

I look to the front. Our teacher, the old professor, repeats: "*Si parva licet...*" with his head held high, eyes closed and hands swirling: he wants me to finish the sentence.

"*Si parva licet componere mag—mag...magnoose*," I say quickly, glancing back at the bombs.

"*Mario!*"

My head snaps back. The professor's eyes are still closed, but now there is a pained expression on his face. "Mario, *si parva licet componere magnis!*" he says fiercely.

I am the only one in class who gets this attention from the Latin professor. Being the priest's nephew, and having attended the seminary—where we had Latin and Greek drummed into us—I am well ahead of the other kids at school. Most don't know what to make of these strange words, and most don't care to know. But I *have* to learn them because of my uncle, making me the target of the Latin professor, which is a good and bad thing. Good because I can get him to read passages when we want to talk or pass notes, and bad because if I make a mistake, even the tiniest one, he jumps on me because he expects me to be the very best at Latin—*perfect* in fact. Because no one else is interested.

I watch him now as he continues reciting his verse, eyes closed, arms outstretched. He moves his arms in lyrical waves as if conducting music or swirling through a magic sea of words. He is dreaming, singing out to the world his beautiful Latin verses, stories and songs. He's not aware of anyone around him. And we've discovered—much to our relief—that even when he opens his eyes and looks at us, as long as he's reciting, he doesn't really *see*. And the funniest thing is that this isn't even a Latin class—we're supposed to be doing the classics—but the Latin professor can't resist drifting off into his Latin...

You see, he's mad. *Everyone* knows it, but no one says it: that the Latin professor is *strano, lunatico*, with *"la testa tra le nuvole"*—his head in the clouds. We think he's *in love* with Latin, as though it was a woman. Cecio believes that if he could, he'd marry it. The professor *looks* normal: a thin little man who dresses in three-piece suits, always with a handkerchief, fob watch and a starched white collar. He has wrinkly hands with brown spots, you can see all the bones in his fingers and thin wrists, and he has watery grayish-blue eyes, but his clothes and the way he stands make him look like a gentleman—except for the wispy gray hair that flies out sideways, or stands vertically from his head.

My uncle—with whom the professor eagerly converses in Latin whenever he can—said he is from an aristocratic family. It must be a *mad* aristocratic family, because his behavior is strange. Not only does he recite his Latin for *ages* with his eyes closed, he even *walks* and recites with his eyes closed. Every so often he gets close to the edge of the stage at the front of the classroom with its one-step drop, and we wait for him to fall off the edge, but he never does. Some part of him keeps him safe while the rest of him is somewhere else.

We quickly discovered that this madness was to our advantage because it means we can do *anything* in class while he recites. He doesn't seem to know, or care when he's in this Latin trance. We talk, swap comics, move seats, fly planes, throw paper balls...but watch out if he finishes a verse and you get caught! The professor is very strict with discipline and quickly deals out punishment to anyone he catches cutting up. Mostly it means standing in the dunce corner at the front of class with your hands behind your back. Now and then you get a stinging slap on your exposed hands from the professor's passing ruler, which is all the worse because you're not expecting it and jump with fright—making the class laugh. I spent many hours in that corner during class until I worked out a strategy.

The idea was simple: I would ask the professor to read a long Latin verse—*one that I knew the end of.* He would no more interrupt or cut short any of his sacred verses than cut off his arm, so, no matter what happened, the professor was not going to come back down to earth until the verse was finished, and he would not be aware of *anything* going on until then. This meant I had a really important job in class: the others would signal me to ask for a verse so that planes could be flown and messages sent. It forced me to brush up on my Latin, because I couldn't always ask for the *same* verse, and it couldn't be *too long* or the professor would not read it, and I always had to know the crucial last lines, so that we all knew when to stop! My uncle could not believe that suddenly, two or three times a week, I was reading up on my Latin: Virgil, Cicero, Seneca. He was *very* pleased. And because most of these writers were philosophers, it made me realize that this philosophy thing was *not* so boring either, that it was sort of . . . ideas—about things like friends, and eating yummy food and beautiful women and love. I was amazed— I never realized they fell in love *two thousand years ago!*

And I discovered something else about Latin: it works magic with girls—with Amelia—especially when I speak of *amore.* It's almost as good as when I describe the cut-out parts from my uncle's movies.

I look across at the other wall of our classroom where the Italian president sits in his frame, along with a crucifix. Beneath them is the old iron fire that we have to run out and get wood for, dropping the large, splintery chunks into the stove's screechy, jamming drawer and trying to slide it back in. Out front is the teacher's huge desk with its solid front—which is a shame because Signora Marinelli, our math teacher, has nice legs. There is also a map of Italy, and the great blackboard that Emilio, the teacher's pet, always gets to clean: we assist by throwing paper balls at his back. I look down at my inky fingers and the little wooden desk I share with Cecio. It has a squeaky lifting bench seat, double inkwell, and worn desktop carved with a tangle of names, dirty words, love messages and initials. I feel for my gum. *It's not there!* Oh, yes it is. My hand was in the wrong place. It's up in the far right corner underneath the desk. I'm going to miss it here.

The bell rings and I shiver: bells still remind me of the seminary.

"Mario, could you stay," calls the professor.

What have I done now? I was only looking at the poster . . . oh, it's all right, he's not frowning at me—must be a message for my uncle. But still, now I have to *wait* . . .

I stand beside the desk as the professor straps his books together.

"So, I hear you're leaving us soon?" he asks without looking up.

"Yes," I say. "I'm going back home to Collemare."

"Where will you go to school?" he asks.

"I will finish high school in L'Aquila," I say. I feel a knot of grief at having said it out loud.

"Ah, childhood leaves us and manhood beckons . . ." He begins saying it in Latin and then stops: "And I hear that you've become a skilled *torero* of late?" He smiles.

He knows about the bull!

"You're skillful with your body, now think about your mind. *Cogito, ergo sum*, Mario—I think, therefore I am. Keep reading the classics: they will improve your Latin and your *thinking*." He leans forward, tapping my chest and whispering: "And they will take you to *other worlds*."

I'm not sure if I want to go to the other worlds the professor goes to.

He thumps several books from the floor up onto his desk until there are two tottering piles: "Ah, we've had good times together, you and I, yes?"

I nod and flash a smirk at my friends Cecio and Adamo, who are waiting for me at the door. We've had more good times than the professor will ever know.

"Pick these up—" he gestures at the books—"and help me carry them home."

I look around the professor's drawing room, which is totally filled with old stuff.

I remember my surprise when I first saw this room almost a year ago: chairs with embroidered cushions and curvy, bowed legs, small polished tables, two covered things with buttons and tassels that look like chairs without a back, large Chinese pots, swords, a fading tapestry on one wall, a moose's head, lots of ornaments in gold and silver from Egypt and the Middle East, he said, ugly wooden masks on the wall that the professor said were from some islands, and books. Lots and lots of books, all along two walls, right up to the ceiling. It's familiar to me now, after coming regularly for private Latin lessons—my uncle never giving up hope that I might become a priest—but I was still not used to this strange man. I would always greet him from a distance, and keep that distance throughout the lesson.

We've only just arrived, and already Adamo's eyes head straight for the bar. Along one wall stands a great *armadio*, ornately carved with a chiseled mirror, but it's what's *on* the *armadio* that interests him. Bottles: bottles of every type, color, shape and size. Bottles filled with magical, forbidden spirits and liqueurs—more than I had *ever* seen. Tearing my eyes away from the liqueurs that first day, I saw that the strangest thing was in the middle of the room: a lectern.

CHEWING GUM IN HOLY WATER

A tall wooden podium that you had to step up onto as if you were about to address a large hall full of people; a podium where you would *stand and recite*.

My lessons here were quiet and sedate—except for the day, some months back, when my friends came with me. The professor had agreed to them joining me; he so loved his Latin that he always hoped my friends—*anyone*—would listen and learn.

"You boys are welcome to stay and have a look around if you wish," the professor had said. "My precious texts are over there: you are welcome to look, *with care*. Help yourselves to anything, and if there is anything you would like me to explain or *read*..."

We knew then we had our bottles of liqueur.

I remember I asked for Virgil's *The Aeneid*, and I said I'd like to hear all of it.

"Well, I don't know about *all*, Mario," the professor responded. "*The Aeneid* runs for four hundred pages. But I will read for as long as you boys are enjoying it." The old man had smiled to himself and placed the book on his podium. Removing his jacket, he stood on the dais straightening his vest and cuffs and flattening his hair, and then gently opened the great book, standing tall as if about to address an audience of thousands...

What an afternoon! The marsala was *fantastic*, the whiskey burned our throats, the *sigaretti* were great, but it was the books—the books were the best thing! Our favorite was the one about a place called Polynesia. It had pictures all through it of half-naked women in grass skirts—it was even better than the artist's book because these were *photographs*! There were fights over this book, and the corner of one page got ripped as Cecio tried to pull it off Adamo, who had been slowly turning the pages for almost an hour...

"*Amicus certus*..."

Oh! The professor's words bring me back to the room: he's begun his reading. He asked me and my friends to stay a while after I helped him carry his books home. He said that he had a reading especially for me, especially *because*—then he stopped and gave a little cough without finishing the sentence. I think he was going to say because this will be my last visit to his house.

Adamo is *still* looking at the bar, at the marsala... *how could he?* Since the barrel incident I can't look at or smell *anything* that resembles wine. Back in Collemare, for the first time ever, I had to stop my *nonno* telling me about the grape harvest and how his fermenting was going, describing the lovely alcoholic fumes that wafted up from his vat as he stirred...

Adamo raises his eyebrows at me and indicates the bottles. I mouth "no." Besides, last time he spilled some: I had to clean the sticky red off the professor's beautiful rug that looks like something from a Persian palace. Adamo had swigged carelessly from the bottle and spilled it all down his front, the *armadio*, and onto the swirls and geometric patterns of the carpet.

"...*Amicus certus in re incerta cernitur*..."

This is *Cicero*! It's that thing about friendship. Something about a true friend is a friend in need...

Oh! Is Adamo in *need*? No, the marsala would only make him sick; I'm doing him a favor. I see Cecio is getting down a book... *that* book. I guess looking at the book won't hurt...

"...*Neque enim fidum potest*...," sings the professor, "...*esse multiplex ingenium et tortuosum*..."

Oh, friendship again. Something about loyalty in friendship not being possible with a person of twisted and complex character. I'm suddenly feeling guilty about that afternoon my friends and I spent here. All the stuff of the professor's that we drank and smoked— we sort of *stole* it, really. Perhaps I'm twisted and complex, and not a loyal friend to the professor! My friends don't care, they don't understand the Latin.

Cecio leaves to go to the bathroom, and I pretend to be paying attention to the professor, just in case he looks up. He did say it was a reading for me. Adamo is now fiddling over near Cecio's chair.

"*Where's the book?*" Cecio asks Adamo fiercely after returning from the bathroom.

"It's not . . . get out, *I'm still reading it!*" Adamo says, pushing Cecio away from where he has hidden the Polynesian beauties under a cushion on the chair. "Get—*get out!*" he screams, grabbing the book as Cecio pulls at it. I can see another page about to—

"*Don't!*" I yell, shoving myself between them. "Let's put it away!"

"But he's not finished," says Adamo, gesturing toward the professor, "I know because you always tell us when—"

"It's finished!" I say, grabbing the book of photographs from Cecio and placing it back on its shelf.

"Cicero was a great philosopher," continues the professor, eyes closed and still in his trance. "He was the one who said if you could fly into the sky and see the whole universe, it would be *nothing* without a friend to share it with. Ah, the universe . . . we must not forget the man who described the universe in the most simple, and beautiful way . . . Lucrezio. It was Lucrezio who described infinity— the universe—in *four simple words* . . ."

"There is no center," I say out loud.

The room stops. The professor stops.

Adamo looks at me: "What are you doing?" he whispers fiercely, knowing I now have the attention of the professor, just as he was helping himself to a cigar to take home. He leans against the half-open drawer of the *armadio* as the professor looks over at us.

"What was that, Mario?" asks the professor.

"Lucrezio said: *There is no center*," I say. "You told us in class and I couldn't stop thinking about it. It made me think about what infinity *is*, and then what it *isn't*, and then how, if there is no center to the universe, then nothing is better or worse or more important to be closer to... like the way some people say the sun is the center—"

"Or God," says the professor.

I stop for a second, and then continue: "And so if nothing is the center, it makes *everything* different... and it just made me think and think and *think*!"

The professor looks at me for a full minute, nodding his head. Then he smiles: "Enough for today," he says, snapping the book shut.

The professor stumbles slightly as he steps down from the podium. I make an instinctive movement to catch him, but I'm across the room. At that moment I realize this fragile old man is not mad. He is not mad at all. This old professor has spent his time trying to open me up to the wonderful worlds that *he* can see and hear.

My friends have already disappeared outside after a quick, guilty goodbye. I hang back, wanting to speak to the professor alone. I put out my hand to him.

"*Grazie* for all your help, Professor. I will keep reading the classics when I go to L'Aquila," I say.

"There is no turning back now, Mario. You are captured. I can see it in your eyes," says the old man, ignoring my hand and embracing me. "Here—for you."

He hands me the book he was reading from: Cicero's book on friendship.

I follow the shuffling professor down the dark hall to his front door. The rain has stopped, and there is the smell of fresh damp as dull sunlight streams in, lighting up an umbrella in a blue and white pot, a pair of neatly placed boots and an enormous pile of old books that look like they were meant to be thrown out but no one's had the heart to do it. I rush toward my friends, who are waiting impatiently in the street, but something doesn't feel right. There is something else I have to say.

"I've decided I want to go to those other worlds," I yell back to the professor, but he has already closed his door.

I turn to see Cecio and Adamo staring at me as if I need to be locked up.

Amore in un Campo di Papaveri Rossi
LOVE IN A FIELD OF RED POPPIES

My aunt has had my bags packed. For two weeks.

It's because I'm leaving—for good. I'm going to Rome.

My mother, my uncle and my aunt *think* I'm going back home to Collemare, but I've decided I'm going to Roma.

It's annoying, because every time I want underpants, a particular shirt or my favorite pair of socks, I have to ask my aunty: lucky she has a good memory. She will say: "Third bag from the left, second layer down," and there it is. At least she hasn't been allowed to pack my under-the-bed things: Uncle forbade her from touching my rocks, insects and comics. And she is *totally* forbidden from touching my cookie tin.

I check it every day just in case—my special tin box where I have put all the precious things from my shelves: the knife from my princess, the stone from the river, my red Madonna, the book the professor gave me, my box of dead beetles, and the picture of Garibaldi.

There was once a picture of a she-wolf stuck to the tin's underlid, but it's long since fallen off, leaving just the yellow tape marks. Uncle still rails about the hole in his favorite magazine. Anyway, I'm happy that—*so far*—my aunt hasn't touched any of my special things, though her packing became so frantic I had to move certain *well-hidden* things out of my room, out of the *house*: my chewing gum and two cigarettes are now in a hiding place where no one will ever look...

I can't go back home to Collemare, at least not for long. I will do the two last years of school that I *have* to do, in nearby L'Aquila, catching the bus each day from my home village with my friends, and then I'm going to Roma.

For good.

Collemare seems too...*small*. Nothing happens there, and they don't sell chewing gum. It's strange how, on that day ten years ago when I was a little boy in my pinafore, I desperately didn't want to leave, and how so many times since I wished I could have been back home with my mother and my brothers. But *now*...

Truth is, I don't want to leave *here*. Everyone has given up on me becoming a priest, and my mother needs my help at home but...now that I've been told I'm going back to Collemare for good—I don't want to. I love my home village and my family and Claudio and my friends, but I love it here too. I cried the night my uncle told me, just as I cried for my mother in my bed when I was four. I'll miss my uncle and all the things he shows and teaches me, and the places he takes me. And I'll no longer be special in Collemare if I live there, unable to tell them exciting stories about my adventures away. And I'll miss my friends: Adamo, Lorenzo, Cecio, and then there's...Amelia. And I might even miss my aunt.

"Mario! *Scostumato!* What are these filthy socks doing near the fire?!" shrieks a voice from the next room.

Oh! My aunt is back early and... I won't miss her.

"I wanted to wear them again...," I begin.

"Wear them again and you'll get the back of my hand!" she spits as I enter the kitchen. "Going around stinking like a *barbone*—what will people think!"

It's only the *tenth* day I've worn the socks: I've kept them hidden so Aunt won't take them for washing... or worse. I decided to air them by the stove while she was out because they were a bit damp, a bit black around the toes and a bit smelly. They're my favorite socks, with a baseball symbol on the side. No one else has a pair like them and they are distinctly—

"*American!* American rubbish! Put on your good Italian socks. What have the Americans done for us except bomb our churches and give our children that rubbish to chew!" she screams.

My aunt never forgave them for Monte Cassino, but chewing gum is *the best* thing the American soldiers gave us! It made us different from the grownups, who had *never* had it. It made us cool. My aunt hated it, because it wasn't Italian and because, she said, chewing showed lack of class and *breeding*. For a long time my uncle, too, tried to talk me out of chewing, but for different reasons. He wondered why I would want to put something in my mouth that was like rubber, that wasn't even *food*, but recently he caught me with my friends in the *piazza*, chewing, and told me that I was allowed as long as it wasn't at home or in public: he said he realized it was our "badge." I sort of understood what he meant, but Adamo— without thinking—denied ever sticking it on his shirt.

And chewing gum was always the best present I could sneak home to my friends in Collemare: I gave them their first taste of it—not only was gum *modern*, it was too frivolous and *unnecessary* to be found on the rickety wooden shelves of the one small *bottega* in my home village—the little shop where you often had to wait for the shopkeeper to come back from his field before he would open up and serve you—and then he'd only sell you the salami or cheese he had already sliced, regardless of whether it was the one you wanted.

In Rome they'll have gum.

"Mario, come with me!" my uncle calls in a serious tone as he sweeps into the kitchen. I had heard one of the local farmers talking excitedly with him in the front room, but I thought it would be nothing more than one of the usual problems my uncle helps people with. "There's been a break-in at the church."

Oh! That's *exciting*... Maybe we can catch—oh, I'm not dressed. I snatch the putrefying socks from under my aunt's gaze and tug them on.

"What's happened?" cries my aunt, tearing her eyes away from my feet. "Has anything been—?"

"Don't know," says my uncle. "A large hole has been knocked through the back of the church. Signore Domenico just saw it as he was passing. Ercolina, could you please notify the *carabinieri?*"

Chains have been taken. Expensive gold and silver chains, and some rings—jewelry that adorned the statues of the saints in the church. These pieces were gifts from the people: from a long tradition of parishioners adorning statues of the saints with a piece, perhaps from their precious family collection, after prayers to this particular saint had saved their child, their mother, their crops. The thieves had knocked a hole in the wall at the back of the locked church and come up through the crypt. My uncle said they knew what they were doing: other churches in the area had reported the same sort of break-in. He said it was sad, because the church in Rome was already suggesting that all these small precious ornaments be taken out of the churches and kept under lock and key somewhere else:

they would no longer be on show for the local congregations. He said it would be the end of a tradition.

The *carabinieri* have arrived. Now there are more than a dozen villagers in the church, including my aunt. Word travels quickly, says my uncle, but I think Aunt calling through *casa* doorways and ducking her head into every shop as she walked back proudly with the *carabinieri* also helped.

The two policemen have been talking to my uncle and are now inspecting the crime scene. I like their uniforms—maybe I'll become a *carabiniere*... It seems the thieves not only took small things, they tried to take some big things too: precious statues that could be sold for a lot of money. We can tell because several statues have been turned around on their marble plinths. My uncle once showed me how they can't easily be moved or knocked off because there are long metal rods up through the center that are locked into the marble base. This means that you have to lift the large statues up very high if you want to remove them from their stands, something that can't be done without several men and a ladder or a crane of some sort.

My uncle said this is why priests sometimes discover a saint's *head* missing: not being able to take the whole statue, the thieves remove its head and sell it at a black market. I thought he meant a market run by black people until he explained *black* meant *illegal*. He told me there were lots of these markets in Italy: I've never seen one. I've been to the fruit market, the fish market, even the large market in Campobasso with my aunt, but I've yet to see a black one. I'll have to look out for saints' heads and chains—

Oh! They've even turned the beautiful, wounded Saint Sebastian around on his stand in the nave. How awful to think they could have taken him! How disgusting—these thieves have no respect!

The police are now inspecting the base of the statue for fingerprints and any other clues—

Oh, no! I've just realized the thieves have turned Saint Peter around!

My uncle and all the other people follow the *carabinieri* as they approach the statue of Saint Peter. They huddle together, getting as close as they can without being a hindrance as the police begin their inspection of the statue. Oh *cavolo!* What should I do? *Run?* This statue is closest to the church entrance, with a recess along its base against the wall that can only be reached with a slender arm, making it very handy for hiding—

"Cigarettes," says one of the *carabinieri*.

"And look here—gum," says the other.

The policeman picks up one of the butts and inspects it, pointing out to his comrade another piece of chewed gum stuck along the hem of the saint's cloak.

The ugly mess at the back of the statue is now exposed for all to see. I can't believe we stubbed out that many butts...

"Oh, Madonna!" cries one woman.

"Disgusting!" chorus two others.

"*Smoking!*" says another. "May the saints strike down those thieves. It is one thing to steal from a church, and quite another to show disrespect by *smoking* in it!"

The policeman drops two butts and two pieces of lumpy gum into his pocket.

This is it. I'll be going to Rome, all right—in the back of a police van.

"Wait!" one of the *carabinieri* says. "There's more." He forces his fingers farther into the recess at the base of the statue, pulling out a new packet of gum and a cigarette box. The *carabiniere* opens it: two beautiful untouched cigarettes sit inside.

Well, my aunt was packing my room... it was the only place! And Saint Peter is normally hard against the wall. It was the perfect hiding spot, until—*oh, Madonna!* When they find out they're mine they'll probably think *I'm* the thief... oh Madonna, I'm going to prison—

"Filter tip," says the *carabiniere* to his partner as he sniffs a cigarette.

My uncle shuffles his feet. I get the feeling he wants to look at me, but he doesn't. My aunt is looking, though. In fact, she looks as if she is about to burst, she's *glaring* so hard at me. Oh God, I hope she doesn't say anything here, I hope she waits until we get home. If she says it here, the *carabinieri* will just handcuff me and take me away...

She can't resist: "Well, *now* we know who it is!" she screams out loud. Everyone is watching her. The police look up.

"Now we know who it is, don't we?" she continues to yell, still glaring at me.

Please, *please*, no...

"*Americans!*" she screams.

What?

"Filter cigarettes and that awful chewing stuff—," continues my aunt: "the thieves are obviously *Americans*. I've told you, Mario, they bring *nothing* good..."

Oh, Americans! I'm so *glad* for Americans! But my uncle is looking at me now, so I don't know *how* I'm going to get out of this one... and there's still a chance the *carabinieri* might find out and take me away...

"They'll handcuff me and chain a ball to my ankles," I am telling Amelia. "I'm a fugitive now, so I *have* to go away."

"Oh no!" she says, dismayed.

Ah, this day is so sad... and so sweet.

I look from Amelia up to the clouds: soft gray and white swirls drifting across the sky. The sharp peaks of the Appennini look as if they will prick them or tangle them around their icy tips if they fly too close...

Today I go away. Away from here, away from my life with my uncle. Forever.

I've said goodbye to my friends, Adamo, Cecio and Lorenzo. Sort of. It was very quick because it was hard, and I thought I was going to cry, and so I said I would come back to tell them about my adventures in Collemare—and my adventures in Rome. But Adamo began to cry. He said I wouldn't come back, that I would forget him and everyone...that I wouldn't come back...

I *am* coming back—when I'm grown up and a famous adventurer. I'll come back to see Adamo—

"Your mother must be very happy," says Amelia.

I turn and look at her on the grass beside me. We planned to meet after I ran into her yesterday—just as I ran out of the church from the *carabinieri*. Amelia and I planned to meet in the field above our village at noon today. Nothing else was said, just "Let's meet in the field at noon."

I put on my best shirt. My best *red* shirt. As I walked up the slopes heading for the field, I noticed how crisp the air was in the bright sunshine, how magnificent the great mountain peaks were in front of me, how beautiful our town looked from above, the size and grandeur of the Norman castle with its well and our great secret, the dashes of yellow, purple and red from new blooms in among the dark green grass that roots itself in patches around the white-gray rock of my beloved Abruzzo mountains. *Everything* suddenly seemed more beautiful now that I was about to leave.

And Amelia seemed more beautiful.

As I strode up the last short slope and onto the flat, my breath was taken away by what I saw in the high field. *Red*. Red poppies. The dark green grass alive with flashes of red from the dance of hundreds and hundreds of tall, flickering poppies. Amelia was already there, in the center, lying down. She stood up. She was dressed in red.

Everything was red: my shirt, her dress, the poppies all around us ... Amelia caught my eye and we laughed. This *must* be love.

"Rusciu has left," I say, suddenly embarrassed by the way Amelia is looking at me. Our large ginger cat, my great friend in the attic, left our house two weeks ago and hasn't returned. "He was old. Uncle said he died, but I think he knew I was going and didn't want to stay with my aunt."

"We'll all miss you ... a *lot*. But your mother must be happy," Amelia says again.

"She won't have me for long. I'm going to Rome," I say.

"Perhaps she'll offer you another cookie ... this time to make you *stay*," says Amelia.

I had told her about my mother giving me a cookie to entice me into the car when I was little and didn't want to leave Collemare. I always got a lot of attention from Amelia when I told her this story.

"This time it will be *her* turn to cry," says Amelia, studying my face.

Sometimes Amelia thinks *too much*. "Gum?" I ask her, scrambling to pull a tatty pack from my pocket. My lighter falls out onto the grass. "I'm sorry I don't have any—"

"I know, I know. The police have them as *evidence*. You don't *really* think they'll arrest you?" she asks.

"Not if I get away. I don't want to involve my uncle and my family here. If I can get away, they'll lose my trail ..." I've heard this line a lot in cowboy movies, and it seems to work here. "I'll be all right just as long as they don't put my photo up on 'WANTED' posters and stick them all over Rome and around all the Abruzzo villages . . ."

I think I've gone too far. Amelia is looking at me strangely. "But I'm sure they won't," I finish.

Silence for a moment as we both stare up at the sky.

"Does *anyone* know? Your uncle . . . ?" Amelia asks.

"I'm sure he knows. He hasn't said anything, but maybe that's because I'm leaving," I reply.

My uncle always surprises me. I was waiting for him to blast me yesterday once the police had left the church and we were alone. He *knows* the gum is mine, and once, when he came out of the church too quietly, he caught me finishing a cigarette—one that I had borrowed from his study drawer at home—on the steps. There was no way of hiding it: I never threw butts on the church steps—that would be disrespectful—and I hadn't had time to stub it out on the saint . . .

The only thing my uncle said yesterday was: "*Mea culpa*, Mario—a few more *mea culpa*s would be good." He paused a moment and then: "So, Mario, these Americans—do you think they are so bad?" I said *no*, looking at him nervously. He went on: "I don't think they're so bad either. They're disrespectful at times, and rebellious, but I think they have good hearts." A gentle smile crept across his face. "And, in a way, the owner of that gum has taught us who live with tradition a little bit about *freedom*." I didn't understand the second part, but I got the first.

My uncle then quickly hugged me to him and said, "I'm going to miss you, Mario." That was all he said.

"So what will you do?" Amelia asks.

"Hide," I reply.

"No, I mean what will you do with your *life*. If you're not going to be a priest, what are you going to be?"

"An adventurer," I reply.

"No one pays people to be adventurers."

I hadn't thought about that.

"And, do you think one day you'll get ... *married?*" Amelia asks shyly.

Married?

I turn and look at Amelia beside me: a breeze has come up and the red poppies above our heads are now dancing violently, flickering and flirting back and forth with the tall grass. Her skin is smooth, her eyes darker than I remember, and she smells so ... so warm and sweet. I notice a tear quickly river down the side of her face. We are hidden from view among the tall green blades and I lean over and kiss her, just like I've seen in the movies ...

"I will come back for you. *One day I will come back for you.* I will drive up the hill to your village in my Ferrari and come back to get you," I say.

She begins to cry. It is the same sort of crying I saw with Adamo ...

At last she speaks: "And how will I know it is you?" she asks, her eyes cast down, too shy to look at me.

"Oh, you'll know it's my Ferrari," I say. "It will be red."

This is the last time I will walk down this slope, the slope above town where I can look out and stand higher than the castle, the cluster of stone houses huddled together with their red-tiled roofs, the activity and noise in the cobbled streets, and the great valley farther down that sweeps across to the magnificent Apennine mountains on the other side.

The last time.

I had to leave my love, Amelia, in the high field, for I depart this afternoon and already I am late back for lunch—and my aunt.

My aunt. I think she's given me a shell.

I had always said I liked this strange-looking shell she had in her bedroom. It has dark patches all over it that look like words and letters, and a pointy cone. It was a precious memento, she said, from a beach holiday once with someone *special*. The shell is so weird looking, I *love* it. Then two days ago I found it in my packed bag with my socks. When I showed my aunt she yelled at me, called me "*Scostumato!*" and told me to leave her things alone. So I left it on the kitchen table. Today, the day I leave, I found the shell back in with my socks.

So my uncle was right. Whenever people fought between themselves in the village, whenever I told my uncle I hated someone at school, whenever my aunt screamed and screeched about communists, atheists, or the people who didn't dress or behave the way she liked, my uncle would always say: "*Siamo tutti figli di Dio*"— "We are all the children of God."

One day a man walking past the church spat on my uncle as I stood beside him. Uncle looked shocked for a few seconds and then waved a calm "*buongiorno*" to the man—I was angry and then I wanted to cry. My uncle told me again what he had always told me: that if I couldn't understand someone, then move to a different place and look at them from there. He said things seem different when you look at them from somewhere else: to not do this was ignorance, he said, and ignorance was a dangerous thing. Which is like what my Latin professor told me: to read and think and think and *think*, to respect the things around me but not follow them blindly. And, when I think about it, Dante, the painter, and my *nonno* were saying this too. Which means my aunty must also be good—*sometimes*. I wonder who gave her the shell. The look on her face when she spoke of it reminded me of a nun in a quiet room a long, long time ago...

We are all the children of God.

I'm not sure I believe in God. I'm not sure if all they say about God is true. I will have to *think* about it, now that I know other things. But I will keep these words with me...

I will keep *his* words with me. Always.

Because I believe in my uncle.

ACKNOWLEDGMENTS

A big thank you to Barry Devlin, whose excited phone call from Ireland, after reading our first stories, gave us that first real boost forward on the book.

Many, many thanks to our agent Pippa Masson at Curtis Brown, and our publisher Jo Paul, who believed in this project from the very start; Alex Nahlous, our fabulous editor; Jo Jarrah, who did a brilliant job with copyediting; and to Elaine Erskine, who assisted us all the way.

Thanks to all those family and friends who encouraged and supported us over the years: Mario's beloved son Tommy Valentini, who inspired him to begin telling these stories; Mario's mother, Pompilia, and brother Luigi, who were of great support and assistance; his late father, Alfonso; his aunt Ercolina; and of course, his adored late uncle Don Ruggero. Cheryl thanks, in particular, her wonderful son Jason Hitchcock, and Emily, Sol, Liam, Kyle and Anikan—the young joys of her life; her brother Mark Hardacre and his wife Janice, who helped her through the toughest times; her darling mother, Margery Mottram, whose phone calls from the U.K. kept her going; and her father, Kevan, who inspired in her a love of words and taught her as a youngster to look for the great and the wondrous in humankind. Thank you also to Vanessa Grace, Stella King, Glen Walton, Kathy Sullivan, Valerie Forestier, David Podmore and all our other supportive friends—you know who you are; and special thanks to all Mario's childhood friends in his beloved Collemare and beyond. This book is for you all, and for every young-at-heart, passionate dreamer.

GLOSSARY

In Italian, as a general rule "a" and "e" at the end of a word indicate feminine singular and plural; "o" and "i" indicate singular and plural masculine.

abate	abbot
acqua	water
aia	communal field outside a village
alpino	mountaineer; alpinist
andiamo	let's go
anima	soul
armadio	sideboard
aspersorio	aspergillum: holy water sprinkler
ateo	atheist
Ave Maria	Hail Mary
bambino	baby; toddler
banditore	town crier

barbone	tramp; hobo
basco	soft cap; beret
battimuro	a children's game in which a coin is ricocheted off a wall
bene	good; all right; okay
bidente	hoe
bigliardino	table soccer; foozeball
birichino	prankster; naughty person
borghesia	bourgeoisie; the middle class
borsa	purse; bag
bottega	shop or workshop
bruschetta	bread toasted with olive oil and then rubbed with garlic and tomatoes
buon pomeriggio	good afternoon
burbero	surly; gruff; someone whose "bark is worse than his bite"
caffettiera	coffeepot
campanile	belltower
cantina	cellar for food and wine storage, usually underneath a house against rock
cappella	chapel
cappello	hat
carabinieri	Italian police
carbonari	coal makers
casa	house
castagna	chestnut
catechismo	catechism
cattivella	naughty girl
cavolo	literally "cabbage"; used as an expletive similar to *damn!*

ceci	chickpeas
chierica	priest's tonsure
chierichetto	altar boy
ciocie	shoes made from rags
cipolla	onion
come sta questo quadrano?	how is this boy?
come stai?	how are you?
conca	large urn for carrying water
confetti	almonds covered in a white sugar coating
conte	count
coppino	ladle
cortile	courtyard
covoni	bundles of wheat tied with straw
cresima	holy communion
cretino	cretin
crosta	crust
crostata	tart
curia	high administrative office of the Catholic Church
curvone	curve in a road/corner
damigiana	large glass bottle that sits in a wickerwork basket/cradle with handles; demijohn
diavolo	devil
Dio sia lodato	God be praised
dolcetto	a sweet apple liqueur
dormitorio	dormitory
edicola	street stand selling newspapers and magazines

eremi	retreats, hermits' caves
eretico	heretic
faggi	beech trees
fascie	bandage or ribbon worn around the body; baby's swaddling clothes
fionda	slingshot
fioretto	small renunciations or promises made by children to God
Fra/Fratello	Brother
frassino	ash tree
fratecercataro	monk who seeks alms
frittata	omelette
fustagno	fustian: thick, twilled cotton fabric
gambale	gaiter: leather or thick fabric worn from ankle to knee
ganascino	affectionate pinching of the cheek
ginestra	gorse: a bush with fragrant yellow flowers
goffo	awkward; uncomfortable
gomme	chewing gum
ladroni	thief
lunatico	lunatic
lupo	wolf
lussuria	lust
mangiapreti	literally "priest-eater": someone opposed to priests
mannaggia	darn! (expletive)

mannaggia la miseria	darn . . . the misery! (expletive)
marachelle	pranks
maremmano	mountain sheepdog
mariolo	prankster
messale	liturgical book containing all texts necessary for the performance of the mass
miscredente	nonbeliever; infidel
moneta	coin
mucchia	group of covoni
mulattiera	donkey track
navata laterale	side aisle of a church
Nazionali	brand of Italian cigarettes
nipote	nephew, niece or grandchild
nocino	a liqueur made from walnuts
non lo so	I don't know
nonna	grandmother
nonno	grandfather
nuvoletta	little cloud; speech bubble in comics
orto	vegetable garden
orzo	barley: in this case roasted and used as a drink; the "coffee of the poor"
pace	peace
paglietta	straw boater
pagnotta	loaf of bread
pala	shovel
palazzo	palace

palmo	outstretched hand
pancetta	tasty cured meat made from the belly of a pig
pane	bread
pane casareccio	rustic, home-baked bread
pannolino	diaper
pantofole	slippers
parnanza	apron worn by rams
passeggiata	walk
Pater noster qui es in caelis	common prayer: "Our father who art in heaven"
pauroso	coward
pellegrinaggio	religious pilgrimage
perpetua	a domestic who serves the priest
pescecani	sharks
pezzi di legna	pieces of firewood
piazza	town or village square
piccioni	pigeons
polenta	thick corn mush
poltrone	lazybones; sloth
pomeriggio	afternoon
pomodori	tomatoes
pompieri	fire fighters
porca miseria	expletive, loosely meaning "misery is a pig"
porchetta	roast pork
porcini	large mushroom regarded as one of the most flavorsome in the world
porco	pig; swine
porco diavolo	expletive, loosely meaning "damned evil"

porta	door
portone	main entrance; or a large house with a great doorway
posta	a group of people on watch, on guard
prugnoli	light-colored mushrooms
putto	little angel/cherub
quadrano	boy (Abruzzese dialect)
ragazzo/a	boy/girl
refectorio	refectory
Regione	region or regional administrative body
Risorgimento	revival; here referring to the movement Garibaldi began
roccia	rock; boulder
rondoni	swifts
rosario	rosary beads or the ritual of saying the rosary
sacrestano	person who maintains the church
scansafatiche	slacker
sciocchezze	stupidity; nonsense
scopa	broom; Italian card game
scostumato	naughty; ill-mannered
scusi	excuse me; sorry
sedere	backside; buttocks
sei un pauroso	you are a chicken/coward
seminarista	student priest
sfrizzoli	pork crackling
sigaretto	small cigar

sorella	sister
stanga	long pole or stick
strano	strange
sugo	tomato puree/sauce
tazza	cup; mug
tettoia	roofed area without walls
tira misu	cake made with mascarpone, coffee, soft cookies and liqueur
tocco	touch
toro	bull
toscano	thick, black cigar originally made in Tuscany
transumanza	seasonal migration of shepherds and their flocks
trapunta	quilt
tratturo	shepherds' road
trebbia	wheat threshing
ubriaco	drunk/drunkard
un	one
uva passita	dried grapes
vecchia caffettiera	old coffeepot: derogatory expression
velocemente	quickly; fast
vestiti	clothes
via crucis	The Way of the Cross: worship that follows the fourteen stages of the Passion of the Christ
vieni	come in!

zizzola	children's game where a pointed stick is flicked up and hit with a bat
zuppa inglese	a cake made from sponge, cream and liqueur